Fire in the Pasture
twenty-first century mormon poets

Fire in the Pasture

twenty-first century mormon poets

Edited by Tyler Chadwick

ꟼP

PECULIAR PAGES

Fire in the Pasture: Twenty-first Century Mormon Poets

Edited by Tyler Chadwick

Initiated by Eric W Jepson

Book design by Scott Hatch
Cover design by Lynsey Jepson
Cover art: *Curious Workmanship* by Casey Jex Smith
Copyright © 2008 Casey Jex Smith

Publisher's Cataloging-In-Publication Data
(Prepared by The Donohue Group, Inc.)

Fire in the pasture : twenty-first century Mormon poets / edited by Tyler Chadwick.

p. : ill. ; cm.

Issued also as an ebook.
ISBN: 978-0-9817696-6-0 (pbk.)

1. Mormon Church--Poetry. 2. Christian life--Poetry. 3. American poetry--Mormon authors. 4. Christian poetry, American. I. Chadwick, Tyler.

PS591.M6 F57 2011
811/.608   2011938437

Paperback ISBN: 978-0-9817696-6-0
eBook ISBN: 978-0-9827812-2-7

Peculiar Pages
115 Ramona Avenue | El Cerrito, CA 94530 | PeculiarPages.com

in collaboration with

B10 Mediaworx
9754 N Ash Avenue #204 | Kansas City, MO 64157 | b10mediaworx.com

CONTENTS

Finding Place

A fire in the pasture undulates
of blue and white and yellow flower,
a fire like a snake, iridescent by sunlight
and undulant in the wind.

Here one will understand the Nazarene's joy,
awash in the lilies of his own field, a spicery
of uncommon radiance in a common hour
rising from the dark, speluncular sod.

Consider, he said. Simply consider. Flowers
catching light like the scales of a serpent's skin,
a yellow apple sun delicious to the taste,
and temptations to joy irrepressible!

The kingdom of heaven found on earth
is like a pasture, a strange, little kingdom
full of spicery, the undulant and speluncular,
and all other words by which we frame it.

In this life we find the peaceable kingdom
within, then above, beneath, and all around.
What can a person driven by grandiosity
know of the quiet, hidden God found here?

—Doug Talley

Preface

Tyler Chadwick

In 1985, *Sunstone*'s poetry editor, Dennis Clark, began a four-part series for the magazine called "Mormon Poetry Now!" Once a year for four years, he surveyed "the state of the art of Mormon poetry" in order to examine "the best of what Mormon poets [were] trying to publish" (6). I'm sure his survey of the field dovetailed nicely with the work he was doing alongside Eugene England, gathering poems for the anthology, *Harvest: Contemporary Mormon Poems*. Together, these projects composed a unique moment in Mormon literary history—an intentional move to place Mormon poets center stage and to definitively represent what England called "the new Mormon tradition of poetry." As England had it, those working within this tradition tend toward "an unusually healthy integration of skillful form and significant content," toward the marriage of formal poetic training and the moral "ideas and values . . . they claim to know through religious experience." It's a union, England concluded, that leads them to "act with energy to communicate those ideas in confidence that they will be understood" and accepted by both their peers within Mormonism and within the field of mainstream American poetry (285).

Twenty-years before *Harvest* hit bookshelves, Mormon poet and playwright Clinton F. Larson spoke to the possibilities of such a union with the prescience of a **poet-seer**. He suggested that "[p]art of the spiritual record that must be kept [by the Latter-day Saints] is the poetry of the people." He warned that without a "body of significant and enduring poetry" to connect the Saints sensually and aesthetically to their religious experiences, Mormonism's cultural heritage would be in jeopardy. But if Mormon poets could, in his words, "take their work as seriously as they should, and by 'seriously' I mean that they become professionally responsible, then a significant and coherent literary movement can begin." In other words, if Mormon poets could meet the demands of their craft even as they faithfully responded to the demands of Mormonism, they would rise to their "literary promise" as a "believing people." They would earn an honored place in the Church, whose authorities would trust and accept them as "conveyors of individualistic truth" and experience (80).

Five years later, in 1974, Richard H. Cracroft and Neal E. Lambert published the first anthology of Mormon literature, *A Believing People: Literature of the Latter-day Saints*. Although designed specifically for a course in Mormon literature at Brigham Young University, Cracroft and Lambert hoped it would be "a good beginning" in the development of a Mormon literary tradition, one worth boasting about as the Church became increasingly international. After all, the collection was intended to represent the growing quality of Mormon letters, which included some "good novels and fine short stories, . . . some stirrings in the personal essay," and, of course, "a body of good poetry." That body ripened over the next fifteen years into *Harvest*, which then became the standard for contemporary Mormon poetry and poetics.

And rightly so: England and Clark had gathered hundreds of poems from fifty-eight poets whose writing careers spanned the half-century before the book was published. The title of *this* anthology, *Fire in the Pasture*, is meant to honor the standard set by these poets while revising *Harvest*'s basic conceit. The scriptural notion of a harvest suggests an eleventh-hour reaping completed in preparation for the Lord's return; thus the title, *Harvest: Contemporary Mormon Poems*, suggests, advertently or not, that the editors' gathering was such an eleventh-hour act, meant to be undertaken once and for all. But farmers sometimes burn their fields post-harvest in preparation for another planting. This is where *Fire in the Pasture* picks up the metaphor.

The phrase comes from Doug Talley's poem, "Finding Place," which I believe speaks to the intersection of religious, spiritual, and moral experience with the aesthetic experience inherent in well-crafted poetry. Through metaphors we often use to describe and to connect with God's kingdom (fire and light, the serpent, wind, gardens, planting, reaping, etc.) the poet takes up language as a form of worship—by which I mean that he uses it, yes, to *praise* God, but also to *emulate* God, whose words make worlds out of chaotic matter. If we think of poetry in etymological terms—*poesis* being the Greek term for the process of making—God, then, is the first Poet. His words and His worlds are constantly inviting us to reconsider our relationship to Him, to language, to the universe. Talley echoes this in "Finding Place" as he drops words like live coals on our tongues and invites us to "[s]imply consider."

The title *Fire in the Pasture* is intended to invoke these associations—and more. But it's not my intention to elaborate fully on these themes. Rather, as the editor of this collection, my intention is to showcase poets who have emerged or established themselves since *Harvest*, with special emphasis on poems written or published since the turn of the millennium. You'll find a range of published and unpublished work from eighty-two poets, including new poems from eight of the younger *Harvest* poets: Susan Elizabeth Howe, Patricia Karamesines, John W. Schouten, Laura Hamblin, Lance Larsen, Philip White, Danielle Beazer Dubrasky, and Timothy Liu. This vanguard joins seventy-four established and up-and-coming poets to provide an expansive look at 21st-century Mormon poetry. The poems range from artfully crafted traditional forms—including sonnets, sestinas, and villanelles—to free verse to prose poems to light verse to dramatic monologues to translations to cowboy poetry. All of these represent the varieties of the contemporary lyric voice; and the range of poets speaking here represents the varieties of the contemporary Mormon experience—a chorus of voices that calls again and again for us to reconsider our relationship to poetry, to the modern world, and to 21st-century Mormonism.

For her help in the early stages of this project I'm indebted to Sarah (E.S.) Jenkins, especially because she introduced me to a number of poets I may not have otherwise discovered. I'm also grateful to Susan Elizabeth Howe, who selected which of my poems to include; to Eric W Jepson, who sparked this anthology's flame; and to my wife, who kept fanning that flame when other obligations threatened to snuff it out.

Works Cited

Clark, Dennis Marden. "Mormon Poetry Now!" *Sunstone* 10.6 (June 1985): 6–13. Print.

Cracroft, Richard H., and Neal E. Lambert. Introduction. *A Believing People: Literature of the Latter-day Saints*. Ed. Cracroft and Lambert. Provo, UT: Brigham Young University Press, 1974. Web. 8 July 2011.

England, Eugene. "Editor's Commentary: New Tradition." England and Clark. 285–8. Print.

England, Eugene, and Dennis Clark, eds. *Harvest: Contemporary Mormon Poems*. Salt Lake City, UT: Signature Books, 1989. Print.

Larson, Clinton F. "A Conversation with Clinton F. Larson." Interview with Edward Geary. *Dialogue: A Journal of Mormon Thought* 4.3 (1969): 74–80. Print.

Foreword

Susan Elizabeth Howe

"give ye them
to eat"
— Fred Axelgard

As I read this impressive anthology from beginning to end, the word that occurred to me again and again was *abundance*. What a pleasure to be in the company of so many excellent poets! The bounty of the anthology reminded me of Christ's generosity in feeding the five thousand (see Matthew 14:15–20). Christ took real substances—a little bread, two small fish—and he created from them far more food than had originally existed, food that nourished the people and made it possible for them to return to their lives both physically and spiritually renewed. Poets take matter (language, emotion, thought, experience) and make of that matter a new creation, a work of art that did not exist before the poet organized it, a work that has the potential (each poet hopes) to nourish—to make readers see what they did not see before, to offer insight, to create empathy, to provoke thought, or to express beauty, soundness, depth. To offer abundance in place of scarcity.

Understood rightly, the writing of even exquisite poems should create humility in the poet, not pride, because poetry itself always exceeds any individual poem, any poet's oeuvre, or even any culture's entire body of poems. Donald Revell writes, "Poetry, the soul of poems, does not reside or rest in them. It goes. We follow" (28). Working poets will tell you that they are always reading, always studying, to learn what other poets can teach them, as well as considering what currents of life and thought they care about enough to embody in poems. Like any lasting human endeavor, poetry is far more important than any single example of a poem and always challenges the poet to greater effort, higher achievement. As Revell comments: "The satisfactions of poetry arise from conduct, not from production" (18).

And so it is for the Mormon poets included in this volume. What is presented here is not all of poetry or even all of Mormon poetry. But that these more than eighty poets care about poetry enough to work at it, to produce engaging and startling poems, is significant. And that they would represent themselves as Mormon in some way—by contributing poems to an anthology identified as Mormon, for instance—gives me great optimism about the LDS culture's participation and growing excellence in this art.

It is useful to ask, what about this poetry is "Mormon"? Are there qualities in these poems that distinguish them from the rest of contemporary American poetry, or are the poems substantially the same as the poetry of the greater American culture? Of course, the answer is both yes and no. At the Sundance Film Festival I once heard Robert Redford say that filmmakers should have the right to put their vision before the viewing public. To apply that notion here, each poet in this anthology has a vision of reality, of what human experience is like (including his/her own), of what matters—including a sense of how Christ's Gospel is present in his or her life. That vision certainly must inform each poet's poems, whether consciously or unconsciously. Reading the poems, I have enjoyed trying to get at that vision: "Gospel philosopher," I identified one poet, and "quirky, pop-culture, family man," "lyrical, serious lover of Utah and pioneer culture," "cynical, lonely urban single," "nature-loving adventurer," "historian," "world traveler," and "curious inquirer about all things," to name a few other characterizations. It is worthwhile for readers to undertake this exercise for themselves. To identify a poet's attitudes and concerns is to make clear which poets are nourishing, which poets to seek out in other books and journals.

It is true that the majority of these poems don't have content that identifies them as specifically Mormon. Many of them might be published (and, indeed, have been published) in the most selective and prestigious American literary journals. Nevertheless, I would claim these poems to be as Mormon as those that deal with specific Mormon experience. I can explain by using the ideas of fiction writer Flannery O'Connor, who wrestled with similar questions from a Catholic perspective. She realized early in her career that she was not going to write stories that the majority of the Catholic faithful would enjoy reading, and she defended her choices by reminding her critics that writing is a gift of the spirit. She said, "The Christian writer particularly will feel that whatever his initial gift is, it comes from God; and no matter how minor a gift it is, he will not be willing to destroy it by trying to use it outside its proper limits" ("Fiction Writer" 27). She also explains, "A vocation is a limiting factor which extends even to the kind of material that the writer is able to apprehend imaginatively" (27). In other words, individuals that we are, bearing unique life experiences, each of us thinks originally and must write in a way that is true to our experience and our interests, in order for our poems to live and breathe and speak to readers.

With this guidance to writers, O'Connor explains how to imbue secular subjects with spiritual truth: "Now none of this is to say that when you write . . . you are supposed to forget or give up any moral position that you hold. Your beliefs will be the light by which you see, but they will not be a substitute for seeing" ("Short Stories" 91). She emphasizes her ideas in another essay: "In the greatest fiction [and poetry, I might add], the writer's moral sense coincides with his dramatic sense, and I see no way for it to do this unless his moral judgment is part of the very act of seeing . . ." ("Fiction Writer" 31).

I find that the content of many poems in this anthology suggests the Mormon identity of the poets, even when that content is not specifically Mormon. More than half the poems are records of personal experience or observations about the experience of others. To record one's experience is a universal human endeavor; Donald Justice notes that "one motive for much if not all art . . . is . . . to keep memorable what deserves to be remembered" (251). But the interest in recording, thinking about, and trying to find meaning in what one observes, suffers, or exults in is of particular significance to us Mormons, believing, as we do, that our time on earth is vital in our growth towards salvation. "Know thou," said God to Joseph Smith, and through him to us all, "that all these things shall give thee experience, and shall be for thy good" (D&C 122:7).

In another large group of poems, the poets imagine the experience of others, including, for example, Marie Curie, Andrew Wyeth, Native Americans, the wife of a sheep rancher. There are many poems set in foreign countries and cultures. Many poems examine a question, a concept, a mystery, in an attempt to come to greater understanding. All of these poems illustrate the poets' appreciation of the Doctrine and Covenants admonition to learn "of things which have been, things which are, things which must shortly come to pass . . . things which are at home, things which are abroad . . . of countries and of kingdoms" (D&C 88:79). Poems about ancestors, spouses, children and grandchildren indicate a deep concern for lineage and family. These poems generally demonstrate a Mormon consciousness, even when the content of the poem is not specifically Mormon.

It strikes me that these poems are largely serious rather than comic, and that even the comic poems grapple with experience in a significant way. To perceive of life as having an eternal purpose and of choices as having eternal consequences leads Mormon poets to serious engagement with their subjects. The poems seldom make use of irony—the rhetorical stance that, in suggesting something other than the actual meaning of the words, often expresses cynicism about or mocks the subject. Those that employ irony use it to question or critique concerns about contemporary American culture and sometimes Mormon culture: for example, seeming to praise the way corporations label employees in order to expose corporate indifference to their actual human needs, or claiming that all is right with Mormon culture to suggest a lack of self-examination and awareness. These are legitimate uses of irony, but the overall lack of irony in the anthology is to our credit because it indicates that we actually engage with the world rather than dismissing it as hopeless or not worth the trouble.

And what of those poems with specifically Mormon or Christian content? They are of major importance in that they demonstrate that Mormon subjects can be treated with the same excellence that might be applied to any other subject. I particularly enjoyed the poems that explore questions about scripture and doctrine: What might Abish's life have been like beyond her small role in the story of Ammon and King Lamoni? How can we reconcile the biblical account of the creation with the scientific evidence of homonids during the Ice Age? Why must the earth of the millenium be crystal when it is magnificent as it is? To whom is forgiveness available?

Of the many poems about biblical and historic LDS figures, it seems significant to me that Adam and Eve recur almost like a motif throughout the collection. Why is that? Because they are the first humans and their struggles represent our own? Because our understanding of their role in God's plan is so different from that of other Christians? Because they are always before us in our temple worship? Or because we are in some ways troubled by the gender implications of their story and feel the need to see it in more depth, to expand it, to tell it with a different emphasis?

There are a number of poems in which poets try to represent their faith, their testimonies. These are a special case in that they are the most difficult of all poems to write successfully. The inadequacy of language is at the heart of the problem, language being an imperfect medium with which to convey any experience, and particularly transcendental experience. The customary language we have for conveying personal testimony has been used so often that it has become clichéd. In our testimony meetings, it is one's presence that allows the spirit to convey one's convictions with power. When language stands in for the self, as it does in a poem, the usual language will not work in this way. In prayer, Moroni noted his weakness in writing: "for Lord thou hast made us mighty in word by faith, but thou hast not made us mighty in writing . . . . Thou hast also made our words powerful and great, even that we cannot write them; wherefore, when we write we behold our weakness, and stumble because of the placing of our words" (Ether 12:23, 25). It is our greatest challenge to find language, imagery, metaphor, rhetoric, and forms that can convey spiritual experience, spiritual truth. Attempting to write such a poem is a courageous and necessary act but very difficult to succeed at. Many of my own poems about the religious experiences most important to me have been identified by my most skilled readers as weaker than my other poems, vague or sentimental. They are the poems I've been told to omit from my collections as I've looked for publishers, but I leave them in because they are important to me. Like some of this anthology's poems that attempt to represent the transcendent, they can help us learn to better embody spiritual experience and truth in the poems

Fire in the Pasture

we will write in the future. And when they succeed, as many in this anthology do, they are of the highest order of poetry.

You may ask why I haven't identified specific poems that I find to be successful in this way. Partly it is because the anthology includes almost four hundred poems, and for each poem I mentioned, I would have to pass over ten other worthy poems. And partly it is to allow for individual taste and preference. Just as poets are individuals, so are readers, and each reader should get to discover the new country of each poem for himself or herself, without prejudice.

Tyler Chadwick has extended a huge effort in compiling and editing this anthology and is to be congratulated for the result. Like Richard H. Cracroft and Neal E. Lambert's *A Believing People: Literature of the Latter-day Saints* in 1974 and Eugene England and Dennis Clark's *Harvest: Contemporary Mormon Poems* in 1989, this collection is a pinnacle in the development of an enduring Mormon poetry worthy of the truths of the Gospel of Jesus Christ.

Works Cited

Justice, Donald. "Meters and Memory." *Twentieth-Century American Poetics: Poets on the Art of Poetry*. Eds. Dana Gioia, David Mason, and Meg Schoerke. Boston: McGraw Hill, 2004. 250–254. Print.

O'Connor, Flannery. "The Fiction Writer and His Country." *Mysteries and Manners*. Eds. Sally and Robert Fitzgerald. New York: Farrar, Straus & Giroux, 1961. 25–35. Print.

———. "Writing Short Stories." *Mysteries and Manners*. 87–106. Print.

Revell, Donald. *Invisible Green: Selected Prose*. Richmond, CA: Omnidawn, 2005. Print.

Fire in the Pasture
twenty-first century mormon poets

Burials

Pulling through Montana in the snow
we cling to the tail lights of the last car
blurring back into the darkness.

"Like the inside of a coffin," my father says,
as if knowing the exact shade the dead see,
lying stiff, frozen eyes peering up through closed lids—

he shifts in his seat, watches the road disappear,
thinks again of dying and the burials we've seen,
his father's simple reduction to ashes.

How small the urn, how light, for a man
that stood 6'3", carried a boy on his shoulders,
lived on trains as a youth, picked apples as a man.

This past summer, watching him thin
to disappearing, blurring out lines between lives,
my father trying to return pieces, fragments, time,

the body burning, the dark smells of crematoriums,
funeral homes, and pale faced lawyers.
Something merges, ends, and begins.

My father placing the ashes back into the air,
offerings to the skies, to the seas,
unaware how Buddhist he is at this moment,

how the faint sound of bagpipes echoes,
how the ashes fall catching light,
reflecting something back into the silence,

the dark birth of the sun coming into view.

Pointer

—a special type of variable that holds the address of another variable

Not the thing itself, but a hand gesturing to where it lies in memory,
like when we say *Hopper* and mean any room viewed from without,

any couple made distant by sulfur light and shadow, the angled turn
of bodies which do not to come face to face, but lean awkwardly on tables,

across keys, at the unopened window where night bends like a palm
under the weight of all that is impossible to touch. A numbered stall

out in the parking lot, in the lower levels of the tower by our building,
between the lines at the side of the road—and what they imply, this insistence

on *fire* and *exhaust,* how smoke rises to our lips. Even now, *ash* speaks to ash,
to the names of my father and his father, to what remains in the wind

and on the waves for days after an eruption, to the week we hid in our homes
after the fall of New York, the trees which break the frosted earth

awash in the color of salt, our hands caught between *lapwing* and *sorrow,*
between *iron vein* and *needle,* between *want* and want.

Conditional

Pray Mr. Babbage, if you put into the machine wrong figures, will the right answers come out?

if they ask for the sky **then** {
        promise only the preset shades of blue,
        do not suggest clouds, however wispy or well-proportioned,
        nor the effect of wind from the east,
        do not imply there will be green-winged birds of any sort,
        nor the dusty evidence of farms, burning fields, plumes of gray smoke
        echoed in the heavens, signatures of the dead or laid off,
        definitely no angels—no visions hovering secretly in corners,
        coded scripts, triggers for events not planned

        if there are to be stars **then**
            cast them as multiple instances of the same fiery eye,
        else
            stitch black thread over black thread till night gleams in absentia

} **else if** they wish for the earth **then** {
    while the world is not null {
            draw ink-black stones from the mountain side
            sketch the long gravel road home, curve after curve,
            or whatever you recall, trees and their forgettable leaves,
            the small burdens of sight

    }
}

Letter Fifty

Someone, I tell you, will remember us
if only by what remains in these letters
grown grey with dust, sunk into the shadow
and depths of boxes, shelves, and drawers.
These lines I meant to give you, if I had
but a place or a name to lay down beside my words.
If longing were enough. The shape of a heart,
or what it leaves. The curve of rain over an arm out
of a window. The sound of trains in the yard, in the fog,
outside the city where the hills rise into darkness.
What I glimpse through the streaked windshield
of my car in the last blows of a storm, before night
opens wide like a sudden view of white flowers
in a dark field. Someone will remember us,
the woman filling her glass in the river, the man
watching the horse drown in the waves.

The Art of Forgetting

How to swim, how to ride a bike—even how to voice
my own name in my mother's tongue, each sound
a hard and pitted salt plum I marry to my teeth,
but cannot break open.

Forgetting is in the blood, something gleaned
from my grandmother—her hate strong enough
to wipe clean the first two years of married life,
the loss of her world, my mother's birth.

When I wake this morning to the cloud-dim Taipei sky
and dress in that early light that filters in somehow
through a hundred shades of smog, it is hard to believe
it has been a year already in this home not quite home.

Here, at the gate of memory, I am not my grandmother
grown transparent with age, but rather some lost son come
in stranger's clothes, the air ripe with incense and ash.
I want to remember this year and the one yet to be.

They say that the muscles have memory, that the body recalls
any motion rehearsed over time. An old horse always returns.
Mile after mile, my body relearns Taiwan the hard way—I feel it
when I move, in the way my calves have hardened, in the scar

on my chest where my muscles split wide when a truck door opened
in front of my bike, in the callouses on my knees where I have knelt
every morning on the cement and tile floors and offered a prayer
full of fire and forgetting for someone come down to loosen my tongue,

to unlock that rusted door and let what beats within go free.

October Plush

This violet, on her way to winter months, waits
beside me at the crosswalk—

her deflated sleeves,

    her shivering waist, too skinny for that dress
so eager
    for every last
    hour of sun.

I cross, she stays.
I can't love one more dying thing.

God Almighty, might this violence
not follow me into the shadows of my home, of winter.

On a Photograph of a Farmer in Småland

There are plots of land he cannot tend.
His slender face turns to the camera, his eyes look aside.
Plots that don't belong to him. Wild things grow there.

His cupped hand is raised, his neck bends
with the seed bucket hanging from it. He's frozen mid-stride.
There are plots of land he cannot tend.

The flung seeds form an arch, descend
like a comet's tail against the pine forest's night—
land that doesn't belong to him. Wild things grow there.

Where's his eyebrowless glance resting if not the lens?
Maybe the ground where his father lies.
There are plots of land he cannot tend.

The tossed seeds hesitate in the air, suspend
themselves for a time, before seed and soil collide.
Not all land belongs to him. Wild things grow where

pine trees thicken, and pastures end,
where toadstools nod drowsy with their own poison inside.
There are plots of land he cannot tend,
that don't belong to him. Wild things grow there.

Chesapeake

Looking up at that vault from underwater
sunlight breaks into something not less than strings
of an instrument, but more liquid, and unstrung.
Waves lift and lower until the motion becomes the meaning.

Whether I now drift in the cloud-crossed sky or sea,
your sleeping body in the eon distance shrinks
to an after-ache. Memories—a stomach cramp.
Had there ever been a sea floor?

How long had I been hovering,
when the screams of children working sand
tolled me back to feel tongue
against the roof of my mouth?

I turn towards the place I left you
napping in Faulkner's drawl,
with your blushing kneecaps.
When I rise from the water,

my soul refills my body, as if
the soul needs something to weigh against.
There isn't a question whether I should find you
and love you: you can't know,

when you touch my wet ankles, how far
out I had been, how little I regretted losing you,
going back to the animal beginning where water
was water, not a metaphor for something else.

Thief in the Night

Look! at the sky—

a plundered flower shop,
its empty shelves and counters.

    Only the moon remains
like a shred of buttercup petal,

      and a handful of stars
like pollen scattered
           across the black floor.

Whose greed, my love, what longing?

House

You played father because you were a head
taller, your hair cut shorter. You'd pull rocks
out of the brook and imagine it was bread.
We'd pretend to bake flat stones like fish, pick
at the gray flesh, and sigh and smack our lips
using lower-pitched voices to sound old.
And when we got thirsty, we cupped and sipped
the mossy air till our lungs were full of cold.
When we first found that tree curved over the brook
hidden from the playground, its hollow little room,
our hair was lighter and smelled musky as wood
from playing house in that elm tree tomb.
The only beds we had were our sweaters,
laid out over the dirt. But you never slept.
You were too anxious about raiding meadows
for the sugar buds of stinging nettles.
We never thought we'd find our old selves in the river's
mirrors. The sky broke through in some places
like rumors of adulthood, with sun slivers
in the dark sieve of branches. We'd trace
the passage of time by the growing stillness
out on the playground. When was the last day
our mother called us out into the silence,
onto the pavement, into the open sky—
a blank canvas, like an empty sheet
we would have to spend the rest of our lives
filling until it covers us once again like trees,
like the roil of a brook, the murmur of hives?

Moose Remembered

This was when we were renting on the west side of town between the Clean Spot
    Laundromat and the red brick house of the mechanic with the ratty goatee
and AC/DC T-shirt who raised hell on Saturday mornings and sent his wife
    and small blond son running out the front door like refugees to the cop cruiser
already at the curb. This was when I was compensating full-time for the little
    I could give you and our baby girl, so early one Saturday morning as you slept
I trapped her in a blanket and carried her out on the driveway to watch a yearling
    moose that had wandered into town from the Teton Basin. Its hide was tacky
brown like an old leather sofa. With a connoisseur's fastidiousness, it nibbled
    from the lilac hedge barricades around La Jolla Apartments. Then the usual
cop car arrived and paused and started shooing the young moose down the road
    with its siren. I carried our girl in her white blanket cocoon around the corner
of the house next door for a better look, and ice drenched my guts when we ran
    into the moose coming back across the mechanic's dandelion-crazed lawn.
I lurched for the sanctuary of the garage, thinking of how I'd killed our child with
    good intentions, when a blast of the cop's siren spooked the moose into the street,
so it skidded on the pebbly asphalt and slammed to the ground with a sickening thud.
    This was everything you missed. Except how the moose loped off like a big
awkward kid down the alley under the pink and aquamarine pulse of The Holiday
    Theater's neon arrow, chased by the cruiser, how I stood in the driveway with
our baby girl and watched the mechanic and his wife and son come out and stand
    and watch, and how we looked at each other, said nothing about how even
though we'd just witnessed a monumental ruckus, things were quieter
    than they'd been in our neighborhood on a Saturday morning for a long time.

The Transient Rains of April Thirteenth

If nothing else, I have this: I once saved a girl's life. Five years back, before our
son was
born, I was walking a street that had grown as familiar as your pulse. January.
Twenty below.
Chestnut trees, stripped of their torches, hardened in the fragile air. Crabapples
blackened satchels of shriveled fruit. One hundred and one crows whetted their
feathers on the
bloodless sky. She wore frayed pajamas: purple stripes. Her hair bristled like
the heart of winter. Her bare feet sloped down driveway frost to the street.
When she raised
her arms to me, I lifted the bundled cornstalks of her bones and took her to
the nearest house. You carry a stranger's child the way you would deliver a pillar
of carved glass. The way you carry the angel fresco dislodged from the cathedral
arch of
your remaining days. I knocked on a screen door. An older girl answered,
examined us through
the ragbag curtain of her bangs. Her brown T-shirt bore a jaguar face with
emerald eyes. "That's ours," she said, pushing the door open. Then wump-wump-
wump. The mother's frantic stampede down the stairs, her face an earthquake,
and her arms
gathering the loose laundry of her daughter's soul to her breast. I walked away,
having learned
something I would realize the day I stood outside for the first time with our
newborn son to taste the glorious rain-gusts of spring: the faces of horror and
ecstasy
are the same. Later someone told me a black sickness had stung the girl's mother
the previous October—stage four cancer was the offhand report. Now her face
is the only thing I see, now that the earth has grown as unfamiliar as your pulse,
and I swing
our baby boy in the deadly basket of my arms under April's unruly caravan of
clouds, each
boisterous plume a mad crusade, the chill of fresh drops rallying blood in our skin.
I see the way she charged the threshold of her home, snatched her golden
hatchling from my
outstretched arms, and slammed the door as if I were not a hero but a terrible
disease.

Daughters and Geese

Only at 5:17 a.m.
could my wife's nursing
our daughter in bed next to me
sound exactly like

Canada geese banking hard
against the moon over the thin
aluminum roofs of the campers
at the Rainbow Lake R.V. Park

off Highway 20. In V-formation,
they batter the sky over
the railroad bridge at
the Jefferson County line, and her

sweet pucker drinks in
the room's blue darkness.
Words alone fail: *suckle, sip*.
She guzzles every future October

breeze whole hog. Her lips
are sugared around with a crust
of constellations and bright plunging
meteorites. Classic white cheeks,

body a barred dark chocolate brown,
feet the color of webbed shadows
with a greenish cast, eyes cut
crescents of midnight, preening

away sleek impossibilities. They seek
the natal home in bulrushes
and cord grass. Her sketchy
swallowing summons the dawn wind.

To listen is to be called insatiable
to an endless supper of names:
Linnaeus, Yahweh, *Branta
canadensis occidentalis*. To be

where the silent curved roar of
the lesser covert feathers divides the air
high above Nova Scotia, where
the wet colostrum-rich seal

kisses the saturated red sand
of the areola, at that estuarine lull
where the salt tide first tips
its tongue to the freshwater current.

Jerusalem Artichoke

After visiting The Religious Reflection Room in the Detroit Metro Airport

In The Squatter's Pub Brewery, two pilots
    (I hope not mine) quaff beer
and devour Black and Bleu Rocket Wraps.
    The label on the Odwalla's bottle
from which I sip green puree says I have
    swallowed Jerusalem artichoke,
a plant that, contrary to what its name
    might suggest, is not an artichoke
and not from Jerusalem. This is
    the equation of life: Nothing is what
it says it is. Despite the high price,
    somehow this is healthy. The Italian,
girasole, means "sunflower."
    After Samuel de Champlain dispatched
shiploads of the bundled tubers
    from Cape Cod to France, people
added "sunroot" and "earth apple"
    to the legend. What is prayer but
a commerce of discoveries? When
    is misunderstanding a pilgrimage?
Some days, the greatest risk
    can be to sit and stare
at the intoxicating flight of daylight
    through two glasses of amber.
This is, after all, the quest of the new world.
    To drink the strange. To explore
without leaving. To grow into the myth
    of one's name and, having exiled
the nomad eye, make a holy city of the heart.

Inch

Three daughters harvest handfuls of inchworms
in the back yard where their mother played as
a girl. Each slim green acrobat twists, squirms,
and rappels down its fine silver essence
through the clean risk of air to be cupped in
hands, clapped in storage jars of criss-cross grass,
the clear lids of Press 'N' Seal cellophane
pierced with fork holes. I speed with it all past
the Dansville Foster-Wheeler plant, Cuba
Coachlight Motel, and Arkport's Hurlbut House,
the medieval hills of Pennsylvania
and New York scrolling along faceless hours
of state highway that link my then to now.
And the world is different where I go.

And the world is different where I go
past the township of Friendship, toward Challenge,
miles from Desire and Panic. The hot orange
flare of oriole speed zigzags solo
between trees split with bronze gashes of sun.
Pale summer dapples ponds with a pollen
as this as mist. Lily pads worship light.
This is the farthest off I have felt—right
now—and the closest I have come by far.
Pinpoint gnats of citrus fire wheel and spar.
The mind snags sticky filaments. The land
clutches the same daylight that fills the jar.
I spool the emptiness around a strand
of soul. There is little we understand.

Of soul, there is little we understand
or parcel out, collect in increments,
the intervals of dusk, glide and descent.
You envision the Seneca crop planned
to perfection here like a loose grid of
stars. The Cornplanter families, one half
in slack semicircles, busily scraped

the bark from red shoots to brew emetics.
The other half stared and traced the complex
theorems of random time and space that would
one evening find spoons of beveled dogwood
and the warped shafts of handmade arrows trapped
in the hard gray mud of love's fossil fern
where thoughts like cloud turrets form and reform.

Where thoughts like cloud turrets form and reform,
noon slants through the college café windows.
The room reels like a stock market forum.
A decade before he drives all those slow
miles to restart his life—a caravan
of native narratives interwoven
with the glimmering tableaux of their three
young girls scampering, arms upraised, to claim
chartreuse worms descending on light beams—
he sits near her and says nothing when she
breaks into his thoughts and life with a word.
He rises, wishes later he'd said more.
They leave. They meet again. Children follow.
The infinite starts and stops with hello.

The infinite starts and stops with hello.
The manner of birth confirms this to them.
First girl: born late on the Susquehanna;
tears the nipple from her mother's full breast;
December moon and skin jaundice yellow;
stork bites; head of hair a razzmatazz flame;
a brusque nurse who stays past her shift, and a
twenty-two hour battle with little rest.
The rictus of pleasure and smile of pain
trade places after hours. Laugh becomes scream.
Dark day and white night cycle in sun-stain-
and-star-smeared circuits of dawn-soaked streams
of curtains too tattered for them to rend.
Beginning begins beginning to end.

Beginning begins beginning. To end
is to deny the circle's open source.
Second girl: a pixie stalk of wheat-blond
that sprouts from the arid banks of the south

fork of the Teton. Sidesteps chance death twice.
One afternoon, the weekend of the Fourth,
north of the township of Sempronius,
he bolts toward the hummingbird feeder poles
across a lakeside cabin's deck and yanks
her back before she falls into a creek's
rocky ravine. Later, she survives an
occluded lung pipe, convalesces on
cherry popsicle sighs and gravel moans
just as ending draws the last starting line.

Just as ending draws the last starting line
another strand ravels out like the first
two. Third girl: August-born, like her mother
and sister, a gaze of retrospection,
wide-eyed and sublime, drama unrehearsed.
She keeps them both searching forward rather
than back—atonal carousel laughter
and calliope grins and three stitches
laced up across a slender slash that rips
open her temple like delicate lips
promising a kiss fourteen years after.
At Tubman's grave, the camera catches
her first steps. On moss-mad stone snail trails sketch
a glinting line or circle, which is which?

A glinting line or circle which is, which
was, and which will be intersects the arc
of days upstate near the Erie Canal
and the home of Susan B. Anthony.
The girl who will one day chase a spry batch
of girls around her house and city park
loves a terrier named Duke and enrolls
in after-school ballet, earns mad money
waitressing summers at The Bluewater.
When asked for a portrait of love and home,
she sits a little more erect, recalls
the stuffed bear from her dad, how he pulled her
in a sled after a lakefront snowfall.
The moment remains more timeless than time.

Fire in the Pasture

The moment remains more timeless than time,
untraceable like 1969,
when his folks bring him, as a newborn, back
from San Francisco General. Zodiac
Killer stabs a cabby. A maverick mutt,
Tasha, all morning and night, barks and trots
above their cheap crackerbox apartment.
He remembers the folklore glamor of
Buffalo Springfield's bassist getting bent
into a hood ornament as one half
of a head-on motorbike-and-bus crash.
It takes ten years after graduation
for life to find him in another town
that delivers forever in a flash.

That delivers forever in a flash.
This extends minutes to millennia.
First night alone, after the mania
of the reception, a drunk guest bangs harsh
encores of "Chopsticks" in a no-host bar
downstairs at The Sherwood Inn. It's not far
to the pier where they huddle in the gray
shriek of a November gale. They are kids
wrapped in college sweatshirts and hope that they
can live off whatever brummagem love
they might dump in handfuls under the lid
of a souvenir mug on a back shelf
with orphan dice, thumbtacks, and spare changes.
Earth forms as much as it rearranges.

Earth forms as much as it rearranges
us. Each lakeside autumn tree exchanges
the cutthroat blaze of monarch drapery
for a skeleton of stripped ebony.
The buzzsaw string quartets of cicadas
drown the spluttering cough of an outboard.
Seagulls grapple. Red deer ascend above
the corn. Boats get stored in dry dock. A hard
plane of gray-green ice mars the shore. It is
the blue heron's basso lament that moves
locals to mourn the influx of resort

kitsch. Headstones bloom. Cafés fold. As strange as
the passage of days, the long age cuts short
the connection between us, whose range runs.

The connection between us, whose range runs
to the blind limit of sense, marks milestones
on the stretched strand of light: The Hofbräuhaus;
Lindisfarne; Aran; Woody's Island; close
to breaking past Rock Springs; Promontory;
Balanced Rock; Moab; no guts, no glory
in Sturgis; lost in Blyth, if nothing else;
thunder and woodchucks at Buttermilk Falls;
Stonehenge's blue sun-scoured palms; the Hub;
the grassy stone bowl of Old Sarum; dab
of Belgium; gig in Nagoya; beebalm
at Yellow Creek; between commitments at Bear
Lake; sunrise in Honduras sends a psalm
head to tail, the span of cosmic measure.

Head to tail, the span of cosmic measure,
plots my observations now where I'm found.
I believe there's no isolation more
exquisite than that which courses around
Fairman's Family Laundromat tonight.
A lone girl smokes and sits cross-legged in
parking space A18, her broken pane
hairstyle bleached the frightening opal-white
of summer lightning. Though I would say that
she has buckled Fate's studded dog collar
around herself, I know we both spin out
of our bellies the frailest lifelines, our
hands cupped for the curious blood of what
we're caught in as prisoner and treasure.

We're caught in, as prisoner and treasure,
this escape and release. A memory: Cheyenne.
Midday, we pulled off to gas up the car
at a truck stop whose name I've forgotten.
A smog of slate rain draped saturated
murals on the ranks of boxcars, their mustard
broadsides spangled in angry comic strip
swarms of pink-orange graffiti from Rocky Top

to Los Angeles. The wheels clanked and screeched
in a way that said *Gather* and *Always*
move on—not in light years but by the inch.
And pause often en route to clear the way
for roadblocks, and for visions and lunch where
three daughters harvest handfuls of inchworms.

Three daughters harvest handfuls of inchworms,
and the world is different. Where I go,
of soul, there is little we understand.
Where thoughts like cloud turrets form and reform,
the infinite starts and stops with hello.
Beginning begins, beginning to end,
just as ending draws the last starting line,
a glinting line or circle. Which is which?
The moment remains more timeless than time
that delivers forever in a flash.
Earth forms as much as it rearranges
the connection between us, whose range runs
head to tail, the span of cosmic measure
we're caught in as prisoner and treasure.

Reliquary

Moving day approaches
The accumulated things of the garage,
        the closets, the basement, under the bed
        even the back of my bottom drawer
Begin to clutter my thoughts too

And moving should be a cleansing ritual
A time to contemplate household objects,
        to purge those not worthy of boxes or bubble wrap,
Making of them an offering to the thrift store
        perhaps or the landfill

But some things I just can't throw away
        gaudy tole-painted Halloween decorations,
        old quilts too shabby it seems even for dogs,
Considering this trash, I entertain the thought
        that some dead ancestor has intervened

Someone who had a body and wants it back;
        perhaps only this kitsch remains from
A houseful of matter organized in the form of
porcelain saucers and cable-knit sweaters and
        a kitchen table of quarter-sawn oak

Someone animated by post-mortal information
A secret about what it means to
        put on this flesh, to exercise dominion
        over even the most inconsequential clod of dirt
A nothing that exerts its own gravitational pull

Or maybe the knowledge that her spirit
        also gave this matter life
Painted it by hand; displayed it every October for years
            this configuration not eligible for resurrection
Making me remember the incorruption to come

Prayer

It was picture day. Me: a first grader. I was all ready.
Hair combed. Shirt tucked in tight. Tie clipped on.
Mom's orders were clear:
    No getting dirty or messing up my hair
    No riding my bike. No playing in the sandpile.
    No playing outside at all.

Those were all the things, especially being forbidden,
I needed to do that day. I had already learned about
The spirit of the law; how it lets us forget the inconvenient parts
    and mostly obey.
So I went to the playhouse, a shed in the backyard,
    furnished with a child-sized pantry, table, chair.

It began to rain consequences:
The things you don't plan for, but choose.
Afraid, hair and clothes already soaked in my mind,
    I said a prayer.
Not a rain prayer I had heard before, not the asking or
    thanking of desert people for moisture.

It was the prayer now most familiar to me:
Let me not bear the bad thing I deserve.

The rain stopped. It stopped abruptly.
The thought "coincidence" might have occurred to an adult,
    logical, sterile-minded.
That adult might have offered tepid thanks:
    "if You did that for me, I am grateful,"
    as a scientific explanation fretted in the mind's back room.

Not me. I knew I had seen the finger of the Lord.
Despite all those farmers' pleas—for me—He stopped that deluge.
I walked across the backyard and inside,
My eyes, like small stones, burned by that revelation.

Sisyphus

The escalator broken again
We climb the adjacent stairs
In wingtips and houndstooth slacks.
I peer into the guts of the silent machine.
It is always the same guy,
Crouched over, sweat on his face,
Wielding a flashlight and cursing,
Pushing the same stubborn rock
Up the same hill. Maybe
It wouldn't be that bad;
With any luck, your hill has some trees,
A view of a lake. A breeze
kicks up and you suck your lungs
full of mountain air. Your arms
have grown strong and the rock
in your hands feels heavy,
satisfying. It is permanent.
Its weight reminds you of its path
Down the face of the ridge,
Rolling all the way to your feet.
It could be a sculpture.
There is already one in there, probably,
Waiting for the right set of hands.
Over lunch you wonder why
The stone needs pushing anyway
And you notice it is almost one o'clock
And you need to get pushing again
If you're going to beat the traffic tonight
And you feel your hands reaching for the flashlight,
Sweat on your face—cursing the escalator.

Ripple Rock

This is where my mind wanders,
Behind this desk, bathed in soft
Monitor light. This is where
I levitate, oscillate, and glide
On five plastic wheels, a pneumatic column,
Lumbar support and everything.
This is where I pour yesterday's lukewarm
Water bottle on my mother-in-law's tongue.
This is where I push buttons
And pile up symbols and consider
The crust of the earth.
This is where my mind
Wanders: How it is thin,
Not a walnut shell or even a cantaloupe rind
But an apple peel,
Three to five miles thick under
Oceans, continents, under twenty-five,
Thin and pregnant and implacable,
Always sending up new mountains,
Earthquakes and volcanoes,
Always pulling high places down.
This is where I concentrate.
Maybe I'm reading something
Or taking a call. I reach
For the rock on the edge
Of my desk, deep red,
The size of a cheap paperback,
Something I picked up last summer
Hiking a shale bowl with my head down,
A bucktoothed puzzle piece, a million
Particles of dust that came to rest
On the floor of an ancient sea.
My hand runs over the ripples
And shallow waves pull me back.

UTopia

Have you ever heard
of a flawless paradise?
Who would tell about it?
There's not much of a story there:
"Life's Perfect, The End."

As it turns out,
you have to live in heaven for a while
before you see what's wrong with it;
before the angel with the flaming sword
swoops down and wrecks your fun.

So, take a place like UTopia,
and throw in a snake.
But don't stop there; add an apple,
a bursting fountain,
heathens, women, and Pandora's Box.

The World's Iagos
all stuffed inside one big bubble.
Shake it around 'til
each one's mad; bared teeth and claws out,
then let them all loose.

Take Care of Your Soul—It's Flapping in the Breeze

My next-door neighbor's going to hell.
I know because his soul
has hung on his clothesline since 1982.

To me, it's like a warning sign:
"Beware of Dog"
but slightly more dangerous because souls are involved.

If he ever does hang up a sign
it should probably say:
"Beware of Vicious Un-souled Man!"

I'm certain it would be better if others could recognize him
as the crafty and elusive man that he is, but
most people ignore his abandoned soul.

One of these days, though, I'll shake it out, and wash it,
then leave it ironed, starched white, and folded on his porch,
just in case he's forgotten about it.

Question about a Sinner

If a sinner falls in the forest, and no one is around, does he make a sound?

If he drives himself there in his truck at night and hikes eight snowy miles to his favorite spot, does he take the time to smoke before pulling out his gun?

If the gun is pointed at his temple, does he say a prayer out loud, or even a small one in his head, or has he already decided that he can't ever be forgiven?

When the shot reverberates, do the animals start or do they all bow their heads and blink away tears as if to say, "Amen. Amen."

When the man doesn't die, but falls on the snow, does he lie peacefully waiting for sweet redemption or does he spread his sins further by squirming and flinging them throughout the forest?

Then, when white snow falls and covers the man, and covers the blood and the trees, can it finally wash away his sins? Can a sinner be forgiven if we refuse to offer him the forgiveness he was looking for?

If another man finds the truck covered in snow, and dogs sniff out the cold tracks, is the dead-black sinner left where he chose to rest or is he taken to a place we know to be better? And because he is black we know every wrong thing that he did, so does he go to hell?

Or, if the man pays his penance and stays under those trees for a summer, a winter, a summer, and the earth swallows his stains, and wildflowers grow up through his time-whitened skull, and dragonflies nap on his ribs, is that God's way of saying that there is mercy enough even for the sinner?

Desert Sheep-herding in the Winter

Thirty coyotes will draw even the best dog
away from his flock.
I stand at the top of the bluff and watch.
Further, further, he chases coyotes. One then another.
Falling prey to their tricks
despite my calls.

Two hundred sheep under juniper scrub
interrupt thin streams of rain with breathy clouds.

I've seen this happen once before, with my grandpa,
but this time I choose not to watch as the wild pack
entices my best dog, of fifteen years, away.
I already know what will happen—he'll fall, exhausted.
So I train my ear on anything else but his yelps.
There. Above the ravine, a magpie calls through the rain.

Our Only Summer in Black Earth, Wisconsin

It was all skinned knees.
The garden mound was a leaning
tower, a hill for just one warrior,
or we wrestled, hungry among the acorns
and mushrooms, wet in the mosquito night.
We sprawled and knew the porch
was a diving board to the grass.

Our olive skin
slept for sunrise and hide-n-go seek,
harbored *Where the Wild Things Are* yearning
for forest monsters, untied shoelaces,
undiscovered streams.

We fed on the blue fire of moonlight,
the gutsy tackling under the stars.
When the red humidity shook,
we dreamt of tombstones, the earth's
cavities filling themselves with the wind and law.

Then
it was as easy as falling off a bike.
Now it is only thinking
about a lost house, counting each brick of it
one at a time, counting
for a moment
beautiful stained shirts.

Joseph Smith

After Robert Hayden

After the pearl shines in the last country,
a ball of spindles, an iron rod,
a dove fashioned from gold plates
belonging to me like skin, free as sky,
after it brightens the unlit corners; after it is banners,
sun, tsunami, grand canyon, undercurrent;
after it sears the antipodes and septentrion;
after it is more than two missionaries
walking from door to door: a vessel, a seer,
a primary schoolboy, a wrestler jailed
in the Missouri reeds, tarred, seeing salt
in distant mountains, in handcarts, in Zion,
a mystic steeped in knowledge and burden,
a translator shall speak at the bar,
and not with Roman toga, not with princes
and medals and crisping pins,
but with Jesus' arms far extending,
his children carrying the asp and lion,
New Jerusalem will start to gleam.

Dear Father, Love, Abish

All those harvests and not a shudder
from you as you rambled
through markets, stopped at wells,
marking the level of water
the way a mason judges stone.
How did we keep
that frightening joy inside?
How did we plug up
the lightning of your vision
when you perceived the tumble
of a moved mountain,
the sip of new wine, or that pillar
of fire purging the floor?

Somehow we said nothing
and still believed, remained silent
as the desert before rain,
closed our mouths so hard
not even a child or neighbor
could tease out our secrets

                              and then
the enemy came with your smile
peppered about his lips, his phrases
after the manner of your tongue,
his tradition and your dogma
bending the crown of the king.
Afterwards I ran with a rising banner
from door to door, and for once flowed
like a waterfall in all its miracle
and danger. How unleashed my mind,
how untethered my lungs—
each breath piling high and clear,
my legs roiling like years
in their speed and astonishment.
This burden's undoing was ice
breaking or a tower about to collapse.

Smoke and steam galloped from my mouth—
people shouted, "King Lamoni and the Queen,"
the Nephite servant simply lay there.

When I came to
your door, you embraced me,
called for Mother, wept.
How your jaw eased a little,
how your shoulders released,
how your beard bristled,
shimmering like the tip of a sword,
your voice gentle but urging,
"Speak."

Swollen

In this soul-side of vision, we sink down,
before and away from the tinsel-tied masses,
lying side by side as if married by sepulcher,
limp in our linen and wrapped
in my long train. Servants hover above us
like the old tending their gardens, cambered
and writhing, then fall through vaulted light
like the husk and sway of cornstalks
already yellow from the harvest, plucked
by the autumn sun. You are the rampart

taking the tide, a vine extending reach,
the diaphanous spirit body more throne-like
in this breach of palette and winter, feeling
once more the range of mountain in its
variety, the steep grade of ascent,
the sweet water nestled in the highlands.
We are ransacked fortification
and first-time chariot, feeling the crumble
of stone and the lava in rock, whirring
like the cymbals of ceremony in this fissure
of firmament and earth, shell and essence.

It is this dying I love, this unreeling,
this hurling rapprochement in a synagogue
of blue. In his voice comes *shofar,*
cornet, flute, *qeren.* In his presence
arises the cypress and cedar, falcon
and dove. His wear is threshed wool
and pure cotton, silk and ash.
But it's his touch that takes the blood
of longing, our severs and cuts, both
given and taken, become his scarlet
in this ineffable dream or vision
lifting us higher than the song of birds
as they dip and soar
knowing what it means to fly.

Fire in the Pasture

Triptych

Journeying

The other nine disciples always knew
what it meant to rise. Treading and treading,
I stumble through the rain, its droplets
drumming me down into a wooded ravine
as the earth bubbles both gurgle and slush.
Clouds stroll to music I can almost hear.
They are like children who won't look away
while I pause for murky footholds

and unknown chords. There are inns
distant in the warming air,
annunciation I have yet to learn about.
Since my descent I am bound
not to let earth press me in its shape
regarding who the smiter is
and who is smitten again. I delay
for the soft trill in brooks, imagine
the running gasp from the coyote's cry.

My children believed it would happen
this way. Perhaps my wife too
as she crossed the last meadow and slipped
beyond herself into bluff and cliff.
Friends feigned to know
what cinders were sure to appear,
what contemplation might burn down
to smolder. The rest tried to conjure
a taunt within my wish to stay alive.
Still, mortal bruises matter
in this story of wanderers and spoiled,

especially when I pull a few through narrows
and hunker with others between the rocks.
I desire soon the horizon that stops.
Its ruby planted within the whisper

of my head. But for tonight I'll sleep
under the aching juniper, its wood a hard
splinter into kindling and logs.
Somewhere inside me is a hidden match,
anxious for the strike fast as a child's eye:
a glimmer for this enduring flesh.

—————————— ————————— —————————

Sorrow for the Sins of the World

never ends, never stops its roll, its drench,
its huff and odd lure, the arc falls at night
back to the tinder of dry earth,
slicks each July scorching,
delves into the strongest, translated flesh.
It is the summons appearing
when what was found becomes lost,
a drowning month after month,
voices and merit upended, wallowing,
crushed, a spillage from deserts
like the mad rush of machine guns, then froth
dripping and dripping. It motors out of
lava stone into cold springs, onto highways,
through the center of plains
and always hasting down the middle
of back roads, rarely clamping on the brakes,
for this dirge won't slow down, not even clowns
and priests can depart from this roistering,
this keening, this King Lear hovel
within and without—
an umbilical cord partially cut.
                                    Again,
the city siren sticks,
shrieks even when time whimpers
at night or when dreams drive it all inward,
isolation amidst momentary celebration
grows deeper, no need to ferret out
what covers then splits the newest leaf

when it hankers after something dry as straw,
when this water falls and returns
during the nearest failed grasp.
The martyr's image re-appears,
more talking-heads search for it
under the next camel's hump,
an overdose of regurgitating blame,
exhaustion laced through last year's surge,
tomorrow's masses tied to its
choking collar—someone's, anyone's
tears sliding through the void of bankruptcy,
this pair of knees ready to break.

———————— ———————— ————————

Caught Up

Word buckler, chary tribe,
inured lamb,

stumped in your cinderblock den, you attempt
to draw up my life—the puns latent

in your knuckles, your shoulders bowed
in perpetual commencement,

though we have never met
at the crossroad of years, you will not

dispense with wondering about the unknown
mountains. Since your teenage grief,

you've heard anecdotes dismounting
the disappearances from cars and vans,

the story twisters passed from cousin
to mother-in-law and back through the lattice

of a friend of a friend of a friend
whose name has been forgotten.

You'd ask, "What are they doing now?"
yet querying through to the speculative,

for you, is another name for foolish.
You want to know and don't want to know,

you are repelled and attracted
by the old natter, the unhatched myth. Yet

I want you to recognize me
even in the surgical winter, a prison

newly rent, this pit recast into a bare-boned
sanctuary. Yes, I've shadowed by

you and your kind, worn something akin
to your collars, a meandering trail

of nighttime water, another fleeing
forebear charged with new blood,

now firm with the yearly weather
of disguising and allaying,

confirming and bearing out
in due course the unadorned into the cloud

and downpour of unspeakable things.
Will you meet us there too?

Beholding the basins and farms,
ridgetop of the vineyard's last stand,

waiting for rending and uplift,
the gusts of ocean, breath and fire.

Wayne

Wayne has an all white trailer
with two paint buckets beneath,
    always one white
    always one black
and every Monday, Wayne is on the roof,
his hot metal canvas, blanking with one brush
then swiping in messages with the black,
some light reading for birds, satellites
like:
    "Spy planes, You rape the Heavens!"
    "End Imminent—Retreat to Space!"
    "I'm waiting for Further Instructions."

I'm his best social worker he tells me
as he spreads out his favorite nude pictures
on the coffee table for me to peruse,
as I help him edit letters to Billy Graham and the Pope.
    "Dear Catholic Tribe,"
because he says we're all in tribes
and I ask him what tribe he's in
    but he makes a wilting face
puts away his paper 'women'
    "you know better"
he says over and over from the bathroom
until I leave.

Wayne eats cold corn from cans
    and tells me true love used to exist
    but the chemicals in soda are killing it
    and one day the leaders of the cities
    will murder the kids with little golden fish hooks
    which They will put in the cafeteria cookies
    and Wayne says he was with a woman once
    but she didn't stay.

Wayne spends four days drawing 600 pages
    of ambulances

with sides painted for different states
to help calm the panicky feeling of being in ambulances.
Happy alligators for Florida,
rain drops for Washington.
Ambulances shaped like a puppy for kids,
an angel for Christians and a heart
for any hospital bound newly-weds.

Wayne is so happy he has to hug himself
    to hold himself in.

One day, I stash a tape recorder
    because no one believes in Wayne.
And he talks and talks about where They've hidden Jesus
and the government's plan to magnetize us
and how they shot down Hale-Bopp
because They are afraid of comets,
which he explains are just whales
drifting through a different ocean
    and the tape clicks.
Wayne, Wayne has a look so broken
he's so betrayed, Wayne, but he keeps it calm:
    "you, oh, not you"
    "I never expected *you'd* wear a wire."

Months turn.
Wayne won't see me
    until one clear night
he yells at me coming down the road
and pulling me up to his message center
    he points to the sky
    "See? Do you see?"
and Wayne stops, eyes shut and straining
and then up, his finger stabbing deep into the black
    "They'll never shoot them down again!"
    "I speak to the comets now!"

Return

for Jan Grzebski, awake after a 16-year coma

What world of choice now.
Gone the walls, the drab komunista goods,
more surprising than to wake up
in your father's body.

You marvel at *a life without rations*
as you set teeth to meat every evening.
You tell us: *the world is prettier now*
and you point out where colors weren't.

But you are less of a miracle
than your wife's silent diligence,
every hour shifting your wax body.
Two decades of just in case.

5,846 times
the world spun around your sleep.
Tonight you'll fear to slumber
convinced this is some Brigadoon day.

For you hear the ocean call
to return, a yawn you can't let take you,
the dope of your hibernation singing
in marrows and corners of your frame.

You wonder if Lazarus ever regretted,
as much as he loved Mary and Martha,
stole away from the revelers, down to the tomb
to breathe in his graveclothes, close his eyes.

Expiration Dates

There was a peeling little grocery on the corner of Rice Lake
where my brother worked between fifteen and seventeen.

A nothing much happens place in a town too big to know anyone.
Robbed once, and solved and nothing even close to scandal.

Sometimes the owner's son would smoke pot behind the dumpster,
and sometimes they could just open and eat whatever they wanted.

And sometimes on simmering nights when the bullfrogs sang that one lonely note,
and the wind was interested elsewhere; they'd close early, running out back with bats

to play baseball with the spoiled fruit, erupting everything over each other.
They'd run, leap into the lake, clothes and all, to swim off pulp and sap and stick.

He said he'd never felt forever more. No moon to click across the sky,
stars as fixed and certain as ever. Nothing but an endless feeling.

The day my brother quit, two weeks before his birthday,
he helped an old man into the store, leaving his rheumatic wife in the Caddy.

The old man bought usuals except milk buying two gallons instead of just one,
the weight stuttering his breath every step my brother helped him back to the car.

The old man handed the gallons to his wife who put them in her lap, leaning over
to smile and wave a shaking hand at my brother as he closed the door.

But when the needle moved to "D" the old man's face seized and his limbs
lashed out against the steering wheel, wipers and blinkers, then the accelerator.

All eight cylinders reared up, and the Caddy shot across the empty stalls
into the only thing in its way, the thick brick walls of Dean's Hardware.

The sound bounced like thunder over the lake. Allen said it was so quick
he was standing there his hand out, not finished waving.

Reality caught up to him running. All he could see was milk
where it had exploded and splashed against the windshield and windows.

But when he was closer he could see pink spots
streaking through the white windshield and oily smoke of the engine.

The door opened, the old man tumbled out like a wet bag of groceries.
The old lady dripping and broken, whiplashed; the whole inside sopped in milk.

This he told me, bereft of meaning, so I tried to make life beautiful, ordered, saying:
all that milk we're given as babies, it's safe somewhere within us, the real life liquid.

But he said: While everyone was outside, I was in the cooler, with a bat,
smashing every gallon with my birthday on it.

Contingency #4: White Out

If you get snowed in, deep locked into your home,
so long the food runs out,
I suggest peeling the walls to find the mice,
or scouring the attics for nests, for beehives.
And when those are gone, even the cold bodies
of ants which taste like raw tabouli,
and you've dug through the crevices, the cushions,
maybe even boiled your leather jacket,
turn next to the wood.
Try the well traveled.
Sauté the banisters, rich with the proteins
of years of hands and arms,
it will taste like strangers and parts of you
which will warm like comfort food.
After the walkways, after the desks and brooms,
save the dining table for last.
And scrape at its surface softly, like a butter dish,
years of meals shared sunk into its lumber.
Waiting for you like a switchboard of memories.

Purpose

My brother builds doors,
sets jambs to lintels.
He can tell by the heft of a doorknob

whether hollow-, stave-, or solid-core.
He tells me where we could kick through,
the kinds of pressure needed to get inside a home.

Odd to see a door apart, freestanding
in the middle of the warehouse.
It defines nothing, leads nowhere.

I ask has he ever stepped through,
he says *not ever, too spooky . . .*
they tell me a guy vanished like he never lived

Sure, it's whisper-talk and voodoo. Still . . .
walls trap a universe, put an edge on space,
but doors are a wormhole, they're built to be.

Craig says *build is a secular way to say conjure.*
Things can't help fulfill their creation.
I don't trust old train tracks, empty riverbeds.

But one night, the world seemed too much
a predictable machine, so I stole into the warehouse,
found an unroomed door and knocked:

Ave verum corpus

This is what I want to understand, this
contemplate: drinking bitterness,

but sweetness nonetheless in the midst.
A branch of almond breaks into flower and leaf.

I remember now the mystery
of incarnation, let him take me,

let him lift me up, let him
consume me for those hours,

let light fall there, and then the dark,
let his smoke fill my mouth and hair,

let him be the god for me:
I learnt the true god, true body,

at his hands: behold! the Christ lifted up
and lain down, tenderly washed

by a woman's hair, with green oils anointed
in their ripe perfumes, rosemary and cloves

folded into his winding sheets; and,
upon rising, discovering his absence

again and again in the centuries,
the callas waiting as if to hear once more

his call; a saving grief, the life in a world
going on, with and without him.

Autumn Sutra

I wanted a leaner, a sparer style.

I wanted birds to be able to fly
through the branches
after the pruning.

In a chastened season,
why my longing,
appearing everywhere?

> on the walk, fallen
>   crabapples smear of ochre
>   crushed under heel

Conundrum to be solved by *techné*,
I thought, though perhaps

I loomed larger:
I wanted to be the altar,
not to kneel there.

Where No One Follows

...because of the nostalgia for dreams...
—Garcia Marquez

Because the bed is crowded with more and more children,
    and the ghosts and angels of their nightclothes are wound
      around and around my arms and hands,
And the press of my husband's longings chokes the river of sleep,
    and no bed is wide enough for the storm of sleep thought,
      and the storm floods the banks which are the walls
Of a room too small for the rage of the river: therefore,
    I wake to a house of walls dissolving in the rush
      of the river where no one follows me, where
I walk alone beside the wide river, and since there are
    no shoes light enough for feet of a woman walking
      to the river alone, and the terrible and
The sorrowful and the lonely there are mine alone, and
    because *mine, alone*, is the name of that river,
      I look back to the bodies of my husband
And children, sleeping deeply, and the stars pour light
    on their foreheads and pillows, where I leave them,
      I leave them every night in dreams.
I look at my hands and feet and the water of the river
    rinses them in darkness. I am a new creature
      of darkness. I am unrecognizable even
To myself: because the moon is only half of itself;
    because the stars multiply; because the fish
      dream of water, the stones dream of fire;
Because my hands each mirror the other, and each rib
    is a bridge to the other side of the body. In the country
      of sleep, the night is sovereign, and a black sky
Is the double of the day. There I will never wake
    again: because the spell I learn by the river is
      my own secret, and I remember it only at night.

Dog Aria

Late, when the sprinklers came on, I'd find myself
listening at the window for our dachshund,
ever surprised into song by the slosh of dishes,
late loads of laundry—
the staccato of his quick sprechgesang,

matching the water's rippling jeux d'eau.
Trained in bel canto, he had perfect pitch.
And as the yard got wetter and wetter,
he swam among the staves
of delphinium and sweet bergamot,

baying adagio at the border
of lemon verbena, his frisky yipe
an allegro of catmint. His elegant snout
lifted to the moon. Each night
he unveiled from his blankets the dog-and-a-half

of his body into the dark rapt air,
and from his big chest, his rapid heart,
he drew the leitmotif of dog, of night,
and the long notes, impossibly long
        —O Sigmund! O song!

Panis Angelicus

In the cathedral, kneeling, I hear a penitent
whispering the prayers of this religion,
finding a way back to God. Above us both,

the light falls, vivid and shimmering.
In one tableau, the angels at the feet
of the Blessed Mother wear robes of green and red,

their wings luxuriant peridot, pyracantha berry.
In another, the arc of angel wings
over the little Family sheds yods of flame,

bright beatitude, leaves from a fiery tree.
In my native religion, angels do not
have wings in color, nor wings at all.

I learned such attributes as pagan embroideries.
Angels do not cross species, are not fantastic
like griffins or unicorns. They are men and women,

as you and I, but with no blood,
and exalted. Though, as I came here today,
even the birds drew nearer than usual.

The iridescent pigeons spread their wings
at my feet before they lifted into flight;
and a little blackbird, with a red eye

at the place where the wing fans out
from the body. A voice is close by,
waiting to be distilled from the vapor of the air.

Sometimes I can hear a word of it,
when I am awakened from a dream,
someone calling my name, into stillness

and the whir of hummingbirds
at the window. Here for a quiet hour
I watch, the windows casting cool fire

upon us all, bread of angels falling
infinite from infinite wings.

Autumn Song for My Hometown

It's always autumn in Boise, Idaho,
sandstone city of my sagebrushed youth,
always in the act of dying,
of fading to a paler shade of prairie grass
where light slants like Dickinson's diction
and paints the foothills like a Hopper beach house.

In the green Midwest,
flat, fat, and wet,
life beats down your patio door,
heavy as the cicada hum,
greedy as a pampered mutt,
too full to sustain an echo,
too deaf to the death knell
of the blackbird in her bare birch tree,
to the apocalypse of southbound geese.

And maybe this
is what it means to be born into death,
born into waning
like the scouring magpies,
the squirrels and the green-gray spruce
who eke out a pretty good life, turns out,
by the sweat of their brow
in this world of golden-brown death.

Every Good Dream

We sat down
together in last night's dream—
just the two of us at a table
at McDonald's because
I guess every good dream needs a good
corporate sponsor.
And since we both knew it
had been a while, I asked how things were
going and waited watching
your fingers admire the
sheer face of the formica.

Odorful, you finally said, which isn't even
a word but I had no reason to doubt the
way you stared into your vacant lap
so I reached for you hand—which seemed the
decent thing to do in a
dream as good as this—and
it was cold and soft like a
trout trembling there on the line but
fit nicely inside of mine which fit
nicely inside our silence
like a sigh or a smile or
a long-distance
phone commercial because

every good dream needs
a good
corporate sponsor.

Moses und Aron

And so it was that God gave us Aaron
for Moses was slow of speech
and didn't look right in a business suit,
for we yanked on his bulrush-bred beard
and mocked him,

mocked him, the man who would that we might meet God,
lab-coated, sulfury-smelling and steaming-mad down from
Mount Sinai.
The master of the shape-shifting serpent pen—
rejected, returned the manila envelope,
advised to apply at the library.

And so it was that God gave his genius to Aaron,
the great dilutor, P.R. man of the Pentateuch,
to trim that burning bush into topiary
and punch-up the prose with a little sports metaphor,
and a little golden calf.

And so it was that we came to prefer the spokesman
while the prophet was buried in an unmarked grave
and was not permitted into our Promised Land,
where we would burn the fat of rams
and would ask God for a king.

A Twenty-Six-Year-Old Virgin Thinks about Sex

It's not so much the making—
the fleshy mechanics that
can't possibly be as good as we hope and
which I'm still not sure even
exist, I've seen so many movies,
always fading to black, always
leaving me to wonder
with Heisenberg and
Holy Grail questers,
to wonder at the possibility
of the particle itself, that
slippery, shiny piece of God,
that simply won't be had
by curiosity or
science.

No, I think it's that afterward that I
ache for the most—
the nestling of cheek bone
into my naked chest,
the rise and fall
of soft, syncopated breathing
in the translucent blueness
of our twilit bedroom,
with time sprawled out
and slowed to a trickle
while the universe applauds us
like the secret heroes we are,
pioneers of passion,
inventors of intimacy itself.

When I Do Go On My Honeymoon

Afraid
but not afraid
to let her touch me,
we'll undress
slowly like
passing the sacrament
and when I see her body,
bare and beautiful
and not ashamed,
I'll kiss her mouth as if
she were the only woman
who ever existed.

SARA BLAISDELL

You Rise from the Exhibit

I move to the modern section—racks of pillows
strung diagonally, sterile floors, a white hospital bed,
somebody's idea of a masterpiece or joke.

At the foot, sideways lightning jolts a screen,
a sign of life continuing. "Look," you say,
in that way the dead do when they aren't really here.

Here you are, sheets pulled back, signature hair.
I could ease in. I'd fit. I kneel, touch the cloth,
break the rules. Mistake the buzz of lights for your pulse.

"Nurses are coming. Get under the bed."
You want them to spare me, which isn't fair.
I'd like to stay here till the line straightens.

You know what goes on here: fraudulent rebirths,
absence of prayers. Even when I touch happiness
I can't stomach it. The art people with walkie talkies
come for me, polite, pointing out the Do Not Touch.

Trial Home Placement

Go easy on the hot sauce, is what we're all thinking
as you finish your eggs, half-ass your chores for the last time,
identify your feelings as "numb" and "number"
and I write it on the white board next to the others:
hostile, optimistic, embarrassed, nonchalant.

A family is taking you today. Toward frilly
scrapbook pages. From what we've heard,
their profiles foreshadow a barn and sky future:
a father to hoist you up on Samaritan shoulders,
a tiny brother who might curl up beside you.

Even if someday the mother tries to wipe
the sass off your face at dinner, we hope you'll
just breathe, slow and hard, on your steamed vegetables,
not bite down on her arm, not try to break her heart,
not let her hurt yours, either.

Closer

For a while I had made up my mind
to die. The grocery clerks will tell you.
I bought strawberry daiquiris, brownie mixes,
all of it. Paid for it with bad checks.

Girls were spreading bathroom stalls
with the type of confused religion
you won't even find on the history channel's
Banned from the Bible: 'hardcore pornography
saved my marriage' or, 'go kill yourself.'

I nearly agreed till you took me
up into the mountains. We realized
where they'd been storing the oxygen
and strangely tolerant elk, the view
of the city like a practical joke.

It made God seem kinder, or at least
I could deal with him: his campaign,
his sly silence, his absurd notions
of giving, and taking away.

You Deserve a Pepsi

He's not in love but spends the night anyway,
since the movie ran late, and the noise from the water heater

in his apartment is driving him mad. He sounds off
about the radiation, the ugliness and beauty.

The women all hate my guts, he says. They do not cherish
my wit, my struggle, my broken wings dragging over

the brown earth. As he pontificates,
he counts your ribs through your shirt. He counts them

like sheep because he is tired, not because he is trying
to know you, not because he is trying to capture this moment

for the rest of his life. He blows his nose and keeps messing
with your toilet seat like he owns the place.

But he won't ever see you as fragile or essential.
He won't, so forget it. When he is finished

walk all the way to Seven-Eleven in your long coat
and yellow night shirt. You can buy anything you want.

When you return, you'll go into the room where
he'll be trying to find things he left on the floor.

I'm going to go, he'll say, or even just, I'm going.

You'll want to say something cold, like, Oh. You'll want to say
something darling from a song, like, You're the magic

that holds the sky up from the ground. You won't, however.
The night will quit existing, fold into itself.

You won't be qualified to question. Each time he speaks,
you'll be so moved, even your fists will break open.

Ophelia

You look so pleased with yourself
and now you think you deserve to be painted,
lying there, drowned, or crowding library shelves.
Your silly suicide cost me 6.95
at an art sale. I get jealous of you each morning
on the wall, resting there below the ferns.
Your arms are open to something, foolishly:
that prick prince isn't coming back.
Still, everyone should have your painting,
a print for every room of the house,
for the bedroom, the bathroom, the kitchen,
for the garage where they get the rope or leave
the motor running—to prove you keep floating,
shining in bright pastels, thoughtful flotsam
till the resurrection.

Orisons

Raw-tipped branches
freeze and unflutter.
Chafed knuckles wince
to bud wadeable leaves,
homesick mulch.

The wind scalped
so the slough
crumbles.

Clutched in trochal
consumption,
the orant, Grief,
spent her worth seasons
ago and stopped
waiting
to rest, her arms
down.

Spindrift

Harpooning—the Undoubtable
Shot from your sea-swept eyes,
Frothing mouths—
Bobbing, billowing
On the world's flood tide.
The spindrift of your good news—
Wholly flung Fervor and Hope
Of Kingdoms, triumphs, doles—
Oil for salt
And brine for wine.
Beyond liminal promises—
Unveiling the Blue
Of seas and skies.
Answers bask on shorelines—
The great and final Receding.
Once heard, once speared—
Caught.
The tissue thickens, binds
Fast-barnacled hooks
Of scarring Divine.

Tonsure

There wasn't
much
to give. The lymph
of my hair,

gone, flyaway
and
yellow-white,
pelts of
scalp visible in
fluorescent light.

But it was

    mine.

And so I

defied, kept
my cornsilk loose,
unhatted,

    wild,

itching

with forced
matted static,
thinking
about thorns.

Rumspringa

Twenty years
too late, I
laced the ruinous
red shoes and
ran
through a fount
of straw and burnt
wine into
a realm of ribboned
soles. I danced
on the table
at supper time,
foamed the milk with
my pointes
dripping sugar,
exposed my
ankles on the
top book shelf,
curled my
toes 'round
the spine of a
broom, hopscotched
on a crack
-ling floe,
scuffed the enamel
of the moon, did a
grande jeté off
the chandelier
of a thousand-
mirrored room.

Pangaea Lost

They never even kissed. Flaming sword at her back, Eve scythed her way through the weedy wilderness, felled milk-bearded trees to their laps, hallooed on the tip of a hoary crag. Her hipbone to hipbone stomach pilled with sweat as she stood on a pelt of aproning vinca, tore spitted meat with her carnal teeth, stacked her topiary hairdo high with whittled bones and deadheaded daisies. Adam stayed closer to home. Tired of routine theophanies, he dug a pit in which to hide, (pestleless mortar of immaculate runoff, prelapsarian soup), till vigilante cherubim ladled, drained, dumped his glabrous curl onto the doorstep of his dewy nursery. Alone, he ate meatless meals on a tray table. (Edenic vegetables in nests of wholesome noodles.) One night as our parents slept, the earth split. Continental seams welted. Adam cupped his pillow. Eve gouged fingernails into her palms. They moaned as glands split. Filaments of cloudy silk from rib cage spinnerets vaulted from their separate beds, collided, tendriled—loomed a pregnant sheet of mist. Children of their fevered dreams, we awoke.

When the Mormons of Orange County Become Shintoists

Red gates grow up like tollbooths amidst the mustard grass of the coastal plains.

Red gates grow up among the shaggy and forsaken orange groves.

Red gates grow up in the shallow places of pungent estuaries.

God steps out of the hiding place called perfection: a gated community on a newly defaced hillside, each house with beige interiors, and a backyard oil drill banging its head against the clay like a mad grasshopper.

God dissolves into dogs.

God dissolves into mountain lions.

God dissolves into eucalyptus trees.

God dissolves into waves.

God dissolves into dolphins.

When my Mormons become Shintoists, they no longer drag their ancestors around like great stalks of beached kelp.

They build their ancestors tiny shrines, topped with little gold angels, in the orange groves. Gnatcatchers watch over them.

When my Mormons become Shintoists their new smiles are not anchored in sentimentality, refined sugar, or capital.

My sister stops dreaming of silicon breast implants.

My other sister stops shopping for a car big enough to carry children living and designed.

My mother visits the shrine of dead children. She has knit a red cap for each of the people she wished we had become. She leaves these beings behind her as she passes through the red gate.

Perfection burns up in a wind-driven wildfire.

Perfection recedes like a long wave, leaving purple spiny urchins crackling in the sun.

Invocation / Benediction

Father, Mother, help me piece together the contradictions of my life:

White cotton, red satin, brown polka dot; torn Sunday dress, Navajo rug, frayed baby blanket.

Make me insistent on every lonely shred, willing to sacrifice no one.

Where there is no pattern, God, give me courage to organize a fearsome beauty.

Where there is unraveling, let me draw broad blanket stitches of sturdy blue yarn.

Mother, Father, give me vision.

Give me strength to work hours past my daughters' bedtime.

Give me an incandescent all-night garage with a quorum of thimble-thumbed grandmothers sitting on borrowed folding chairs.

We will gather all the lost scraps and stitch them together:

A quilt big enough to warm all our generations: all the lost, found, rich, poor, good, bad, in, out, old, new, country, city, dusty, shiny ones;

A quilt big enough to cover all the alfalfa fields in the Great Basin.

Bigger. We are piecing together a quilt with no edges.

God, make me brave enough to love my people.

How wonderful it is to have a people to love.

I Promise

I'll wake you with the mouths of flowers wet
against your warmer skin. I'll brush the smoke
of waking with the voices we forget
too well, too soon. Not long from now the clock
of humid summer heat will swallow us.
The tadpoles of regret might wriggle loose
the mason lid; we may no longer trust
our wrinkled hands to finger well the noose
around the constellations, bulging whites
that bleed the sunlight pebbling through the arch
of nights against which flocks in arrows fight,
their straining necks half reaching to the stars.
I will remember lying here with you,
as though the water swallowed other truths.

Her fingers knew the alphabets of rain,
the spilling heavens, spelling as they fell
among the hollyhocks. Her lips could tell
the droplets' pacing as their rhythm framed
crescendos to be felt but never named
by children watching sidewalk gutters swell
against their borders. She could sound the well
of noons' humidities until the drained
and flaccid clouds retreated to the east
beyond the tearing mountain summits. This,
her testimony of the moistened light,
and this, the calm recession of the beast.
A marbled moment, braided with her kiss
along the shining edges of the night.

Red Wheelbarrow

After William Carlos Williams

So much depends upon the window pane
above the double sink that frames the yard
where she is watching as the evening wanes.
The light is growing heavy, thick, and hard.
The wheelbarrow is sitting on its side,
its rust invisible against the mist,
the tire caked with mud. She stays inside
and sometimes wipes her forehead with her wrist.
The chickens do not seem to feel the rain
or hear it tap the metal barrow's edge.
She tries to see how little day remains
by peering from her kitchen's little ledge.
    So much depends upon the glazing wet
    arrangement inked in silty silhouette.

Beacon

Attending to the wounds again. The sky
undressed unclotting, losing moons. The sea
congealing, thatching thick its womb, its sluice
of sudden signs disgorging magma sighs,
the gorged and gouging constellations speed
to dissolution, marked and marking loose
parentheses, apologies unfit
for numbered sparrows, preening pawns, for us.
This bandaging the hemispheres, this small
absorption, mist along the cheek, this spit
and clay and mealy middle blindness, truss
and timber, crucifix and shepherd's stall
and all the sodden sympathies again.
Be this, be here, be whole, the veil is rent.

Salt and Blood

He lets it fall. It falls, descending pall,
grey drape that mutes and dims and dampens all
that burning morning bursting hot-white call
of crimson dazzling awe, wide world unwalled.
And yet He lets that peace in pieces shatter,
and what had glowed a grace-fierce fire, sputter.
The heat of birth reduced to smoky matter,
the whole of Holy Ghost a distant flutter.
Cold desert, colder night, stark sky a stone.
A thirst inside a hunger, trembling bones.
This splintering from heaven and from home—
my God who kept me, leaves me all alone
to shake, to scrape, to kneel and stutter-speak;
to taste the salt and blood of Him I seek.

Goodbye

In my family, it is the word that says everything:
I love you; I want you to come back.

Only in her later years did Mother use the word
proud. That sounded as frothy as *love*.

Once I didn't say *Goodbye* when my parents left
for a long day and into the night for Salt Lake.

As usual, Mother had washed and ironed the temple clothes
before layering them lightly into the two suitcases.

Later, with my sisters and brother, I watched
from the kitchen window for headlights to announce them.

When they didn't come, I knew I wouldn't forgive myself.
Salt Lake was as far away as we'd go then.

State Street was a long corridor of sirens.
Once I grew up, I didn't fret so much.

How many times had I practiced, unnecessarily,
being an orphan? Then before she left finally

after all the rehearsals that unhealthy year,
when the family knew she would go and not come back,

we cast unnatural words around casually,
profusely, avoiding our own *Goodbye,*

fearing, perhaps, it would snap the coffin's latch.
We should have owned the word, released its syllables

from our tight tongues like genetic valentines,
the word both warmly complete, and open-ended.

Nothing We Needed to Know

And then, to show how it was done,
Mrs. Jackson, the home ec teacher,
bent down the way you drink from a tap
and demonstrated how to let one's breasts
drop into a brassiere. How each
should fall into its cup—
right and left—
for a perfect fit,
no adjustment needed.
She reached behind her back,
hinging her elbows,
and locked the fastener shut,
slid each arm into its loop of strap
and straightened: twin bulks
at the front of the room,
she with squat brown shoes, brown hose,
hair graying and tight,
the dress form headless and bare,
tomato aspic firming in the fridge.
An institution of baked eggs and etiquette,
a reputation as the toughest teacher in school
and the mother of two girls we knew,
in odd shapes of afternoon light,
a white brassiere on the outside
of her mildew-dark dress.
And no one dared laugh, not then,
nor later, when we sat, our chairs in a half-circle,
as she read, cover to cover,
voice pasty, lids low,
a church book on chastity
that filled the eighth-grade requirement,
but kept sex itself
an itchy gray blur.

Prayer for a Grandchild

For Holden at two

Let bells come
from porches and throats
of brown cows

and whistles be
handmade from weeds.
Let shock be

from stands of mint
in a ditch and pansies
bearded with ice.

Let him find
four-leaf clovers,
his name in a pond

of soup. Breathe leaves,
eat snow, harvest
"cheesies," hear

ducks on the roof.
Give him knowledge
of horses, calluses,

women in aprons,
the smack of a ball
in a pasture, yarn,

copper dirt.
Let him hear
music alone,

plain words.

The Smell of a Baby

Mom, she says,
this is my first one who has died.

I'd seen her cadaver
that first semester of medical school—
a sallow withered purse,
one used long enough,
then given to science,
an old woman's choice.

I remembered my daughter's attention to arm and leg,
to muscles, nerves, tendons, blood vessels, ligaments,
to the opened abdomen and chest
and especially to the uncovered face:
she'd honored it until the very end.

This time, at the delivery, the head and face are what showed first.

In that luminous weatherless room of bodies, biting odors,
the other students said they thought her cadaver
had the faint smell of a baby,
somehow the faint smell of a baby!

She tells me how she laid, in the mother's arms,
the cocoon of warm flannel,
still breathing then,
its face plump as a breast, as pink;
how she nearly forgot the confusion inside,
nearly forgot how its legs
were fused together like a mermaid's.
Later, the autopsy would show it was a daughter.

My daughter, awakened by a fresh life crowning—
one whose cycle would complete itself
in the time of a hospital TV drama—
tells of scrubbing her hands in the night,
of sheltering the mother, father, and baby
behind the heavy door
in a caliginous bottomless room.

Of saying,
Take all the time you need.
You can look if you want.

So She Wouldn't Fail

So she wouldn't fail at something big,
she kept busy doing average things,

things she wasn't ashamed to talk about,
exactly, things she could always say
were temporary, and just until she found
what it was she was really meant to do, or be.

Even the most desirable calling
had its drawbacks, and what if
once she'd made it there, she didn't like it
after all, and there was no escape.

She could see herself shut inside
an office, skin wrung out and gray,
feet itching inside three-inch heels.

Or traveling from one town to the next
selling something that at first felt fabulous
and then inconsequential.

She placed her belief in things
that could be inventoried: dishes, round-trip tickets,
brand-name blouses she'd find on sale.

Had she been a reader, she'd have liked fiction.

Her comforts required good taste,
but how exotic can exotic taste on a kitchen plate?

That was what she wanted—
to count on things that kept her busy
and beyond harm's way.

Most of her big dreams had been interrupted
or ended badly. Others simply passed her by.

But dreams kept pressing, and at their best

would feature her dexterous hands,
her brain with all its songs,
her kind compromising heart.

It was hard to live like this, she thought.
If only dreams had timers telling when
or could be scanned to expose the flaws—

some *signal,*
like a purple handkerchief in a breast pocket
or an emissary waving a white placard,
her name blocked boldly in.

  —*after Stephen Dunn*

ALEX CALDIERO

it occurs to me as I gaze on the splendid work that the maker too
stood in the very space I stand in unfolding for all time

Almost a Song

something near the wave
yearns to taste the sea—

if it has a name
it is your name.

if it has a face
it resembles me.

something near the wave
yearns to taste the sea—

there's no telling who
it is waiting for.

if it were a tongue
it would surely speak.

something near the wave
yearns to taste the sea—

Love adoration amour devotion eros infatuation passion
admiration esteem philos regard respect ágape altruism
charity kindness benevolence consideration generosity
tenderness thoughtfulness attentive chivalrous considerate
courteous solicitous contemplative meditation pensive
reflective speculative conjecture guess surmise theorize
consider meditate ponder reflect ruminate chance gamble
hazard risk venture adventure endeavor enterprise
investment undertaking attempt experiment try bet dare
danger jeopardy menace peril threat

Keep listening
as if at any moment
a voice would utter
an extraordinary answer
and consequently
leave us clear and wholesome
ready to acknowledge *us*
as full service beings

Analfabetismo

You speak
differently
when you read
than when you talk.

Words move
your lips in ways
that defy the logic and rhythm
you are used to.

I clearly
remember
not being able to read
my native language;

how the language
I learned to speak in school
mysteriously became
the one I speak every day.

>   You speak
>   differently
>   when you need
>   than when you got.
>
>   Words move
>   your lips in ways
>   that defy the head and heart
>   that you were born with.
>
>   I clearly
>   remember
>   not being able to name
>   my wants and desires;
>
>   how the language
>   I learned to speak to others
>   mysteriously became
>   the one I speak in my dreams.

You speak
differently
when you talk
than when you listen.

Words move
your lips in ways
that disconnect your tongue and mouth
from your breathing.

I clearly
remember
not being able to give meaning
to what I was saying;

how the language
I learned to speak in my head
mysteriously became
the one I whisper in my room.

> You speak
> differently
> when you think
> than when you know.

> Words move
> your lips in ways
> that resist thought and reason
> and then abandon you.

> I clearly
> remember
> not being able to recall
> what was already on my mind;

> how the language
> I learned to speak in childhood
> mysteriously became
> the one I speak only to the dead.

You speak
differently
to your own body
than to the body next to you.

Words move
your lips in ways
that are unrecognizable
when you see them in the mirror.

I clearly
remember
reaching out
to reach within;

how the language
I learned to speak in secret
mysteriously became
my own scream.

We Think We Know the World When We Divide

We think we know the world when we divide
raven from dove, the evening from its end,
but truth is not static; it collides.

Prying osprey from flight, we struggle to decide
how the wind differs from things it bends.
We think we know the world when we divide.

Each year in March the run-off has defined
a ruptured path as stone and stream contend
to name the edge where rock and doubt collide.

In hollow June, the month my sister died,
I hope to see forget-me-nots and death as friends;
their fragile blue from her I can't divide.

Beneath the August stars I try to hide
in roots and grass my heavy wish to rend
rebirth from God, to see spirit collide

with earth. But even God's omniscience cried
when he watched his son like snow descend.
We think we know the world when we divide,
but like Jacob and the angel—we collide.

The Eternity of Abraham's Children

eternity was our covering and our rock
—Abraham 2:16

Dearly Beloved, we are gathered
to face immortality,
the welding of flesh to flesh.

Stained glass should raise the crush
of church stone, the foibles of humanity,
but in the glass we see spilled milk and feathers—

in the window's lead lines, the striations
of gull primaries cast off and collected
to adorn sand in the semblance of castles.

In weddings and temples, eternity is our
covering. But it must also be our rock.
Amid principalities, growing as insatiably as our universe,

somewhere the center is still the splay of lichens on granite,
or the way the errant curl, dark and glossy,
runs across the bride's neck.

Fire in the Pasture

Perplexed by the Revelator's Heaven

The earth in its sanctified and immortal state will be made like unto crystal
—Doctrine and Covenants 130: 9

Aren't leaves crumbling against the edge
of Autumn, the fibrous tangle
of the lesser shrew's heart, and a prophet curled
in the belly of night, shaking like a reed fragile enough?

Why transmute Alps or Andes into Spanish crystal
or celestialize black forests into a clarity
that can shatter?

Won't porcelain branches snap
like the camel's leg, the donkey's left ear,
the Christ child's outstretched
wrist, glued and glued but always somewhat scarred?

I have seen too much of crystalline nativity to wish
the world's rebirth a sea of glass.

Grandmother Naming

In the passenger seat she rubs her belly
like a good idea, reads billboards out loud.
She is looking to name the baby. Dick's Café.
St. George Inn. She thinks it's a boy
she's naming, having read the paper clip
dangling from kite string over her wrist: left
to right, a boy—circling, a girl.
She pats the warm fluttering, thinks
my little man, my sweet boy-baby.

At this point, I am no one's idea,
though it's my mother's fingers grown smooth
in the thin sac. When she's laid out
on the white-sheeted bed, she will not know
they are sad for her
girl parts, but will already be full
of her allotted eggs.

Inspecting her, Grandfather will call her good
and name her after himself—also
after Jerry Lee's Used Car Lot.
Later she will imagine me, first brilliant
daughter. She'll close her eyes to a dream
of my face, believe I love my name
and my body. Why shouldn't she? She doesn't know
who she's dreaming. For now I am bright
arms and glimmering feet, I am
little sun-dried white dresses.

After Her Stroke

Above this cold chair
they say *vegetable*. Voices like calves
bawling for their mother's teats.
I think yellow squash, summer,
radish the shade of my lips
in sun, all the ways to be beautiful.
Even after five dull children,
my breasts really never sagged.
I cradle them days when he nods
across from me. He spreads his cold palms
on my cheeks, looks deep
though he thinks it's just his face
he sees in my blue irises.
I want to say Lawrence
you never held me right. And when
did you see my legs never sprouted
one blue vein? The kind wandering
down a thigh like a wet blue trail of mud.
You can't kiss a thigh like that.
What I love is my skin, how cool
it presses me. They watch scared.
I breathe to say it and everyone circles
my face. *Scared* I whisper, and they think
I mean me, and who knows
how long they'll weep, pray me out
of my body, when it's what I want to keep.

After Matisse's *Basket of Oranges*

First a basket of oranges, almost
centered. And behind the table, a door—
half avocado, half red wine, and maybe not a door
to the artist's yard grown full with hibiscus, but a cupboard
or trapdoor to his lover's favorite window.
He doesn't want guessing, though.
Just oranges. As in *here, have an orange,*
or simply, *look—oranges. What I dream of
in art* he wrote *is something like a good armchair,
a thing to please writers and businessmen.*
But (this noted on the back
of my calendar) he liked bodies: eyes,
lips, angles of wrists and fingers. None of that
stayed clear, though—someone always asking
what it means, a face this yellow.
Behind this picture's door some body might be waiting—
some *she,* maybe—tapping her nails
on her teeth. When he taps his brush
to his painted oranges one last time, he might reach
for the real basket and carry her
one in his palm. She might smile
and peel, lick juice from her thumbs.
In his painting, the oranges aren't large enough,
the room busy and cramped, as if he wants
what's behind this picture.

Telling My Husband His Death

I wouldn't plan mine. But for you—and others—
I've wondered. The first time on my mother's bed
with my brother, two months old. And so many pillows.
Just one might have fallen, might have pressed
his soft face. So simple, he wouldn't have cried.
I loved him, pink and smooth-elbowed, but I wanted to think
how fragile, how easy to die and to feel quiet
after. Take the foal we found drowned in the river. One night
you're wishing her birth—next morning she's stiff
as damp canvas, water rinsing her hooves. Her mother empty
but light again and nuzzling my palm. What if you
could go that easily? Not that I want you dead, but I'd like
the guessing over: what day? what time? will it hurt?
I dream countless ways, but this comes back:
you fishing the river—water deep and sparkling
on your skin like a thousand kisses. A little much, but I want it
beautiful. No late-night pile-up driving home
past the roller mills, your clothes cut off you
in the ambulance. Nobody holding you up at the Amoco.
Never me pressing your wrists, begging please, don't go.
I need it a blessing, as they say—cliché all over.
Nothing for you to see but raspberries, tangled wild
on the river bank. Nothing to think but raspberries,
washed and bottled in a mason jar. The scent of sugar.
White cloth covering. A thing that soft.

My Father, Keeping the Backyard

With the lump in his back there's more
to think about. My father, still
in a wicker lawn chair, scans his aspen
and thinks of morning—of the smooth blade
that will open his new scar for the second time in May.

When I visit like this, he corners me
with endings, says he's ten years
past the age his father reached
when a '62 Chevy split him wide
against a blunt curb. Two days later
the town mortician, tonic-haired
and grey-suited, shook my sixteen
year-old father's hand. He said,

"We almost couldn't view your dad
he was torn so bad. But I wrapped
his side with the same stuff
the ladies save Sunday dinner in.
Some days all you can do is keep
these bodies together."

Of course my father has become
the mortician. Each time he performs him
the last words change. Tonight
it was blood, the thin wrap seeping,
and, "The inside always wants out."

Later, viewing my father
from the sliding glass door,
I know the mortician is who he believes.
Even with my mother, brown-legged
and deep in her tomatoes, fuchsia nodding
from their pots on the deck, promising
love in each round flower, he dreams

his way out. Lips straight, a long finger
circling the chilled rim of a juice glass,

he eyes this yard till dark. When he creeps
to the house I can't tell his arms
from the warm, rich black.

TYLER CHADWICK

By reason of breakings they purify themselves.
So Job. So flesh flung in leviathan's wake,
rolled loose soul in the infinite boil. So leviathan
riffing off the riptide, cacophonous staves
upwelling from the Good Book's selvage swart
with the fingerprints of sin's compulsive caress.
Sins legion as the ridge and whorl of waves
spread horizonward from leviathan's violent
weave. Sins thin as spindrift—lustrous spit
and prism—spun from the tango of scale and sea.
Sins brazen as scales down compulsion's backside:
Weathertight. Weather trim. Weathered
shiv and shimmer breaking on bodies blanched
in the rush and boil of birth.

—*after Job 41:25*

Fruit

1. First

"She's like an apple
in a water balloon,"
the doctor says. They watch

their fruit unfold across
the screen in light movements.
Submerged beneath her sea

enclosed by silent walls,
slow fluid breaths inspire
her ripening, baptize

the room in innocence.
Within this matrix
of tranquility,

they sense her beckoning
through sound's translucent waves,
calling from her still place

into time's raging sea
for a Return. Then Light
ripples from around her world

as from the Garden tree
the autumn God called Adam
and questioned why his seed
had grown so ripe with blood.

2. Last

In their yellowing tree
atop an autumn hill,
shades of spring

shadow their fruit. Night rain
stagnates in micro-seas
about the stems, drops

dew across his face as he
climbs to pluck the apples
and drop them

to her waiting hands.
Bruises soften
the golden skin: some

from the gathering, some
from careless branches
and birds, and some

from larval codling
churning flesh
from the inside-out.

Breath caught in a gust,
he palms the last fruit
as branches strip blood
from his cold hand.

3. Return

The pair returns
to their paradise, straining
for shades of green

in withered gold.
Arm in arm, they step
beneath their tree

and rest against the trunk.
His eyes pursue the land
into a blurry field

and hers wash his hands
in reminiscent strokes.
As the sun beds down,

dusk winds
swell fruit pooled
around their feet. He sighs;

she leans against his arm
and waits with him as night
settles on the hill.

Their breath swells with the fruit,
diffusing through Earth's skin
into the pulse
of their generations' veins.

On J. Kirk Richards' *Stand of Trees*

I've been neglecting what it takes
to piece together dawn from old
snapshots and reminiscence faded
as the blush from Adam's skin

when God's question stunned
the garden and he slipped with Eve into
the shadow of God's voice, their shame
a stand of trees backlit by cherubim

come hounds a-bay to flush them into
death, sin, recognition, solitude,
a blood-drunk field mantle deep with sweat
and sorrow, soil thick with the afterbirth

of myth and tectonic histories, pieces
of a puzzle that shift in bed as I
try to number them *one, two, three,*
no, *one, two . . . one*

edges ragged as the blanket Cain has
carried since Eve weaned him from the teat
and he found his thumb to replace it,
but not enough to fill his hunger, not

enough to keep serpents from burrowing
into his need, from shedding that rag
like yesterday's skin, from slipping him
the switchblade he used to quarter the fruit

he knew had ripened in Mother's womb,
the harvest he'll never find as he works
his spittle and excrement field into bodies
with his hands red as stygian clay.

Two Poems on Fatherhood

I. Two Kitchen Floors and a Tea Party

1.

Scrubbing the kitchen floor
on my hands and knees:

Dad walks in, looks down, says,
You'll make someone a good wife

someday, then grins. I
shake my head,

laugh back, and return
to searching for my reflection

in linoleum.

2.

Our six-month daughter strapped to my chest,
our three-year-old downstairs

in front of Sesame Street: I
mop the kitchen floor,

watching crumpets rise
in the oven because

she's playing tea party and I thought
we'd try them for real

this time.

II. At the Grocery Store on a Mid-week Afternoon

My cart loaded, infant
and toddler in tow, I step
to the check-out stand. *You*

playing Mom today?
the cashier asks. Looking up
then down, I'm tempted to

strip myself, say, *Did I*
wear my wife's breasts today
by accident? Slip on her

twice-episiotomied sex
with my underwear, her
labor-wide hips with my jeans?

No wonder nothing fits.
I must have missed the mirror
on our way out the door. Instead,

while unloading groceries
on the conveyor belt,
I patronize her smile with mine,

and tell her, *Something like that,*
though it's really
nothing like that (Dragoti's

Jack Butler got my arc wrong);
then wait for the price,
pay, reload the cart,

and gather my girls
into the flaming circle
of our mundanity.

For the Man in the Red Jacket

...the waters are come in ...
—Psalm 69:1

His word, more than his face, remains,
trailing me as the rain that stuck
to my glasses and soaked my clothes,

seeping through
my windows, my façade into
the crawlspace of memory.

I see now he was serious: as we'd
passed on the street, each moving
the other way, he'd pulled off

his red jacket hood and tried
to make eye contact. *Have you
necessarily taken the time,*

he'd asked, *to find out
what grace is for?* Reluctant
to break the rhythm of my run,

I'd turned just enough to see him
in my periphery, standing alone
on the corner as the rain started,

and said nothing. If he'd asked for money
or the time, I might have slowed, at least
to tell him I didn't have any or

It's six twenty-two. But grace, I
remember thinking. *Get serious, brother,
and out of the rain. It's early. I'm*

*running. We're about to be wet
and our garments as heavy as Genesis.
Of course I've made time for grace.*

Tornado

We were swimming, my sister and I,
the only way one survives summer in Kansas,
trying to stand on our hands in the shallow end,
toes pointed above the water line,
when everything—
children's voices, splashing,
mothers calling, the lifeguard's whistle—stopped.

In slow motion I turned my head
and saw it, coming fast, a funnel cloud
twisting, writhing,
the entire horizon to the east having risen up behind it,
black and evil.

What I'd heard was true,
nothing in that whole flat world moved,
or sang, or whimpered,
even the water that lapped the pool went still.
Earth sucked in her breath,
forgot how to inch forward.
The wheel, notched and greased wouldn't catch,
wouldn't shift to the next inviolable beat.
Never had I seen black like that black.

Years later when I lay on the ultrasound table
nine months pregnant
thinking, *I am still that same summer girl,*
and the nurse couldn't find a heartbeat on the screen,
yet he was there floating inside me,
my stomach stretched with his shape,
I knew,
once before,
I'd felt the earth stop.

I was able to run then,
my sister and I, our wet towels plastered against us,
our bare feet slapping the sidewalk.

Sermon on Manchac Swamp

Here, where duckweed coats the water
like green algae,

where Spanish moss curls
like an old man's beard, crisp and wiry,

where cypress lean into the swamp,
their pointed knees praying for roothold

along the bank,
here, where heat is wet,

where palmetto fronds have long forgotten
how to move their delicate fingers,

only the alligator stirs, sliding
like cream into the coffee colored bayou,

where spotted gar and catfish hang
just below the surface, too lazy to swim,

where greened-browns and khaki-grays
camouflage the earth,

where only the trumpet vine splashes red,
where cottonmouths cradle in tupelo gums

and spiders sprawl in their littered webs,
here, if we listen, is the sermon on idleness,

how it smells,
how it smiles

its immense satisfaction
at our boat slipping happily into the shade.

For Helga

*Andrew Wyeth painted more than 240 canvases of this
one model, keeping his work hidden from the public.*

He paints her face in secret:
the wide-spaced eyes, blue-gray,
clouding his nights, his days,
each lash, delicate as his finest brush,
the brows, broad, stroked hair by hair
like brown grass on Kuerner's Hill,
her skin, coarse, familiar as his own,
    each burst vessel,
    each small line etched
    in oil or tempera.

For fifteen years he frames her face in every light:
    beneath old tight-fisted trees,
    against winter-bleak grass,
profiles blurred in rain,
in snow—cold, half finished sketches,
in Karl's loft, where shadows
and black iron meat hooks hang
from smoke-stained rafters.

In *Crown of Flowers* he wreathes her in daisies and sun,
like some goddess come from the hunt,
golden strands of hair backlit in disarray,
needing to be smoothed from that face
only he touches,
hoarded on hundreds of canvases hidden
like holy treasure.
    She hints at a smile with rough,
ruddy lips he draws over and over,
until he can paint their savor
with his eyes closed,
with no light at all.

Fire in the Pasture

Still Life

This jigsaw puzzle of twelve sunflowers
keeps me sane. Each petaled
piece holds off the dark that threatens.
I search for edges first,
then beginning with the line that divides
the table from the blue background,
(a serene, calming blue)
I work my way to the signature: Vincent.
He arranged the flowers early that morning,
painted furiously before they lost their shape,
before their color bled into brown.
Centered on a cloth, the same shade
of old gold as the fattest flowers,
they eyed him from a yellowed crockery.

He wrote his brother
there were six shades of yellow
in this painting. I chose it because the flowers
and pot and table top all looked the same to me,
and the puzzle would be difficult.
He knew that. He knew how fast yellows could fade,
and the pain it would cost to preserve them.
I see them now, the bright yellow of opening,
the curled copper of facing the sun,
the bronzing of too much heat,
the drooping of passion sipped thirstily all day.

That summer he cut off part of his ear,
studied its furled edge,
its coiled cartilage against his palm,
fingering the lobe,
soft and delicate as the flower dust he brushed
so many times from his fingertips.

With each piece I put in place,
he whispers to me,
The madness is making it all fit,
before the yellows twist and fade,
before the blue turns to black.

A Little Night Music

She stands at the sill in her Battenberg lace
that took hours of steam to iron.
She feels the gown billow out behind her,
night's cool breath on her legs.
She flies.
Arms extended on either side,
she skims above the ground,
up over Sievert's Hill,
down the other side.
Like a glider, she slips between the trees
tilting right, then left,
moon-made shadows flicking beneath her,
never having to pull in her arms.

In a clearing nearby, a string quartet
plays *Clair de Lune*, the notes
and five line staff rising in spirals off the bows
of the four men,
all wrists and white cuffs in the moonlight.
She hovers on the edge of the scene,
her toes knotting in the tall grass.
The cellist sees her,
puts down his instrument
and comes towards her, bow in hand.
He will play me now, she thinks.
Between his knees, I will be the cello.
And from the tiny pleats across the bodice of her gown
the notes begin to sound, slipping out
into the surrounding shadows of the trees,
thin and strained at first,
almost dissonant.
Then, on a deep sigh,
they flower from her throat.
These are the notes of my soul, she thinks.
And the pearl buttons
down the front of her gown glimmer
like stars spilled across the sky.

For Grace Isabella

The Crown without the Conflict
14 May 2003

I saw you once . . . and last,
As I wrapped you in white
And lay you beside your toys . . .
Teddy Bear, Bunny, Locket,
Recording of your father's
Voice that you had never heard.

I saw you then . . . counted
Toes and fingers, saw the tip
Of a tiny nose, as much
Intuited as saw eyelids in
Sleep. Not much more . . .
The hygromas (ugly word,
Uglier in life than in the
Read) and the hydrops
Blanketed all else in their
Insatiable greed to
Absorb fluids, tissues.

Still, I saw you . . . in the arc
Of nose, the slit of
Eyelids, the curve of
Spine against the sheet
The hospital had wrapped
You in. And it sufficed.

You remain part of my son
And of his love
And of his parents
And of hers throughout
Long links and chains
Of genes and cells
And Spirit throughout
Time.

Pomegranates

Birds have plucked ripe pomegranates
hollow,

split/pricked ruby-leather
shells,

pried ruby-blooded seeds
loose

from flesh-tint membranous
moorings

and swallowed—cocked heads back,
throats

quivering . . . and pomegranates
hang—

empty Death-Star hulls—from upper
limbs.

Damon Again

Milton felt no frost when Damon died,
No chill eclipsed the hot Italian sun
Or touched his neck and drew an icy line
Into his heart—he did not know the pulse
Had softly stilled, the breath, the voice, the mind.

> *If we dwelt in Arcadia,*
> *His flocks would weep with mine*

Nor I, working in my roses, cutting
Canker from thorny limbs, twisting back
An errant branch and twining it again
Where it belonged—heat poured its June in May
And I worked silently, unaware.

> *If we dwelt in Arcadia,*
> *His flocks would weep with mine*

Five decades now—and we have drawn upon
Each other time and again for strength, for joy,
In sorrow, in pain—five decades . . . and still,
As if standing alone, I did not feel
You pass. I should have.

> *If we dwelt in Arcadia,*
> *His flocks would weep with mine*

I should have felt earth shake, air weep, fire chill
To ash, water freeze to solid—all
Infinites at once time-bounded, space-
Constrained. And did not. It took a phone call
From your son for me to know.

> *If we dwelt in Arcadia,*
> *His flocks would weep with mine*

At Midnight

She watched the night-news re-cap,
Last gasping cable from LA,
Watched the channel
Fade to angry starstorm static.
The video place had upped its price that day—
Five-fifty for a first-run film,
And she was too incensed by the blatant rip-off
(It was the only rental outlet in this burg)
To waste her money there.

So she sat and smoked and drank and stared
At nothingness enfleshed in patterns on
Fake-oak paneling in the rented room.
The static grew insistently.

She stretched, she let her nubbly robe
Drift open, and the snow of breasts
And waist and thighs
Matched flurries on the set
That coalesced, extruded, blended
With the dark-oak backdrop,
And he stood cloaked and silent—then
With a whisper, naked by her knees,
And she leaned back and smoked and stared
At watermarks that marred hypnotic
Cartographies of cheap ceiling tiles.
She bared her eager throat.
Once she moaned and bit her lip.
Once she cried.

At dawn she woke. Exhausted. Sore.
Bloody. Depleted fullness and
Dampened fears. The channel flickered
Its test pattern, giving birth to some
Charlatan selling ginsu knives or cars.
She did not know or care which one.

Cosmology

I cannot help it.

I see Wanderers and Long-Tailed Stars,
Not planets, comets.

Orion is for me a jewel of ice-locked light.
Not hot and distant suns.

Scorpio curves brilliant venom
Across the marges of my mind.

The moon waxes, wanes, breathes saffron-silver warmth,
Alive, not dead.

I study, define, compute, manipulate—
And still I cannot see objective stars.

Kinetic Sculpture

Perhaps my first experience
with kinetic sculpture
was at a recital
(violin and piano)
when marcato or accented notes
broke, from the violinist's bow,
several strands of horsehair
in the middle or near the frog
and the passage went on so furiously
that she must ignore them and let them dance wildly,
caught bright in the light,
whipping a sinuous halo
around instrument and player,
jouncing and squiggling—
not quite in time with the music, just behind—
until there was enough of a moment
in the music to stop,
hold the instrument with chin only,
feel to the end and then the tip of the bow
to snap the loose hairs off and let them fall,
before beginning again to play.

Quarterly Report

      leafless but loaded,
         laboring,
     bowed branches
      could crack
           or
              spring's running again,
                  under glass,
                  roots slither,
                shoots writhe,
             glistens of green,
                          some are here for the first time
                          we teach creaking
                          of porch swings
                          and tree-climbing
                          so clever you never
                falling softly,
           leaves bare forest rafters.
                 birds
               leave.
            branches
           chatter
        in the wind.
      all
    pulls
   in
  for
winter.

Dove-gray Evening

Beyond the shadows you stand,
wondering if I meant what I said.
In the darkness I shiver
and pull my sweater closer.

The streetlight hits your tense shoulders.
If I looked, I couldn't read your eyes;
you shadow them from me.

Mine was a sneak attack—
almost a mutiny—
I agree.

My anger and my love seep out
into the silence
and soak into the wet lawn.

I gather the small shards—
pieces of me you had been keeping—
and say a soft goodbye.

Wilmette

This brightness blinds, this fortress surrounds
slow life.
I remember the old place with a tingle.
Quick memories of
       leaf-nests hiding lost mittens,
       races to shatter gutter-ice on cold mornings,
       felt-leafed books on thick summer nights,
       paper jets in the gym after long meetings,
       magic in the yard on moonlit snow-nights.
Scattered now.
Gathered at Christmas
and during new summer nights;
                      cool, and muslined.

I am kept from returning
by laws that keep
mouse-stalkers from becoming once more
string-chasers—
able to pretend the memory

and nothing more.

Maybes at Sixty

Maybe, after all, my life will count for something;
maybe a letter in a sentence in a paragraph
    in mortality's long essay.

Maybe I will gather age, frail as yellowed paper
in crumbled leather, hard of sight and sound.

Maybe I don't have much time, a lurking illness,
a car passing in the wrong lane, a falling plane.

Maybe the world will end first—a comet, Armageddon,
the Second Coming—and we will all go together, or,

maybe my light will fade out quietly
with a million others on the same day
the lights blink on,

accompanied by loud wails of protest or joy,
from a million more coming in.

Building on Ruins

A response to Brad Kahlhamer's exhibit, "Let's Walk West"

1

For the young ones, past and present collide,
    in a conflagration of time.
Pieces fly everywhere.
In their heads, only remnants of the stories
    that tell them who they are.
Shelters of buffalo hide, terraced adobe, mesquite
    give way to government housing.
Sacred maize, squash and beans are replaced
    by Fritos and Coca Cola.
They grow up with one foot on the land,
the other in Albuquerque, St. Louis, Cheyenne.
They have Mexican, Irish, and cowboy grandfathers.
Who can tell them which skewed path to follow?

2

The old ones got lost, too.
Nobody knows where they went
    except Mountain,
and Coyote, maybe he knows.
The archaeologists dig in the mounds
    and under the crumbled walls.
They dust the past from fragments they find:
    agate points, potsherds, scraps of moccasin,
and spread them on the ground.
Then pack them off to museums
to be stored in drawers and closets.
Do they think the pieces will grow back together
    there in the dark?

3

Some things we do know.

When the eagles disappeared carrying legends
in their beaked jaws, they returned
on paper bills and coins in slot machines.

In each of us the heart drum chants
of buffalo and bear, squirrel and javalina
even if we are not listening.

When we leave the land the Walkers follow
and haunt us with visions of stone mesas
stained with our blood.

And we know this:
The bones of death are always there,
just under the skin.

4

The Acoma makers search crevices
in the malpais for ancient pots.
They say the spirits are still in them.
If they powder the shards and add them to the clay
the new pots will be stronger.
That is what they say.

Veils

Lord, this mutable veil between Thee and me
agitates thick and thin like fitful clouds
gusting between earth and sky.

Sometimes I, ground bound, weave
and toss dense curtains of ponderous doubt
that fall back to chide and smother me.

Sometimes it is Thy mantle, formed
of gossamer so frangible that your finger
presses through to light a pile of stones.

Sometimes I feel my spirit lift
with the flurry of doves from a wire
as they shimmer silver, swerve,
veer and disappear, flush white
further on then vanish again
in the tangled translucence of air, where

I search for a tear in the folds of sky
flailing to feel the clutch of your hand
grasp, rescue, then lead me gently through.

.

I. Reflections on Darkness and Light

After having retired to the place I had designed to go, having looked around me, and finding myself alone, I kneeled down and began to offer up the desires of my heart. I had scarcely done so, when immediately I was seized upon by some power which entirely overcame me, and had such an astonishing influence over me as to bind my tongue so that I could not speak. Thick darkness gathered around me, and it seemed to me for a time as if I were doomed to sudden destruction. But, exerting all my powers to call upon God to deliver me out of the power of this enemy which had seized upon me, and at the very moment when I was ready to sink into despair and abandon myself to destruction—not to an imaginary ruin, but to the power of some actual being from the unseen world, who had such marvelous power as I had never before felt in any being—just at this moment of great alarm, I saw a pillar of light exactly over my head, above the brightness of the sun, which descended gradually until it fell upon me. It no sooner appeared than I found myself delivered from the enemy which held me bound.
—Joseph Smith History 1:15-17

The Asking

All that has gone before makes the now, somehow.
Whys are sucked deep into the darkened spirit's
black hole where desperate reaching retrieves
distraught questions from God's battered children.
Response comes in increments,
not *yes* or *no*, but *maybe, no matter, not yet.*

Born through a veiled past
we experiment upon the Word,
begin the long quest to fade shadow into light
only to realize, when the tests
and pleadings for help are done,
that we have to write our own answers.

II. How long will you choose darkness rather than light?
    —Helaman 13:29

The Play

Disembodied in darkness
    sightless
        there is only what we feel
            what we grapple for

Actors, chained to fear,
    flailing ourselves with other's lives
        performing
            on an unlit stage,

the curtains closed
    Voices
        of an invisible audience
            taunting

III. The people who walked in darkness have seen a great light
    —Isaiah 9:2

The Awakening

Let us chant a litany to day
with its certainty of sun
its lavishness of light;
to fires that appease the specter of night
to the spark within
that is the hugeness of us all
that lights our dreams, our visions
and causes us to yearn
for an unfathomable love.

IV. The light which is in all things, which giveth life to all, which is the law by which all things are governed.

　　　—*D&C 88:13*

The Testing

Why not a passion for the source
to counter dark's obsession?
See how lightning lashes at the night,
how the prudent carry lanterns into caves
to wrestle both angels and demons,
how focused beams transform matter.

Wave, particle, quantum,
aspects of the whole.
In a universe made of
shards of shattered stars
the shadow proves the light.

V. Double Helix

> *We were in the beginning. Intelligence, or the light of truth, was not created or made, neither indeed can be. The body filled with light comprehends all things.*
> —*D&C 88:67*

We come knowing
　　　but don't know we know
　　　　　eons encrypted, spiraled
　　　　　　　inside us, encoded in an
　　　　　　　　　infinitude of atomic light
　　　　　　　　　　　Intervolved between shadow
　　　　and sun, life breeds in darkness
　　　Intaglioed leaves dying
their golden death crumble
　　　and decay into the entropic
　　　　　dregs that infuse nascent
　　　　　　　roots with opposed force
　　　　　　　　　to push stems, leaves
　　　　　　　flowers towards visible
　　　　　light, while we, in the

night, like blossoms
triggered by dusk
ef. floresce dreams and
visions illumined from
within to bloom in the
gardens in our minds
Let there be light and
there was . . . is . . . in
all things, through
all things, brilliant, bright

Early Harvest

Midsummer. Eventide. Live waters.

You: broad-backed bundle of golden sheaves

      hewn down,

        washed,

          rushed

headlong through death's threshing current.

You: pre-ripe, holy harvest

      wrested from these, your people;

        gathered to those, your people

who attend from iridescent pastures.

You: Firstborn son,

      First fruits of my womb,

        Firstling of our flock,

          First raised of our labors. . .

            Enfolded now in the arms of the

        First raised from the dead,

      First lover of the flock,

    First fruits of the tomb,

  Firstborn Son. . .

        O, Son!

Sweet, sacrificial fruit of my flesh,

Preserved in spirit

'Til that first morn when you, our first reborn,

Shoot forth

'Mid spring.   'Mid song.

Sailing to Manti

To my husband, on the 22nd anniversary of our
December marriage in the Manti temple

We sail the vein:
Perforated, gray southbound highway
Down
From dawn's perch
We approach,
Splaying this languid stage of sagebrush
    In two
Vast contours, undulating,
Old rocky chronology seeping left to right,
Largo to fermata . . .
Bending beyond peripheral vision
          curling,
      wrapping,
   enfolding
Heaven,
Her mist-mottled crepe curtain
Whispers,
       Torn,
As ragged hem reveals enough:
Mountains, their triple depth in
Slate then ash then dust
Hang an ageless opaque canvas.

Drawn, we aim.

Trusting, we offer
Hands stretched through a veil.

We sail.

Pietà

Toth was his name, Laszlo Toth: the death man
who one midmorning charged Saint Peter's sanctum
lunged with frenzied hammer at the polished Madonna
frothing at the mouth
       shouting he wanted Him as his own
cracking with mallet swing the curves of submission
    breaking her soft hold on the dead Son.
The camera crowd gaped then contracted
wrestled him to the stone floor sentenced him
deported him declared him deranged.

Have pity on him.

Hard it is, to insanity hard, to behold a son's graceful bow
in the hold of another (doctor, technician, nurse, mortician)
to glimpse quite by mistake through the sanctum doorway
as another cradles the warm form wilting, folding under death's weight
as the gurney sheets must be removed from this side
and the tubes extracted from that side
and the limbs placed neatly at his sides
and machines are rolled away into shadows
as the muscles melt
    twisting the stone sturdy man in the
ultimate capitulation:
deference to death.

Hard it is, to derangement hard,
to not swing a mallet or hammer, to not fling oneself
onto the stone floor,
to not break into sharp marbled shards.

Have pity on me.

Bottled Fruit

For Donna Charlene Glazier Dalton and T.S. Eliot and Langston Hughes

There are museums alive under my mother's house, quiet
life-giving mausoleums, loden and loaded with their chilled secrets,
cement-walled vaults with jugs of holy jewels,
amber pendants round as halos lining the walls.
Crystal caskets crowded with dense-fleshed
soldiers, *salute!*
Cheek-to-topaz-cheek they nearly breathe
in their neat ranks, awaiting orders.
No withered raisins in the sun here,
no, but muscled suns afire in blackness: promising,
pulsing practically,
still half alive,
still life.

Let us go then, you and I, to visit those cellars
of all my mothers and their mothers and mothers,
who considered shelf life over self life, who
frankly shelved their life to bear and bind themselves with
that fleshy, sinewy fruit of the womb.

Let us see them at the kitchen sink which heaves with sultry harvest,
let us watch them ply their mothers' genes, cradling fruit
like a bronze planet in each palm, slicing its dense flesh at equator,
making two hemispheres with silk-slick skin
taut against engorged roundness.
Plump little breasts.
These, they slip two-and-two down the throats of jars
until they cannot fit a single other,
and baptize them en masse:
a ladle of sweet, pectiny waters.

In such rooms the women come and go, talking of Mason jars, Ball and Kerr.
And none dares eat a peach. But to satisfy her hunger, postpones it,
puts up for the eventual quelling of a someday craving,
saves, replants the pit, stocks this immediate abundance,
preserving it, holding on to life.

Man, with his wristwatch, might claim there will be time,
there will be time, indeed there will be time
for all the works and days of hands,
time to know and gather enough
the tender seasonal berries of our fragile human yield.

But the mothers are unconvinced.
They weep and fast and weep and pray
against the measured minutes left together
while all the late afternoon long they hear the voices dying
and the music from a farther room.

Gone too soon from their slippery hold, these dazzling passion fruits
with their ever pungent plushness and immediate delice,
these pears with their translucent skin the color of liquid bone
and veins of laced filigree.
Firmest fruit like buffed and bottled riverstones:
these are their proving rocks
touchstone testaments of existence
their innermost fruits
which fill deepest chambers against the time
when they might nourish—or might outlive—
the mothers.

House for Rent:

To George MacDonald and C.S. Lewis,
Response to MacDonald's "living house" allegory, as quoted by Lewis in Mere Christianity

Imagine, they suggest.
Imagine yourself as a living house
and God comes in (here comes the allegory),
God comes in to rebuild that house
and to rebuild, He destroys you.
Splits you wide open.
Knocks you down to shape you up. Blows you away to bring you forth
       as mansion, His dwelling.

Imagine?

Imagine: a structure well beyond any
apt literary construct;
Imagine the literal natal invasion,
factual inhabitation, indwelling, the magnifying internment;
this alive thing with its lush, essential interior,
nautilus of distended tension,
gourd-like terrarium, loamy abode,
an incubation for cumulus nimbus,
spirit under my ribs
      or cosmos
        in the veiled universe of my belly.

What, kindest sirs, might you imagine about a living house
but what woman need never imagine?
Tell: can you conceive of it?

I am the aquarium,
have known (four times) the thrumming oceanic drag,
      fulsome tidepool slosh in pelvis,
      sweetest ferocious confined Leviathan
      stomping inner tympani,
      boom-boom-blooming to omega.
      Four times nine moons—
(a moon myself, pneumatic)
holding that glowing orb
or the finest delicacy: shrimp-on-wafer hors d'oeuvre in salty brine

burrowing in our shared cell.
    Most intimate inmate.

I am the accommodation, the occupied real estate
(most *real* of all states)
a fleshly floorplan, walls torn down for the guest wing thrown up,
placental planting, deluxe plumbing, organic annexing for the increase.

I am that natural habitat for humanity,
an address for razing and raising,
strung taut with that sturdy umbilical pull until (and after)
      birth.
      Now, that's *some* moving day:

Nude little lord, prodigious squatter, long since incorporated, moves out
trailing furnishings, clutching soul (whose? my own?)
in bloody wash,
the old self eviscerated, inverted, and that
humanangel image *(past imagining)*
      multiplying upon itself forever
      ever
      ever
      ever . . .

To *be* such a sanctuary of conception,
to *be* asylum for small gods and sovereigns, who swell, crown,
rise to rule and risk life!
      At such risk. At such risk as one can never . . .

Can one imagine those same living quarters drawn and quartered
when son-brother-cell mate—
      (the one who moved within,
      then out of you,
      your heart still raw in his hold)
when that oblation grown lustrous, thunderous, launch-ready,
      is ripped   (*with*   *that*   *riiiiipping*   *sound*)
away?

Hard, benevolent wounding, whose frayed fibers hang,
sodden shreds post-rupture,
and you, true house, are rent
the cloven enclave,
      rent in two, or into

two billion splinters:
tattered scraps of love's sabotage.

Imagine yourself as this living house, haunted in its
boney scaffolds where memory whistles its blue wind
and you are apart-ment
living house split leveled: he there,
you here,
          fetal-curled in your own basin;
or a bunker: hunkered in poetry;
or a ranch: speck on the shadowless prairie, barren and boundless;
or a lean-to: whole halved to make a whole, now wholly halved.

          And *now* . . .
God moves in
though there is no palace for Him here
only rubble round the crater,
wreckage ringing the hollow.

But He, soft-handed (the hands gored)
comes inside (the side gashed)
to silently,
          sacramentally
recreate from laceration Lazarus
          and is at home.

WILLIAM DEFORD

St. Teresa of Avila as Middle Manager

It is a room without shadows.
Around a conference table, seven souls,
Seven cold coffee cups, legal pads,

Uncapped pens, one pencil
Sharpened like a spear, like the Holy Spirit.
There is a sublime flatness here,

A Giotto madonna stripped of goldleaf.
Teresa, from HR, isn't taking notes.
The meeting goes on without her.
Her eyes are fixed on the ceiling,

She feels a cool breath
From the vent overhead:
Spirits must still brood
On the faces of things, she thinks.

                    *

The maintenance man is on his way.
God has entered a sputtering light bulb,
Blinking a numerology echoed
In the mouse-clicks of the oblivious AV guy.

There is too much symmetry here,
Too many glazed-over eyes.
At last she raises her pencil, a gesture

Of sorrow and amusement.
She speaks a parable
That sends concentric ripples
Through everyone's coffee cups.

Fire in the Pasture

A Story of Two Raindrops and a Wooden Frame

they fall drop by drop
—*Tadeusz Róziwicz*

Falling, she knew it would come to this. She had lived a long life, with few secret sins: she was sometimes bored in church, she once had a mild crush on the bishop, a married man, she nearly always told the truth. In the spring, a chariot of fire came for her as she had hoped. It started to rain. She bustled around her house dusting furniture, straightening lampshades already straight. She wrote a final entry in her diary and placed it in a desk drawer where her sister was sure to find it. By the time she got to the curb, the chariot flames sputtered in the downpour. Gabriel stood by the coach, sodden, without an umbrella, holding his hat in his hands. They lifted off, and halfway to the Gates the flames sighed and went out. Nothing of the chariot was left except a soggy, charred frame. She hurtled down, faster than she thought possible, shrugging at her usual luck, trying to make out the patchwork of her town below, steering herself to someplace inconspicuous. Soon she and Gabriel were lost among the raindrops falling alongside them—so many souls! she thought—while smoke from the plummeting chariot rose like incense, like prayer.

Stripping the Kitchen Floor

I peel up linoleum like juniper bark,
Scrape at the glue, sand to discover
The white pine of this kitchen floor.

Black streaks scatter like bugs.
Four generations dissipate to dust
And settle in cracks between boards.

Since nineteen-five, these planks
have born the scuffs of children's shoes,
Blackened nail holes stained with paint.

I sand through the houses this house has been:
Patched-up three-family tenement;
A condemned pile near the street's dead end,

Hovel of spiders and stray cats;
A hobo stop by the tracks,
Leaves heaped at the foot of the stairs;

A dowry and a family home;
A farmhouse in alfalfa fields . . .
I feel the lines, the amber grain

Of pines that stood in the canyon
When this valley spread out
Birdloud and empty of towns.

Moon Over Power Lines

And a cloud received him out of their sight.
—Acts 1:9

There is a swath cut to the soul
Of the woods. Across the road,
White houses are growing blue, holding
Breath with the emaciated trees.
The sun remembers us and vice versa.
Once again, Earth has become our dark sun;
The cold comes down. It stirs like a spider
Beneath our shirts. At twilight, nothing can surprise us:
There are tambourines shaking in the woods,
Goldfish sparkling in the windows of houses,
Their pectoral fins tufting like flamenco skirts,
Nothing can surprise us
But Earth's ghost haunting itself
Low and gold—its eyes sewn shut—whispering,
It is not for you to know the times or the seasons,
Breaking humbly, terribly, over the stitches
We have stretched across the ground.

Placenta

Snow glistens in its instant in the air.
—Wallace Stevens

I picture it, a milky glass teardrop
Just large enough to fill my cupped hand.
It floats in an almost-dark cave;
It lights the cave but slightly, casting
Wan shadows, a vessel of music and logic
Unknown among us.

I saw it as a dark circle on the ultrasound,
Saw it conspicuously empty.
It's common, the doctor said, for it to end this way.
But it hasn't ended, even after the procedure,
After bringing you grape juice in a paper cup,
And watching you lift it to your mouth, trailing
An IV tube from your wrist.

The dark teardrop is still there
Not a thing but a place, as the name suggests,
A place that cannot be given or taken,
That does not live or die.

Legacy

Her afghans and roses give her day a pattern
that will untighten her mouth pursed by a memory—
how her mother would fatten the favored son with milk,
claiming only boys needed calcium, not girls.

My grandmother's bones brittle, in pain,
her voice still bitter as she purls,
"She gave me weak bones."
She remains after eighty years

that girl thirsting for milk
in her quiet house scented with roses, talc,
as September light darkens over the Dresden shepherdess—
a gift from her brother while stationed in Germany—

the folds of her china skirt milk-white,
the rose canes turning brittle outside.

Poem for my Daughter

I left behind a childhood in storms that woke me years ago,
pelting the glass panes with exploding stars.
It returns to me tonight in the desert teasing Kentucky blue grass with rain.
If we are made of truth and light, I want truth the color of twilight—
a whale's back cresting the water so swiftly,
we can't say if we saw whale or wave.
Each month a sea has been rising inside me
where my daughter breathes water and sleeps near my heart.

The sky will flood dry washes for her,
churn rivers into muddy flames, soak the foreign grass.
I step into thunderheads
our hearts an untrembling wall.
But sagebrush roots drink quietly
from an inland sea the earth has always held.

Great Basin

I am no nearer to what the sea tries to loosen wedged in rock—
a sorrow slipped between a trapped metal cap
and glass shattered along another coast.
The truth is I don't live near the ocean
but in a desert town I refuse to see
built on an alluvial fan of gypsum soil shifting
beneath cracked plaster and skewed door frames;
beneath miles of silver sage, rabbit brush, dry lakes

and wind trembling through pinyon rooted along the highway.
I leave my own trace by planting wisteria and honeysuckle,
Southern foreigners thirsting for water.
I blink and the town is gone, drowned in a sea of fossils.
What that sea left behind is the desert I walk through,
a sorrow slipped between shale and trilobites.

The Meadow

Night the trees trill
at the edge of my ear,
a seven-year sleep unraveling
from husks honeyed to bark.

There was a night like this—
leaves slowly falling,
or really a year opening,
into rings and rings.

We skipped stones across them,
across the maple's reflection:
its fallen crown
is a ghost of leaves.

I took you into the waterfall
where we kissed.
I pulled off my shirt
sunned myself against a rock,

you beside me—and on that day
while northward spring
startled forsythia, I dreamed
of the locked drawer of childhood

when we dropped a world
of spun glass—blue-green marbles—
into the deep pocket
of a bird's nest.

Descent

He holds them in his hands
as if holding the sea—
my first gift in a strange place—
six blue china horses
a wilderness in their eyes.

Take them, he says.
I touch their cool hooves.
He binds my hands between his palms.
Now you must always return.

I smash the horses into
a foam of blue shards.
Deeper into the earth
I carry the sea with me.

Oceanside

By water, I mean the waves
cradling the shore
near the place I grew up.

My mother would drive us along the coast
past sand and those peach-colored
vacation beach homes.

I sat in the passenger seat of
our beige Buick station wagon,
the window rolled down as far as

it would go—salty wind gusting on my face
and the sound of ocean static like a radio
playing something I couldn't quite distinguish.

It was a sound like the shh-ing of silence,
a sound like noise that is the absence
of noise. My mother entranced.

Me studying sunlight setting on waves:
some spots turquoise, others sea foam green,
the rest almost black, or dark blue.

The only time she spent with me—
before her father died—before my father
took that job across the U.S.—before she remembered

she was missing a part of her life, the part
that comes after adolescence, before marriage
when you listen

to the sound of the ocean, when you wish for the noise
that is the absence of noise—for the silence
of the mind before it crashes, and crashes, and crashes.

Albatross

I was shot.
But the mariner's curse now hangs
on me.

A bird or a poet?
Only Baudelaire can answer
this exile.

Help me now
find a use for these
giant wings.

Dragonfly

I.

I first read about you
in Dante Gabriel's *Silent
Noon*, hovering over lovers.

You were that blue thread,
ethereal and connected
to the celestial realm,
sent to seal their moment.

II.

Traveling 70 miles per hour
in a car at the close of day
across black to blue strata (black-
top, plains, and sky), I find
your body stuck between
windshield and wiper blade
on the other side of glass.

Your colors fade from
peacock to landfill
as the sun sets on us.

III.

Like you, I am caught
between metal and glass—
between what I can see
and what remains to be seen.

You leave me
stuck in words material,
nearsighted.

Human Dispenser

I wanted you to sanctify what merely needed reconciling.
You, my human savior, sent to justify my morals and this world
With yours. And why
You? As if you were a type of savior.
As if you actually wanted to.

I thought you did.
                    That's what I get for thinking.

It was all in the cards. The Devil. The Fool.
And that heart. Pierced with swords. Stabbed.

Knowing is inevitable.
Especially when you ask for it.

I wanted both: ignorance and enlightenment. And you
Graciously dispensed them.

You, some kind of dispenser of knowledge.
Your contents measured out in vats
Large enough to swallow me whole.

My Translation of the 1st Half of 2nd Corinthians 1

Paul and Timothy, by God's will, to Corinth:

Grace and peace from God and the Lord
(Bless) the Father of mercies, the God of all
comfort. Who comforts in (tribulation)
so we can comfort in trouble
with the comfort that we comforted
of God.

For the sufferings of Christ in us
abounding,
so our consolation by Christ
abounds.
Our affliction for your consolation.
Our comfort for the same two "-tions."
And our hope of you is steadfast, knowing
that as you suffer, so you will
be consoled.

We wouldn't have you ignorant
of our trouble in Asia:
We were pressed out of measure
above strength, so much
that we despaired
(even life).
But the sentence of death was in
us—to not trust ourselves, but
God who raises the dead,
who delivered us from death
and delivers, who we trust
will still deliver us.

Thanks for your prayers.

We (rejoice) because of:

1. the testimony of our conscience that:
in simplicity and godly sincerity
(not with fleshy wisdom)
but by God's grace

> we've had our conversation in the world.
>> No—with the world.

All That Possessed Us

Bobcat sits crouched on a flat granite rock,
unfurls her yellow haunches and springs.
The little girl screams. Bobcat, with white braids
and a crown (toyrone berries, recently gleaned), stalks
Indians with rocks, as they crush acorns and
berries bursting with poisonous white powder.
She circles the teepee where it stands—a pyramid skeleton
of long sticks covered with dollar-size leaves.
There are tunnels full of pale crumpled foliage
where we three lie, suffocated and swelling with
pink war paint from breastbone to widow's peak, and consider all that

                                               drew us.

Predator becomes prey, with red half-moons on her
pale forearms.
Let's go down, she says, to the fence
and walk through that tunnel we should stay away from,
and dig in the big anthill until we turn orange.
We'll duck under the bushes until we come to that
green chapel with the tree that fell
and climb on its flailing octopus limbs, high over
our heads. We feel them rising and bucking, and we wonder over all that

                                               moved us.

A hillside is for sparring bobcats
with plenty of daffodil prey
and crocus prey, and stickers that choke our socks
and give us thoughtful pause.
We lay, looking up, and feel ourselves falling
endlessly forward and Drowning. We snake our way
along the un-mown grass and slide through the
tearing underbrush, until we find that pine,
that massive trunk that towers like Babel, and
soon we see above the green canopy. We look down,
far, far down, and for the first time, question all that

                                             possessed us.

Ode to a Leather Jacket

That day I walked away from you, I dreamt
of the first time when you crouched against
the wall, waiting. And stills. Yes, *stills*; your breath
was furred with that (faint) rosary scent.
Oh, Gabriel, with dark hair springing away
from that classic brow. A break in time
means you and I could tumble in a mess
of haylofts. Who could say
what I am. What you are. Whether we're the same
or just faltering in our own relentlessness.

I slide my arms into those cobalt sleeves.
It falls, a villainous cape clear to my shins
and I dig in those pockets for those dimes
and my number—all escaped to heaven. (*Please.*)
The kiss. Do you taste chocolate on my tongue?
It was in the pocket, as smooth and warm
as skin which melted it—melted me.
My fingers cling
to those lapels without my leave. I'm torn
with what I mean and what I wish I see.

It's cold, you said. *It's cold.* What a cliché.
There I turned, and found your eyes again:
a threadbare look will keep my soul agape
and silence every question with a sin.
What milk, what beehives I should wish to know
at a cost too high to name in numbers.
Glory, glory, glory on the nerves, in
priestly clothes.
What I can't forget, *sure*, God remembers
and names. Believing you? *Believing me*,
and leaving.

Morning Low

There's a shoe pile, propped
against a sandy log, seventeen heel-prints away
from where the tides are changing hands between the beaches.
Up on the sand, the bone-shells bleach
white, out of the rip-tide's way.
My black heels break

open; the grit on my feet swirls out
through stinging, cloudy water. I climb over
the resurrection (Inert. Alive. Awake!) and arch my soles
to keep my skin from grating against their beaks. I see
mussels sway, spread sharp lips in spray,
and breathe, too slow to see.
The shivers break

along gulf-stream nerve beds in
a coral pattern. An arm there—a claw hand.
Warm licks on my ankles. Cucumbers; they bare their Jelly
in the morning low. They lie in wait while water rises.
A fish head, eyes alive, moves with the tide.
A swell breaks and ices my knees.
My leg hairs undulate.

Taxi

Call us another biplane. We'll go rocketing off, along some
ice-cobbled street, following the lights that run
in long lines along the pavements.
 As we rise they bloom and brighten: azure and ultra
on the way to puddles of deep, sweet silence.
There's a turn here that leads to Ursa Major and
the implosion of depth. I turn and find you in the
sudden gleam of your glasses-rims.
The whorl of stars rushing past; there—above the
zaggish dark shapes, towers and church bells impinging
damply upon the clear canvass—there it is, a belfry full of
sparkling golden things, whirring and swirling up around
the sickle-blue crescent. You and I. . . .

on the ground, we have an awful tendency to
stare down wells, looking for blue faces and giant dippers,
while above us a bear may chase a bowman in a
cacophony of flutterings.
Even now. It's the wing, the fuselage, the nose of our vehicle

that frightens and fails us. Don't look. Instead, let's stand face to face
with ice and moon rocks, and keep our heads up, drunk in the
starkness of space.

Gaius

I cannot look at moths.
One seizes himself from
spade to spade, in
the haggard mat of grass roots, and
I feel impatient with the
inefficiency of frenetic,
blind antennae.

Still it is my lawn,
great, or small and disturbed.
It's all my glorious mix of crab
and Florida blue;
roaring ant lions,
and creaking night crawler.
Even the scat of a neighborhood pet
that wandered off the street.

And those triangular wings—
the wings of a folded airplane—
I flinch away from the thick fuzz
of antennae, and even in flinching
I confess it to myself
and to the kingdom of heaven:

If I wish to claim a piece of nature,
I cannot, then, shudder at
the badgering about my night lights,
the cloud that erupts from
my stalest firewood boxes.

I must admire even the needlenozzle, with
its fan of wasted breath, and listen
to the dull buzz of electricity.
I keep my switches flicked for the
wash of heat that warms and lights
a squat little body,
hovering on a windmill of wingbeats.

I seriously consider the Gaius
along the edge of a swat-tool,
(white matter, suffused with mucosa).
I spend an hour to watch them agitate;
and when night falls—shiver me lunar—
I acknowledge the face there,
the blue chin clockwise of
the eyeless features; more than a medallion
inside my worn jewelry basket.

In the end it might be that I must even
stretch my own chin on the chance—
even the slightest chance, that I myself,
with my peach-fuzz skin and saltwater breath
could be the perfect, warm perch
to calm the lost moth
and tame its seizing.

I Teach Six-Year-Olds about Jesus in Sunday School

A girl I've never met meets me at the door,
whines at my leg until I hold her. Thin arms,
thin mouth, a sour smell I overlook while fetching
crayons, glue sticks, snacks. She lifts her dress,
exposes the top of her baggy white tights, looks at me.
We both sing: "Faith is knowing the sun will rise . . ."
I sit next to her, tap her hands, whisper no.

Kyle, on the front row, holds a cardboard
box on his lap, a green scrawl on the lid.
It's his turn to toss the bean bag and recite
a miracle, but he stops, looks at me, says,
"This is my box," like I have to meet it
before he can toss. He places it on the chair,
doesn't know the miracle, returns it to his lap.

Michael sucks on his plastic bat, swings it so
I'm showered in spit. "What's the bat's name?"
I ask, taking two fingers to slow it. "Jesus."
When I end the bat business, he howls and I hold
him like the Pietà, his sweaty back sticking to my arms.
I rock him, pray in his ear until he sleeps,
his tears soaking my blouse, his bat tucked in my bag

In the Hall While They Take Chest X-Rays

A chubby boy wearing green sweats whines to his father,
"But *when* do I get my snack?"

I'm impatient for the pleasant part, too.
I stare at a silver cart full of gauze, cotton, bandages.
It's sleek and pretty in fluorescent light.

After they buzz around, sticking and stabbing you,
comes the part where morphine makes your voice thick.
And I can sit on the edge of your bed, my arm across your torso,

as long as I don't swim around in the nurse's assumption
that we're something, that we're *we*.

Banded Claws

At dinner with your husband,
a plaid sofa crashes
through the ceiling, shatters
the lobster aquarium.

While busboys corner lobsters,
you leave your bowl of mulligatawny
and a thick conversation with your husband,
so you can look a lobster square in its spiny face.

Its rubber-banded claws droop over the bar,
and you tuck your arms, stiffen like you did
at the zoo's butterfly house. Butterflies are
nothing but tiny hairy lobsters with pretty wings.

Behind you, the maitre d' and Fire Marshall
rule out termites and a waiter plucks a lobster
as it ascends a collection of fancy hotel soaps.
He tucks it under his arm, like you used to cart your cat.

At the zoo, when a Blue Morpho settled
in a woman's hair, and she delicately extracted
a camera, begging a picture, you said, "I think it's stuck.
Really. It's pawing your hair and I think it's stuck."

Now all the lobsters are corralled in a quilt basket,
plodding against one another. You think: boiled
shells are brighter red. You think: iridescent pink
butterfly eggs in her hair. She had bragged,
"A good fertility omen."

You're thinking this instead of sperm counts, instead
of seeing the bright coiled TV guts splayed beside
the dumbwaiter, instead of sitting back down,
arranging your skirt, and telling your husband,
he's right after all: you don't want a child.

The Unfortunate Marriage

Sun does Moon's laundry each morning,
wrings night from his coat,
tucks him under her bright blanket.
All day he'll sleep, she'll burn.
At dusk, she'll sink.
All night he'll pluck the linty stars, fling them.

Bioluminesce

Once we watched deep-sea creatures
bioluminesce in shimmering sheets.
Sirens outside, an orange haze from
street lights, strobe of the TV screen.
He held me and a manta flapped by,
graceful in marine snow, larger than a car.

And now a strange nonchalance, quiet car
rides and all that, laundry spats, creatures
tripping into habit, keeping both sheets
crisp, clean. 7 a.m., he calls from
Milwaukee and we talk through screens
and we know it. By the time we say goodbye

I'm licking a spoon of peanut butter by
the fishtank. I forgot to ask about the car
payment, forgot to say we're just creatures
tripping into habit, that his half of the sheets
seemed cold. The fish are darting from
one fleck of food to the other behind screens

of algae and glass. Maybe I need to screen
my calls today, lounge nude, take my bi-
quarterly mental health day. The car
won't start? I'm ill? Some creature
that I care deeply about ate dryer sheets
and croaked? If I can drag myself away from

peanut butter, perhaps I can keep from
calling him back. On the window screen,
a moth lands, flattens its wings. Out by
the mailbox, the newspaper waits. My car
is covered in dew and bird shit. You create your
niche, right? We're issued blank sheets

and fill them? I pluck the moth from the screen,
hold it by wing tips. A car starts. I cup the creature
in my hands, carry it in, settle it on his half of the sheets.

Felucca at Maadi

Along the Nile cornice, royal purple jacaranda
and flame red acacia petals winnow down,
flake the late May river path, swirl and fluff
about the ankles of the early evening strollers,
part like sparrows fluttering to seed or crumb.
    None come underfoot.

Along the river, we move north in a felucca,
rhythmed about by music tinning out from
black dog woofer boxes on the shore—
a large, white ficus leaf feathering
before the west-leaning wind as it spreads
    itself flat across the water.

Above, loose cotton-thread clouds perceive
themselves into the calligraphy of an Arabic script.
Read from the right, as the texts between the
whirling mosaic illuminations I once saw
on the Koran's pages at Rumi's green tomb
    in Konya, they raise a question:

"And who will explain this steep path to you?"

The bland wind billows the sail edge into a left-handed
crescent, a cloth trace of the waxing early moon above.
On coming about, the angle line wavers, the wind
    lufts and teases the charity of its blue border.

It whaps like a wet sheet hung to stop
a Utah canyon breeze near Wildwood,
after noon, when it reverses on itself, valley bound
along the river, running to kiss the rising
    desert valley heat below.

The diminishing Akhenaten sun gilds a path on the river,
as thin and golden as the leaf on Tutankhamun's masks.
It lays the way to sail straight to those triangles at Giza,

where Cheops's barge awaits, earth-bound,
    to companion us into the after.

No need to come about again this evening,
the angles of Ra right themselves on the river.
We can keep on sailing, straight on together
    for an eternity.

poetry on the 'fridge door

#1, v.1

my mother is madly licking
at the languid red peach,
screaming at life and
the rust crush of death.
an angry winter knife cuts
toward the smooth white summer light.
a thousand gorgeous whispers
chant away at the black shadows.
she senses that it is nearly over.

alzheimer's

my mother licks languidly
at a dried red peach,
clinging to her life still,
and the rust crush of age.

she cannot taste the delicate
gray winter knife tearing
at the smooth white summer light.
she cannot feel the
black autumn shadow
chasing away a thousand
green spring wisps.

she cannot smell the
slippery blue summer dew
dripping on to the brown
prism-edged autumn sand.
she cannot see the silver
merry-go-round winter wind
chasing itself and roaring
in the purple evening spring sky.

she cannot hear the fiery,
yellow-orange autumn fumes
enveloping the emerald hews
of the spring ice chunks.

my mother cannot sense
that her seasons are nearly over.
her senses say they are just beginning.

again.

Lisa Gherardini Might Be Pregnant

Seated in a gray-clad museum wheelchair,
my father's brown eyes look skinny,
slowly disappearing from view as he ages,
    wanders toward a dream in the afternoon.
He ignores the art in the room, has not read the guide,
    has no desire to know who is here.
His thoughts are elsewhere.
He is thinking, in his nap scene, what it would be like
    if Venus had arms and could softly embrace him.
He wants to catch a ride out of the room to see her,
    again.

Across the room, Leonardo's *Mona Lisa* leans
    against her wall, beyond the reach of slashing fists.
Hands folded, soft *sfumato* eyes sleep weary,
    she smiles, bemused, down on him,
wonders why, unlike others, he is not paying
    attention to *her*.

The mystique of her middled age mocks him
with gossamer sweetness and velvet, a moment of
self-satisfaction turns the edges of her thin-lipped mouth,
    barely.
Lower, in the silk folds of her black gown, she hides
    some soft secret.
She waits for him to guess it, or her true name, then she
    will let him turn and go, even if to see another.
Strict as a schoolmarm, she will give no hint to help him.
She will hold her laconic smile until he makes his
    suggestive guess or just gives up and leaves.

Someone should whisper "Lisa Gherardini might be pregnant"
    in his ear.
Someone should tell her my father prefers Venus.

Then they can stop bothering each other.

Twelve Questions in One Long Sentence

I have smelled the perfume of a thousand tonca beans hovering in the night air just above the forest path, and wondered what they could possibly add to the bitter taste of the cocoa, heard the paired green parrots chattering in the afternoon as they fly against the blue sky, and wondered what they were saying to each other and how long they would fly, waited for the crimson red of the ginger lilies to appear in the corner of the back yard, and wondered what pain provoked their deep, confused color, tasted the sense of the cherry-coconut ice cream, and wondered how to thank who ever thought of the mix, watched the yellow poui bloom all across the hillside, and wondered when the cooling rains would come, kissed the bites on my arm torn by the thorny branches of the red-purple bougainvillea along the driveway, and wondered who appointed them guard-dog sentinels, sucked on the rich yellow-orange flesh of the julie mango, and wondered how they got to be so sweet, opened the coconut and drunk its opaque water, and wondered where it got its coolness, danced the full brown cocoa beans around the box, oiling them up carefully for the 100 kilo bag, and wondered how many it would take to make a Hershey's Kiss, stripped the meager white flesh from the cocorite seed, and wondered how long it took to grow so little, healed the razor tears on my hand from the blade of a sharpened cutlass, and wondered how stupid I could be to blindly take it from the dark interior of the black knap sack, leaned toward the double rainbows over the Northern Range, and wondered who painted and hung them there?

Things Missed

Every now and then I make it a point to go
without knowing to these places, try to discover
a view of my own, be surprised, have
an experience uncluttered by history or the facts.
I try to imagine my way to a bit of truth or the
answer to some awkward childhood riddle.

I went to Giza once this way, entered the wind-dusted
space, dodged the thronging hawkers, slid sideways
past the harried shirtsleeve tugs of the pleading guides,
as they offered to sell me a day or two of knowing.

I lingered at Cheop's boat, counted the oars,
thought of his trip to the longer side of eternity.
I measured step by step the footprint of the pyramids
and climbed on a few of the metered blocks—
wondered how long they'd been there,
how much longer they would stand.
I considered the angles and the sides, tried
to recall their geometry and physics, as explained
by Mrs. de Jong at Brigham Young Junior High.

With my shoe I shuffled the underside of the sand.
I exchanged smiles with the camels, complained
with them about our thirst. I curled my lips,
bared my teeth, made a low bellow as they do,
and thought of the crumpled, sepia portrait
of my grandparents riding theirs fifty years before.
Then, I squinted into the west-leaning sun
as the day began telling me to leave.
I went to Giza once this way and failed to find
the nose-broken Sphinx haunching coyly
just beyond the brown edge of the afternoon
shadows there, a little down and to the left
of where ignorance had taken me that day.

The User's Guide to Onomatopoetic Elegies

And should we die before our journey's through,
Happy day! All is well!
—William Clayton

it's viewings, not funerals I won't attend anymore
and what bothers me is not the trail of people who
have to touch a clammy hand to satisfy this head knell
      but it is this: my eight-year-old brother still blonde

with finger-length curls started meowing
at me when I should have been terrified of the boxed body
      across the room. (and not in any normal fashion) he mewed
with clarity and volume against shuffling masses
reading the audience card in whispers, "he was a good man,"
and piercing, like god, so only I could hear it, and maybe my mother
who only shifted in her floral-print whatever it was.
      my brother, now a small cat padding across the room in full march, *come,*
come ye saints, the actual tune equated to meow mix, he
leaned his head on my knee and at my reddening only meowed
softer, approximating a kitten gondolier for the dead, *come, come ye,*
      paced a warbling line between the bodied room and a row
of folding chairs, *no toil nor labor fear*, he looked at me coyly
and started verse three, with his back toward my now
      shushing mother, and so quietly again to the chair, to my

legs, to the ground and the underground and the hell under,
he meowed, *happy day, all is well*, the part for parts left to
beetles, cockroaches, companions of crypts is this too much
here too much to say, that i hope they clicked their little
antennae in time, they mulched in the dirge of earth, rhythmically
praising the newly blessed place and company

abandonment for two

for Trent Johnson

you gave me a bike,
a cruiser with a light that
shines when you peddle

it's black, the better
of two; you named the red one
like a proud father

and swear they were left
for rust at the rack, locked and
abandoned to us

I finger the dents,
wonder who misses my gift,
whether you meant it.

arms upon arms to an earth

for Trent Johnson

you called your Eden
desert, immutable wayplace
of God, pulsing, still.

I called, newly
staked, and dusted your ear, pressed
together the hum.

the tree's square hands
punctured our shine's reddening cracks,
its loud birth swallowed

the overfolded
map whole in temporary
green, first bush, dune, hill.

May 18, 2006

Dear T——,

yesterday I fell and bludgeoned both of my ankles into oblivion.

(first we remember our broken
bodies)(the breaking of
something that feels like body)
(this bread tastes like)(your
broken body)(like
surfaced blood)

you'd run your fingers over the open lip of skin,
lay your mouth along the line of blue blood
airborne and black, draw a careful line up the length of my shin.
I'd give you a blood orange.

Yours,
B——

hollow-boned scaffolding

in church I draw wings
held on with backpack straps,
a transfiguration

they unfold,
fill like parachutes, slow us
into our inky new lives

The Delivery Room

I see myself
    daughter
inside your rhythmic breathing
    hair pushed back,
        your full young face,
the familiar swim
    of pain and heaviness.

While you in the water
    ride the waves
that rise and dip
    toward
that final crescendo
    of pain and holiness.

when our familiar
    gates swing open
when we
    like Eve
taste the salty fruit
    and choose
        to swim.

Mother in Law

At the edge of the yard
the very corner
where the garden used to be
a rhubarb spreads full blossom.
The gate behind still tied closed
with a rope—
a worn woody backdrop
to blood red stalks
fanning in the sun
when all else is diminishing.

There is little left of your former life
so bountiful and busy,
but this feisty little plant
you many times turned into pie.

It is redder than I remember
shiny as if polished
by the years
spent in growing and raising
boys and plants
Wyoming wind and all

I remember
the way your short frame
stretched in shadow across rows of beans,
how you'd kneel in a ball to check kohlrabi bulbs,
and snap cabbage heads from their cradles.

But rhubarb was left
to grow hearty against the wind
prolific in the spring and summer
it grew back every time it was picked
becoming redder, shinier too
as if sacrifice had a taste,
a name and a hue.

To Kent, My Brother

Strange after forty-one years
I should think of you

a picture
white as an angle

plump bread dough
baby

lazy in the palsy
that captured your body

and made you pure
and dead at ten months

the silent first
we all followed,

oblivious you
encircled our world

with some
blessed halo

linking eternity
with one imperfect wreath.

Sagebrush and Sand

Take me,
so unfamiliar.
my light,
your dark,
incongruous
as sagebrush and sea,
I the morning blast,
you a whispered night,
we are no mirrored pair
and yet,
we meet along the edges,
where the water strokes the land
    where crabs dig like dogs
      as they sink into the sand.

The Blue Jacket

That day the vein burst
    in your head
you wore blue,
periwinkle crisp
as snow
glazed by wind,

While damp sheets tossed in the dryer,
children quarreled in the car,
You, glittering in blue,
reached out a slim hand

that had the day before
shaped loaves, applied lipstick,
reached for the right piano key—
but now grasped the honor,

the applause, the coming together
of dreams kneaded into bread,
the everyday warmth of all that is real
and sharp
as your jewelry
handed to me in an envelope,
the suit waded in a plastic bag.

You asked as life slipped out of you
whether they cut the jacket off,
whether I'd seen the
shade,
the way it caught the light
as you burst through the door.

Atlanta to Salt Lake

for Sally

Prose will not capture some people, the way
they drift. You can only see them dragging
their furniture through Wyoming night,
down a dark throat of road, the ice
clear and slick. We stopped to sleep in a solitary
town: Rawlins, Wyoming. Ahead:

a slow hundred miles of snow. (Things ahead
are always murky, but we go anyway,
forward.) Oklahoma was first, the solitary
landscape scarred with arthritic trees, as if dragged
up by their bones. We stopped only twice,
once at a motel with "crap" on the walls, and all night

she couldn't sleep, fearing what other nights
("hookers and pimps") had left in the sheets. And still ahead
of us, Nebraska flats and the Wyoming ice
a vast white cliché. It wasn't the way
I expected, but an easier slope for dragging
that U-haul than I-70. Just solitary.

Only a semi every few miles. We played laptop solitaire
by turns—her black skirt in the window shading her like night,
blocking the sun, while my toes went numb—dragging
the load away from failed relationships, hoping ahead
for clarity, like Thelma and Louise. But that's not the way
it works. Still, we ate at that truck stop the night before. Ice

shrapneled our faces; her Dad phoned to warn us of icy
roads that could lead to cliffs and a solitary
death where our car might "blow up. That would suck." His way
of cheering her up—and it worked. That night
we laughed through the rattlesnake backscratchers, Dead Head
T-shirts, Jesus figures, stuffed pigs dressed in camo, dragging

ourselves to warm beds in a decent motel. Then that dragging
day through whitewash, WY, horizons of ice,
to Rock Springs, shouts, and a Pizza Hut buffet. Ahead

was Utah, final destination for her solitary
path without men, though every night
she would think of the same one. But that's the way

it works—in circles. The way she came dragging
back home, still obscured by night, months later, the ice
still thick inside. More solitary. Less looking ahead.

Adjusting

Somewhere in the pile of plastic wrap, stacks
of yellow bowls, blue-lidded Pyrex, the metal-slick clink

of gifts we hope will last for years and several children,
is the woman you married, the girl you loved

before she became Woman of the House, Your
House, the garage too crowded

for two cars. Her arm stretches across your bed like Iowa
before she touches flesh. And you reach out

with closed eyes, hold her bone warmth, not knowing
she is still outside, trying to think of words

to name it all. Remembering: it was Adam
who got the naming power, made Eve

Mother before she could be Girl. How long
would it take for her to turn

toward that sound? Did she sense the girl
inside, the muted memory, the leaves

in her periphery twitching? Or just
hunger, a stomach growling

for self, a woman with all things given to her
who wanted. And when she ate the fruit,

she devoured the Memory in its flesh—
her elusive Daughter-ness—

sucked her History from its pit,
licked clean her sticky palms,

her living fingertips, stretched them out behind her
to touch God's hand.

In the Mountains of Gilead: Jephthah's Daughter

My father, if thou hast opened thy mouth unto the Lord, do to me according to that which hath proceeded out of thy mouth; forasmuch as the Lord hath taken vengeance for thee of thine enemies, even of the children of Ammon. . . . Let this thing be done for me: let me alone two months, that I may go up and down upon the mountains, and bewail my virginity, I and my fellows.
—Judges 11:36-7

I have known no man. I have only
known their black bead gazes, some flickering
moths in firelight, others burning coals.
Those still singe my skin, my insides sore
with emptiness. *Jehovah-yir'eh.*
In this high place, thorns of balsam tear
my skirts, my flesh when I forget my steps.
How cruel underbrush could heal a wound
I do not know, only that my mother
smoothed its balm, once soothed affliction
in her hands. *Jehovah-yir'eh.*
Tomorrow I descend to ceremony,
ascend the altar, await the angel
to stop my father's hand. *Jehovah-yir'eh.*

The Semantics of Blessings

Do not steal my fire and ice, make null
my trial, void it with another name
than pain. The cut of a blade opening to bright red
is revelation, not in later epiphany,
but present sense, the now of living, now of
lava coursing down my throat to scorch my
inside self. I know on my tongue the later coal
will make me glow, the later scar will disappear
as skin stretches old. But that should not erase
the instigation, surprise of not healings,
solitude in grocery stores, noise of
one's own breathing. Joy is not inserting
catheters in bathrooms I'm too tired
to clean, and I am not immortal yet.

God as Intern

I.

Twilight: a great scab
crusted over the land,

a red line
seething, an end

of oozing, deceptive
stillness. We itch

to make it palpable,
this waiting, caught

between end and beginning.
Did the first of these

bring nostalgia, a yearning
more for past worlds

or the next? We think always
of endings in this half

light, of loss, forgetting
that evening came first,

darkness before
the light, the morning

wrapping up the great
project, God's gray head

napping on a crooked elbow,
dreaming of formulas.

II.

Before declaring
it was good, eons before

there was a before,
how many scraps did it take

to learn measure twice,
cut once?

And what paternal tips given:
Water down the marble

to cool the spinning blade.
(We don't want explosions.)

How many crooked bookshelves
of redwood, grooves that fit

in only one combination,
one leaning post that needed

propping, how many drafts
of diagram to dissect, recalculate,

the paper rubbed transparent
from erasures, and how much forgiveness

before mastering perpetual motion of rivers,
the great slow pendulum of moon rock?

Raison d'être

They say the closest
distance
between two
points
is a straight line.

But tell me—
in real life
does anything
(save the hypothetical crow)
travel straight?

water ripples
light undulates
sound moves in waves.

Perhaps experience too
is best transmitted
not straight on
but through a twist,
a loop, a spiral.

Such convolution,
some think,
is called for,
makes more sense;
hence,

Poetry.

Ye Shall Be as the Gods

How far from Eden's shadow must we go
foundlings banished, sick with nameless dread
looking always backward, ne'er ahead
longing for the lushness, for the flow
of Gihon's honeyed waters. Now we know.
Our seeing eyes perceive we were misled—
promised knowledge; given pain instead.
How far? How far from Eden must we go?
Blood-smeared sweat-bleared we toil to bring forth fruit
from earth, from loin. Then what this sudden rapture?
From whence the breeze, and how so sweet the gall?
Surprised by Joy, we feel our souls uproot
and soar toward that holy armature
upraised in honor of the blessed fall.

Somewhere

She strains toward heaven
arms outstretched
like a child wanting to be held
then falls back, outdone
subdued by gravity's ponderous sway

How long must she stay
suspended as she is
between fire and air
between here and there
incarnation and release?

Do not rage, mother
(leave the raging to the poet
and his father, now both long dead
despite the raging)
Go gently. Go.
Let go.

we did not know.

we did not know it was so hard
so hard to go

Ceremonial,
we bathe the body
that gave us life
        and gave
              and gave

we watch
and wait
stroke the sapless cheek
match breath for fitful breath

and then

a transmutation
as imperceptible
as hushed

as a sigh
       or the absence thereof

The silent inrush
of imponderable light

And now it is we
who are suspended
dangling as we are
between grief and relief
holding on and letting go
the notion of Death
and the reality of having been left—
       the widest distance of them all

Blood and Milk

I dreamed of Oxford . . .
    (spires, a thousand spires, endless lectures, musty halls
    a solitary self in a Bodleian expanse
    A good life my dear Wormwood. An orderly life.)

then awakened to laundry
    and things to be wiped
       (countertops, noses, bottoms)

How did this happen? And when, exactly?

Time flows, it flows, it flows
and there are choices to be made:

      left or right?
      paper or plastic?

      blood or milk?

There's freedom in the bleeding;
bondage in the milk
Do not be deceived.
Ah, but it's an empty freedom;
A holy bondage,
A sweet and holy bondage.

Five times I chose the chains, those tender chains,
    (though once will bind you just as well!)
and checked the crimson flow.
Suckled while dreaming of Trinity Term
but awakened, always awakened, to the laundry
and to that small and cherished captor at my breast.

Tonkas

the real M.A.S.H fiction
forests colonials raped
harsh *Ilbon-nohm-dil*
Hankuk and *Chosun* were bald
all native trees Japan burned

rice paddy foxhole   battle-scarred country
red soil frozen becomes gray   plants long rows of small scotch pines
waiting for spring rain   green and gray at night
disappears under night snow   grows into hilltop forests
smells of life it will create line by line in row by row

Uijongbu Station   mornings wet or dry
shaved bald gray gourd bonging monk crowded busy and quiet
surrounded by meat   in one direction
breaths *bundaegi* cooked silkworms the crowds flow like small tired fish
beats to blue subway's rhythm straggle home at night *meulchi*

uniformed students   a modern nation
scramble through streets baggy eyed stomps to a united thought
books pens pencils bags   apartment forests
pause just a moment to eat   below *Uijongbu's* hills fade
spiced finger thick rice noodles I pour my cold spring water

sitting on my rock   an old man sits down
on my day off before church   legs cross pours water on head
I watch the subway   dreamy eyes look down
snake through the thin corridor his leather face confesses
a thousand armies marched through long days worked in the paddies

Hankuk now transformed
M.A.S.H California copies
not scrabby desert
once it was plush verdant green
now stark urban concrete gray

Physeter Macrocephalus

The dive's alike descents to ocean's grave
the deep forereef to sand that's spread as far
as murk allows to see the sparks, the stars,
the things I misconstrue that swim like waves,
like *Amphiprion Ocellaris*, lights,
or grains of inspiration, sprites, that cringe,
ignore my grasp. My plexiglass syringe,
collection tube I use to siphon bright

and interesting fish extracts, it draws
a lambent dream from silt, the gloom. I see,
perceive him: *Physeter*. His sable skin
reflects the flashes wriggling out from jaws,
his teeth, defaced and scarred by squid. Then he
enigmites, grins the midnight brine the din

below the flippring snorklers catching theirs
in topreef shoals incognizant. My cares,

concerns, are asphalt bound today. The dive,
nostalgic denizen of daydreams, piped
orgasmic fantasy, eludes the hive
of cubic fabric covered life and gripes,
like *Dendrochirus Zebra*, blazes and flares.
The glowlight caught in scuba hunts for muse,
afflatus, genius, daemon, font, the air
I pumped in tanks to breath at depth and use
in small amounts contained in crystal tube,
my phial holding *Physeter*'s largesse,
the photon, ember heating hands I cube
around enshrouding fire while I confess.

Atchison, Topeka & Santa Fe Railway
(AT & SF) General Motors EMD type F7

The cellar stairs beside the fold-down board
where I transplant small cuttings, pot-up blooms
of citrus—limes and lemons—plants I hoard
in colorful containers for my rooms
descend and land on bricks surrounded by
a hedge of lilacs opposite, beside
a Tudor arch and pointed doorway. My
old key is bellicose, caustic, decides
the lock and leads me in. The room is bare.
The lights are dim. Exposed, old river-stone
foundation walls are mildewed, cobwebbed. Spare
decor amounts to trash and ashen bones.
The cellar, key, and cabin—new to me,
but mine: a place—my place to set me free.

The former owners blocked the inside door.
I excavate, restore casements to wed
the saucy arches, doors with carved and bored
symmetric keystone roses tinted red.
The arch upstairs descends to cottage womb below
concupiscent. I scrub and sweep and seal
the cellar. Tables, shelves that hold and stow
my tools, I reinforce anew with zeal.
I build a corner workshop storing saws
and sanders, clamps and gigs all used to build
a model rail-road. Painted engines draw
the twenty miles of cars my joy has filled.
And dreaming, whistles blow. The whistles blow.
Asleep, I hear the diesel's whistles low.

Sister Myra-Kate O'Donnell

It's rotten Myra's clever. Rotten for
instructions from the social worker: "Count
and itemize and inventory your
belongings. Please explain, prioritize
what is important, what you want to keep,
and why, all on a single, paper sheet.
And what does not fit, we will discard and give
away, donate to DI, Saver's, sell
on EBay, KSL, or Craig's or burn."
So Myra searches the three hundred stacks
of colored paper that coordinates
by shade and tone along her home's west wall,
records their auras, names and pedigrees;
the alphabeticalized tinfoil wraps;
the forty-seven television sets;
top-loading VCRs; eight betamax
recorders; magazines; the coupons; ads;
the Valentines she sent to thirty-three
orange and marmaladish cats who cannot
escape because they need to practice songs
of love, piano, war-games, Parcheesi,
the mashed potato, knitting, mopping, catch,
and chasing butterflies; the Christmas cards
unsent but filled with dandelions, peas,
and ballpoint pens the postman says will rip
envelopes saved incase the kids stop by
or something; books that sing and dance at night;
the land-lord's ghost who can't put down the one
old comic book; the ant farm; China bowls;
the childbirth handbook; teeth; the curling irons;
chinchillas hiding from the cats; tea cups
she sings to but will never use; the years
supply of tampons not used but who knows;
the postered frog-prince lining bathrooms, halls,
and bedroom walls. The list, her life, she types—
a hundred foot unperforated page

of plain-old paper towel—cannot stop
the hoarding senior taskforce, firemen, cops,
the social worker nor the trip away
uptown to germ-o-phobes and sanitized
and linolumized, catless, soulless rooms.

The Ruin of Loneliness

It is not the emptiness
as silent as night sky.
Not the ash. Not the buried
sherds. It is not the people
who once walked these
ruins with the confidence—
the pleasure of those who
know not. I do not know their
bright sorrows or their fears
red, like wild poppies. Once
I stood in a doorway,
painted a faded sea-blue,
and thought how easy it is
not knowing, not knowing
you'll ever leave. Oh,
for loneliness like that.

Thursday Is the End

Of the week, in this country;
women in various scarves
face the wall of their future's face,
blank as an opaque night.
Even the image of themselves is not
reflected. Nothing will outlive
the memory of their two sad rivers.

Friday is a holiday.
But for the cigarette sales
woman inside her black abaya,
every day is a holy day
as she spreads her shameless
good of expired cigarettes.
Just over the mountain—
at Earth's lowest land is
a sea whose shore has salt
enough to wash her wounds.

Saturday is Saturday.
Day off. But who will sift through
the rubble searching for the missing
shoe—the missing leg?
Who will form the lines in this
country, day after day, every
day? Who will still pray
to the refugee god?

Sunday begins
the work week. At dawn
a flock of birds cover
the tree like ripe fruit.
In the full sun, they disappear.

Celibacy at Forty-two (III)

what is love like
love is like the eyes of a flounder
grown on one side of its head

what is the night like
the night is like my long arms,
my long fingers

what are you afraid of
I'm afraid of baby
bats hanging upside down

what is the saddest thing you know
a political prisoner in China lived
40 years in solitary confinement

what do you miss
I miss good lies, keeping
time by another's breath, guilt

what is the softest thing you have touched
the long nose of a horse,
the small concave between crossed legs

what will you wear tomorrow
tomorrow I will wear the touch of a masseur,
a grey scarf, the stain of pomegranates

where have you been
inside of magenta,
outside of enough

what did you forget
I forgot to have a daughter
I forgot to have a daughter

what do you love
I love orange lichen, getting
the second line, silence flowing back in

where do you live
I live in a marsh wren's nest
in a room made of poetry

how do you decorate
I decorate in silence,
in gauze and red beads

what do you celebrate
the smell of coffee, the inside of my
mouth, shampooing with a bucket of rain

what will you give back
I will give back two silver earrings,
enough covers, my insecurity

what is so difficult
differentials equations, a habit
of closure, returning to the body

Red-tailed Outside Scipio

On a seared cedar
post the red-
tailed hawk lights

still as the seventh
day, still but
for the black tack

of its singular eye,
alive and focused as sin.
With a quick bob

and a down-
slurred cry she
rises on a riot

of air—high up—
through the gyre,
circling far above all,

calm and silent circling:
there—up there, in the blue
of the nave of the poem.

To Baptize

They want to baptize my son,
take his slight body,
immerse him in the wetness
of water, make him stainless,
wash from him sins
he did not commit, sins
that belong to no one.
They want to stand him
in the water, have him
shudder and pimple,
soak his paleness
in a pool of solvent,
dilute him into a true person,
bleach him to the dry
white of dead sailor's bones.
They want to bend him
backwards—nose, eyes closed,
fist holding wrist,
bend him back as the moon
bends the tide, then
pulls it forth again.
They want to cover him
completely, hold him under till
he knows deep, Atlantic loneliness,
while he waits for the pull
of human mercy to save him
from being human, the faith
of dry men allowing him
terrible air again,
to bring him forth as something new,
as if there were shades of white,
as if he weren't already water-born.

Mud Flap Girl on Being Hard to Get

Who can afford to fool around? If I
let every man have what he thinks he sees,
I'd be broke and highly diseased—so my
policy calls for commitment. To tease

isn't easy—I work hard to maintain
your delusions: never grow old, never
be seen with another man. I remain
out of reach, but barely, and forever

promise the impossible: I came here
for you. And what illusions you'll believe—
mirrors that say I'm close, that I'll appear
from a cloud of cigarette smoke. This love

is the easiest ruse: a woman who
exists without need, is perfect for you.

Mud Flap Girl on Birth and Venus

His cookie cutter meets a sheet of chrome,
and I'm born to mod Hephaestus, his truck.
Sure, your entrance was sexy—rise from foam,
vamp in Botticelli's shell, best of luck

with your golden apples. Can't make me trade
places, though; revenge plots don't thrill me, your
costumes would kill me, and I wasn't made
to co-star. You go peddle Grecian lore.

As for me and my low profile? Time to
flash this mettle and pluck. Think revelry,
not rivalry; think transcendence. A view
that's new, from nowhere near the top; where three

dimensions is out of the question, and
a metalshop spokesmodel tips her hand.

Living Alone

Living Alone
don't undress my love
you might find a mannequin:
don't undress the mannequin
you might find
my love.
—Charles Bukowski, "Trapped"

At lunch with Charles Bukowski
I order a Pellegrino; Hank brings several
bottles of something red, and delicious.
It's not just you, I say. About the mannequins,
I mean. The reason I go back
to work in the afternoon
is three identical men made in the image
of a man made in the image of a god
without a head or arms;
the way cashmere comes to life
sliding the sleek black line from shoulder
to hip; the rapture of silk
in the break of a trouser leg;
the way my cheekbone rests
against a shoulder blade, right breast
finding home in the valley of a backbone groove
as I snap, zip, straighten, and smooth.
People gather in ones outside the plate glass,
lean into the Pygmalion promise
of taste and touch, the exquisite ritual
of button and buckle. The closeness of this
body if I close my eyes is nearly
close enough, designed like all
mankind to leave us
both comforted and wanting.

Made for TV

In the movie version, my problem
is something no one talks about; so I take
pills or yoga or strangers home
to bed. I'm obsessed with needy men
or cleaning the bathroom until
the smell of bleach makes sleeping
dreamless. I used to cut myself
but kabbalah and Dr. Drew have put me back
on track, except I'm oh so lonely
alone with my heart of gold.
In the movie version, he's a detective
who's lost his edge and drinks
from a flask hidden in the bottom drawer
of his desk; or he suffers from survivor guilt
and doesn't know how to sleep anymore.
Maybe a certain case broke
something inside and no one can fix it
especially his partner
who keeps renting *Lethal Weapon*, hoping
for an epiphany and better action scenes.

After the writers have established
all of the above, there's a call from the sergeant,
who says an accident rolled
my car over a cliff. Mysteriously. He says
there was no body, no identification.
And just maybe it was no accident
after all. Instead of tracing the license plate,
the detective follows a hunch,
because in order to get to know her,
or should I say me,
and to increase the dramatic tension,
he must carefully examine what was found:

earrings, Austrian beads circa 1940,
mint dental floss, a three-pocket apron
filled with small bills; an empty piggy bank,

one banana (still green). "Talk Nerdy To Me" t-shirt,
rhinestone Elvis belt buckle,
and a roadside emergency flare. And then
there were three tubes Bobbi Brown
lip gloss, two pairs ballroom dance shoes,
one postcard Love, E. Ethelbert Miller.

A window sticker from The Bayou Restaurant
(palm readings Monday); Eva Luna
with a broken spine; American Airlines
Bistro Meal, empty Kit Kat wrapper,
two packs Trident Cinnamon gum. Al at AT&T
left his business card, and one
lavender feather boa.

The detective smiles for the first time
since the opening credits—
the director not allowing anyone to miss
his epiphany: this is the girl who could make any man's
heart remember beating. The detective vows
to find her, or should I say me,
but these clues, carefully catalogued, don't lead
to a one-armed man, or the bed of a river
where I'm not busy reed-breathing
under waterscum and algae,
or to an abandoned barn where I'm not
recovering from a headwound with the help
of a recently escaped convict, or suffering
from amnesia, or both. The third act
is dedicated to the mystery
of what will happen when he finds I'm just a girl
who forgot to set the emergency brake.

Lost and Found

My younger father wasted his inheritance,
drove a convertible while standing

for the national anthem—baptized then
in the cloying damp

night of a DC summer, free at last
from the consequence of his mother's

most recent drink. And later, immersed in this
bible, this blessing—given faith

enough to make a missionary
from a boy, bring him into the white

Wyoming snow—to have and to heal,
to hold what covenants abide

in each translucent verse. Decades
later, in spite of thou shalt not, I stole

my father's bible, seeking a miracle
within the redolent scent of my second-grade

Sundays: wanting a scene like Patty Duke
in a flood of well-water, *w*'s wrapped in a fist

and joy pouring down like a forty-night rain;
wanting my prayers to ascend like manna

returning to heaven, a reward
for this thieving kind of love.

WARREN HATCH

The Fine and Dying Art
of Shaping Light into Words

*For my daughters, who argue an extended sense of backyard,
to whom "sleeping out" has grown to mean packing sleeping bags,
Ramen noodles, and Pop-Tarts, and curving their way like martens
up their steep round hill above our neighborhood.*

How light in cool air bends inward smoother, focused
through a spotting scope; how the neighborhood below
lies enfolded in dusk, and light no longer roils
on convecting air. I zoom up the magnification
and sweep down through our neighborhood.
Lingering on my house, the porch light. And down.
And down. Past the park, its swings and jogging path,
then wetlands.

On the wetlands, in that dead willow, the redtail hawks settle,
their bodies a mere darkness on the willow's bleached bones.
I scan the park more carefully. Each walking shape
melting into gloom. And that unmoving shape—
what spectral remains of light say *woman*?

What essence shaped on dying light says *beloved*?
I aim a flashlight and tap out *c*, like a cat,
stalking and pouncing, twice (dash-dot-dash-dot),
l; and so on: *c-l-a-i-r-e*, *hello*, shaping light.

And she in the hollow of the park among the last settling frisbees
and first kick-the-can games and dull glinting swing chains.
She sees on the hill's lip my sudden blink of light—I am here.
And she knows with the first blink all the following stabs
and stutters of light. And she blinks back *steven*.
She scans this dusklit hill above the valley floor,
bright above the enfolding night of the park but already
melting back into the mountains above. Then, *the darlings*?

Wait, I say. And we wait. And we talk on in the tenuous language,
each blinked word wrapped in the glimmering thread
of waiting for one's children, for their days' unfolding arcs.
Only tonight is certain; tonight they will come down
from the dark and thicketed scrub oak;

Fire in the Pasture

tonight they will keep safe. On the mountain above,
the two martens crouch in gamble oak,
coaxing chukars in voices that skip like flint down shale draws,
teasing the hunched doubting birds from their guzzler pools.

Eventually the girls think of the valley and peer down,
then reshape their lips tightly to that pulsing light,
whistling dashes and dots. The chukars' voices fall still,
the crickets and katydids, still. I answer, whistling,
and they slip down to our hill, and I send:
darlings cuddled down as they curl together
under the faint stars. Above us all,
the peaks of the Three Sisters rise like a heavy sea,
each peak cresting, veined with blue shale in faint town light.
And if waves, then the final dwelling places of starlight.
The Eumenides, the beckoning fates.

Northern Cross

Teach me the Northern Cross, you say, kneeling,
and I touch collarbone on each side of your neck
and following my fingers you turn, mapping galaxy
with the curve of bones. Find the milky Way first;
face west, and spread your arms north and south,
I say. You breathe deep once and your neck arches,
your head then in the crook of my arm, east, here
in August and after midnight. Then, this is Deneb,
and this is Altair, mapping those blue-white stars
to the softness and awakening hardness of flesh.
These stars of Cygnus and Aquila, swan flying
after eagle, south and west. Follow my hand;
trace their spreading wings, the chill dewfall,
arc of swan's neck along ribs and medial line;
you know the stories of swans. And this Vega.
Your spine arcs. Oh, you say, rising to the star,
another eagle swooping in Lyra, faint trapezoid
like one knee bending away from the other. Oh.
You see we will have a daughter who will watch
an eagle hunt, stoop, devour prey. Oh, she says;
you see the cross, have always known your way
among these stars at the top of summer sky,
the great hunting birds, their stories bone-
deep and white in the arc of pelvis.

Red Shift

I take the chess board in my lap
and dust it off with my shirt tails,
and I set it out between us.
His eyes narrow.
The dumped chessmen clattering
across board and table,
"Let's sort this out."
                After ninety years
he's started to see red shifting time,
how it bends his mind like spreading taffy
between the crowding dendritic advance of shadows.
So find deep roots, and hold on. We rebuild
nearly everything among shadows of what was.
He remembers pawn, rook, bishop,
but not altogether their moves.
We hunch in the sloping afternoon light,
and I hold my breath over his surprises—
like, a pawn should move straight ahead one square
but attack diagonally, although if the pawn wishes,
his first move may be two squares. Quixotic.
I probe his memory of the en passant.
He says, "Look," jabs at my chest,
We both watch his hand wither into a fist.
His face softens, and he settles back
to stoop over the board.
                He knows
the knight's dog-legged permutations.
I try the Sicilian defense, such old shared things,
maybe he'll remember, But he hasn't just forgotten.
He remembers differently, the gravity of soul
bending beyond his grasp, maybe bending
the far walls of the universe.
                He's still relentless,
like we played evening after evening back then.
So I stand up and my son sits, and they play on.
And the next son. Gentle boys

knowing how to act, hour after hour.
"Shit:" he says softly, "Son of a bitch,"
trying to work it out. Sometimes they giggle.
The late news comes on. He draws the rocker up
to the fire, stares into it. "A lot of company
in a fire," he says.

Sparrows and Boys

Those giant ditchbank cottonwoods in our front yards,
a Spring storm rolling across the lake and salt marshes,
breaking in the groaning, brittle trees. Thunderous.
We awoke to front yards thicketed in branches,
splintered ends sap-scented. We climbed
and wiggled until we stood in arbors
of dappled light
     And the bird nests.
                    Those little birds in your hand,
all that unfledged life. "You can't keep it. It's wild. It'll die,"
Jay Anderson said. He wore an eye patch
from a jackknife-on-a-swingset encounter
like a mother's cautionary folktale that no boy ever fears.
Except in our neighborhood.
Jay said, "If you touch it, the parents won't have it:"
One-eyed, and older, and right—but I couldn't *not* touch it.
The birds craned and gaped. Featherless. All mouth and stomach.
So the Williams boys got the idea to stuff Blackcat firecrackers
down the birds' throats and light them. Kind of a dare.
And when that first fledgling sparrow blew apart,
those pieces still twitching with life
right in front of you and your buddies,
you had to say, "Wow. Cool." You gotta work
to get that.
          I climbed out of the arbor.
Jay Anderson, sitting on the ditchbank.
So I jumped across and sat. And we waited,
our unfolding lives minus what we had just left.
How to redeem that thumbsmudge of viscera
              "I didn't know," I said.
"I know," he said.

The Voice of Water Here

Imlay Barrus built our neighborhood, started with this chapel,
    dun brick, hunched under a vault of hewn ribs as if cast from ocean.
From the chapel, the homes sprawl across the lay of the land.
Decades later, we find no two pair of joists equidistant, and cuss him.
He is deaf to most tones, although not to certain passages of water.

    He lives still in the smallest of these homes
    at the brink of houses, outsheds, gardens.
He lives where alfalfa flows into sage,
    then into dry lake beds crowding the north horizon,
        folding into sky.
Has lived there, seen the proof of life in its cycles and pauses,
    the possible depth of encroaching dark.

    In evening, sitting before the desert, he longs for his wife,
    mourns his great-grandson Rainey,
    still sees the boy running under his orchards.
I live on, I live on, he says, measuring a loss
    grown deep against the frail joys left him.

    On his walks, he hears the irrigation water in ditches
    like a child's voice, or at times like stones turning deep in earth,
speaking through the wood of his cane.
    He passes between giant trees in his yard, an ash and an elm.
The trees have grown beyond parable
    from a sermon he no longer remembers,
    one straight, the other warped, huge over the yard.
A stream writhes past Imlay's yard the way a serpent
    undercuts and lays claim on the giant trees.

    He returns each day to the corner home where he raised his family
    and now Michelle Chaudoine raises hers.
He sits in her kitchen for its morning light,
sun on a Singer sewing machine in rivulets on ebony
    or composed under the cast-metal pattern of the treadle.

    Together they consider the orchards beyond the kitchen window.
Peaches, crescent shards of autumn sun

from trees Imlay Barrus and his sons had planted against winter.
Trees wizened, frozen, groping like lightning startled out of earth.
They struggle, he explains. They, far north of their climate.
Grafts among them are Castilian, brought up the Rio Arriba
          by Franciscans a half millennium ago.
     These grafts too know time.

          Having grown comfortable together,
Imlay and Michelle seldom talk. They see coming years
we would define by the darkness of their winters,
like the Chaudoine border collie's chain path around the woodshed,

     winding him short to his post. One of her sons falls,
mind darkened by alcohol or such gifts.
Some farm the land or traverse the world,
missionaries in strange countries.
Her husband leaves her and returns.

          Imlay Barrus no longer goes up into the chapel,
     no longer stands in the shadows of its Scandinavian gables.
Sabbath, a priest and a deacon bring sacrament to his home.
In the kitchen, the deacon pours water
into pleated white paper thimbles,
     brings a tray of these to the coffee table.
They sing hymns that to Imlay are like wind trembling
among taut ropes. Then the priest breaks bread into a tray.
He kneels over the bread, sanctifies it,
     remembering the Son, His Body broken.
They pass bread among themselves.
He prays again, remembering His blood,
shed for them.
     They share water.

          After, they visit on the porch into evening.
An ash-scented breeze ebbs around the great trees.
Imlay cannot hear the trees,
     cannot hear meadowlarks in sage
or the deacon's frail, shouted talk.

Imlay listens for the tones left him:
the kitchen-tap drips,
water in a porcelain bowl, half-full.

What? the water asks. *What?*
Rainey's voice, *What?*
until Michelle Chaudoine walks between the cottonwoods
  with two children made solemn by twilight.
The children hold bread wrapped in a towel
  and a quart jar of peaches.

Faith Healing

And there she was, Kathryn Kuhlman strolling the stage at the Civic,
parting a sea of applause, her gown like an angel that got away,
so pure it might have been empty but for the Holy Ghost preening
in her body as she paced the floral proscenium, lifting her hands
in a sign language I knew only God understood.

Sinners ascended on heavy legs, a janitor, a waitress, then more,
stark and drooping till Kathryn said the word and illness stripped
from their bones like skin from an apple and clean praise ran
from our mouths, the aisles breaking into dance jagged as levees
in a storm washing us down to Jesus' enormous boat.

It was the night she became the miracle I believed in the way a bird
believes in air and branches, all the premises of life and limb.
She was open windows blowing in my blood, a lake of promises
you might only reach by falling into them.

That summer I lived in my father's trailer, slept on a fold-out bed
beside a line of rustler boots, the allemande left and "Oh, Johnny, Oh!"
being the stray passions he took up with wife number three, who cajoled
me one night into coming to a regional square dance where I sneaked
out with a blonde freshman who was ditching her mom.

We wandered through porchlights, her cheeks perfect crescents
under the slouching moon, sky crossing its legs all around us, her chest
sloping in white angora, a silver cross playing in her fingers, grace raining
from the stars, our words and the quiet between them as balanced
as planets, a private equinox we presumed to live in a two-hour walk.

And there I was, at fourteen, wondering if she and this sentiment
would apportion the shape of my life from then on. They might have
—who knows—but for her mom waiting, arms crossed, at the double doors
and my dad with a broken boot-heel, sitting out the late dances,
cursing and drinking black coffee from a thermos.

                                        That night,
fifteen miles from the Civic, the shadows let go of my shoulders
and the angels settled in my eyes, a gauze I could barely see through,
and everything I knew went up in a cloud of hope, which seemed
the world's way of relinquishing the thought that I should ever die.

Family Tree

Adam: The wind hissed
in the branches,
green tongues
whispering
a secret I could
never peel open.

Moses: When I raised my staff
the sea split like a log
opening its chapters
into a story
a whole nation could
walk through.

Elijah: Ravens gathered berries
and dropped them
into my mouth
as if to plant
their dark cries
in my voice.

Jesus: Come closer.
Taste the wood,
feel it splinter
your tongue
into praise.

Joseph Smith: I bowed my head
onto a stump,
as if to a martyr's axe
and when I looked up
I saw the whole grove
burning down.

Jesus' Final Oration at The Last Supper

You interpret my clenched jaw
into geometry,
an angle leaned into stars, a law
for accidents. Not me.
Truth is, you know me less
than you know the sea, coral-hearted,
strung with weed and nets, fish
blossoming, caught, gutted,
salt drying in your fingernails.
That's the truth, confess.
But I am vaguer than your sails.
I am off course,
broken-compassed, adrift
on cures and indiscretion.
Turn right, I'm there, turn left,
still there, an obsession,
like trying to strap a harness to
a cloud. So just believe
in me as you believe in paintings,
oiled cloth, fraying weave,
poses tightening
around a table like this one,
corners chipped, backlit
as though it were a question.
Then interpret,
survey the scene, its damage
and its joy. Observe what's lost
in perspective: the rage
staining my lips, the blast
of ocean hitting land, the moon
still vivid in blue sky,
floating stone
resonant with the cry
of doves and anxious lambs,
wine dripping on the bottle's neck,
that line of ants who lift some crumbs,
trudge to their hole, come back.

Museum of Ancient Life

A leaf grins in a rock's face
as if concealing secrets:
the quiet of tree hardening to stone
or amber cupping light, careful
as water in a child's hands.
The shelves of debris proceed
by age—Pleistocene, Eocene,
Paleocene—a glass geometry cooled
by the fluorescent hum of
the Ice Age. Beside them a version
of a bird leans from his pedestal,
wings canopied as if caught in
the updraft of the past tense.
As we walk the gallery, I am
holding my son's hand the way
homonids do in this mural of a family
crossing the Bering Straits,
trudging from one era to the next
on the complicitous ocean.
They totter on feet still learning
to bear the upright beast all
the way to this place where today
my boy ascends the carpet slope
toward a forest of bones with
wonder still blowing through them,
here, where unpronounceable
names struggle to survive.
Where could Eden ever have been
but here, with no map but
ourselves, here, where the only
cost of remembrance is death.

Deluge

Even before the flood
Noah's life capsized,
his heart felled like a tree
in the stiff wind of the spirit.
Weathering the neighbors' complaints,
scraping pitch from his feet,
checking the groins of beasts
whose names he didn't know yet—
it was as if his world were
already submerged in inanity.
And in the end, when the riverbeds
turned to seas, he longed to see
dogs and horses swimming,
fish leaping over treetops,
anything but the stew of carcasses
that would fill his eyes.

How could he have known
what to expect from the
requisite madness of following
the foghorn voice in your head?
Maybe we can never know,
when the world falls upside down
and we swim in the skies,
holding our breath against tides of
everyday sense. But we are still
the living cargo of our dreams,
trapped—two by two if we are lucky—
awaiting the creak of the tentative door,
the splash of puddles, the odd
mischief of starting over.
Like doves to the ark,
our hearts return to
the only windows we know.

Blessing the Baby

We are low church—a plain chapel, unadorned pews and pulpit,
dahlias on the organ the only image of God. Come today
to give my brother's infant daughter a name and a blessing.

"The purpose of life," says the bishop, "is to gain
a tabernacle of flesh and bone," and I wonder
what my granddaughter imagines, having visited

the great hall on Temple Square but not
the house of metaphor. "He's explaining
our bodies," I tell her. "Why we love them."

But it is a tabernacle, a tabernacle of men
held by the priesthood as planets are held by the sun
who take this infant in their arms. Too many to form

a circle around the child, they make an ellipse. In the name
of Jesus Christ, says my brother, and gives his baby
his great grandmother's name, Julia Brooke Howe.

She sleeps through her blessing, a white bow honeyed
to the crown of her head, the clouds of her dress floating
over the arms of the men who hold her. The congregation,

though happy for the parents, swirl in their personal orbits.
A boy lifts his throbbing hand in its cast. A neighbor reads
a novel hidden in his Bible. A grandmother can't remember

where she is or why she's come. Two teens thumb wrestle,
eyes closed. They are all of the earth, earthy. Julia, awake now,
is given from the arms of her father to the arms of her mother,

her eyes ocean-blue, just as she dirties her diaper.
She, too, belongs to this soiled Earth
that is sometimes washed, renewed, sweet-scented.

Andrew

wants me to stay home,
build him a zoo,
scare the elephant
with the black plastic ant.

He throws himself to the carpet
will not be consoled.

But something outside

time circles as
I lift this sad boy
in dinosaur pajamas
into the rain.

Shivering like a spray
of apple blossoms in cold wind,
he stops crying, holds on
to my neck. I show him

five deer, bunched
under the poplars.

He twists toward them
as a sunflower turns
to the sun. The deer

stare at us, waiting,
then suddenly wary,
take the fence one by one.

"Jump," he says,
 "jump, jump, jump, jump."

Toy-sized
in the far field
when we reach the poplars,

they leave footprints,
a tuft of hide
Andrew carries back

to make the deer nibble
his carpet, tip over his blocks,

leap onto his bed
while the boundless world
follows inside.

Both the Fragrance and the Color

"What good is the name Florence," she asked,
if I never set foot in Italy?" Longing for beauty,
she turned to flowers: bulbs and corms
in every corner of her yard. As her arms
and legs enlarged, she ordered her flowers

to flourish. Jonquils shivering in snow banks.
Lilacs with thoughts so heavy
they couldn't lift their heads. A chorus line
of fire-colored poppies, flimsy skirts
over black and green underthings.

Frivolous flowers, though she was our stern
grandmother, not given to generous outbursts.
Despite her weight, "a condition of the thyroid,"
she knew the discipline beauty exacts.
Roses obeyed her: deep red

Mister Lincolns, Charisma, Peace.
Had her hair washed in beer and tinted
the shade of violets in her violet tree.
She read always, "for mental stimulation,"
as if books were orchids she could eat.

I offered *Dandelion Wine*, its new-cut lawn
fresh as her own even though its flowers
were weeds. She sent it back enraged
and wouldn't say why, her anger
a question that hovers

over her grave. And when I lay
roses there I ask what noxious plant
grew out of that novel?
Did it say grandmothers die?
That desire withers but remains desire?

My only clue is the black and white
photo she tucked inside: a young woman
I'd never seen, hair swept up, striking

eyes. Eyes she had water-painted
iris-blue, just her shade, her color.

Losing My Mother

At three a wave almost swept her
into the Pacific, and eight decades later her mind
flounders, swirls in the eddies.

In her childhood, when girls didn't play
sports, the boys picked her for catcher
or first base, or the hard white dreams
she knocked every time over the left field fence.

Tall, a natural for women's
vice president, she gave the position up
to drop out and marry my father.

Pregnant seven years, mother
of nine, she offered us children
her legs, her public speaking voice,
her Saturday morning bowling league, her salt.

She has never been sorry
she drifted away from that last year
of college to have me, and then into the
vast sea of her family's needs, has she.

Today she's awash in the jars of peaches,
cherries, and apples in the fruit room,
floating in syrup in the dark, hundreds
of jars a year for forty-five years,

what she might have asked for herself
dissolved in sweetness. She doesn't know
what she wants but wants

to feed us and asks, *Are you hungry?*
Do you need anything to drink?
Are you hungry? Are you hungry?

Inadvertent Elegy

*I write his three poems in /
memory.*

1.

Cliffs of Eden, burning / red / under God's thumb. The woman in the desert. The woman / the man / created he them / the beginning of days. / Remember the soil, red and thick / of the dust of the ground waiting / for the garden.

2.

Pomegranates and persimmons and I / can never remember the difference—, which one you wrote and which you held in your hands, fingers pressing the skin, before offering—

3.

I always care. Today is Monday. Today is / June. He tells me you are like a god, golden and godlike. / *I don't always know.* What can I / remember? There is a face that looks like you, but it is voiceless. I pray your voice, pray / your voice, pray until my words are / yours and I remember.

Weary

I counted them as they
came—sons and daughters
who didn't count.

I counted their limbs, perfect
limbs, like their father's—
nothing so imperfect.

I found him perfect, my one
week of us, my one weak
husband. I knew, walking

steps behind him, that we
were only that week, that I would
give him and forgive him

as my father gave him
to her. I forgave, but forget
her name, beautiful sister,

in the names of my children,
in the name of the Lord
who heard me.

Eve, the apple was a pomegranate—

Exhausting, the tear and pull
of scabrous flesh, exposing pale
pulp, the seeds sleek pulse.

Her fingers bleed red and

Adam takes the peel, pulls away

the arils. Two in his hand, two on her tongue.

       You want them to see you, to offer you
your share. You expect Eve to thank you,
Adam to take your hand, take away the pen,
write the last words:

How many times will you write
       redemption without being

    redeemed?

Elegy

The breaking
of tulips
through frost

and the hart's teeth at the roots.

It is the morning, or the windows on the bus are black with ice, or our insignificant names crowd the London streets. A cherry tree rising from a man's ear. The man searching for the woman sitting next to him. Lilies in the shadows around our ankles, wilting. The anger ubiquitous in that. The anticipation. The hesitation. And our wings spread

like hands in the shadow.

We never know. We only make it halfway there.

Song

In the early spring, every word opens
          yellow, opens red

and he is singing.

Maybe it's only myth, the man leaning over the river. The river startled by its own reflection. Its own measure. The ice breaking to become face, become pulse. The cadence under his skin. You've sung this story before: *Vanity, vanity, all is——.* So easy to say *vanity,* and mean *Every measure is the same.* Mean *I stand on the bridge next to the man who knows my every name.* You believe every bridge I give you, every face the river takes.

    You're about to overhear a voice. Don't be alarmed.

Tonight You Died

Orion stands above me
in the blackness of this night
belted in three stars,
club drawn in my defense.
It matters that he is there
as you have shown me
countless times, your arms
around my waist.

The moon, now shadowed
to the crescent of a bowl,
holds other worlds in space.
Glitter of stars spills down
to dust my shoulders
with your presence.
Alone, I feel you racing up
through heaven's shattered skies.

Memorial Service

for Leslie Norris

Loosed red balloon
tethered by my eye
glides unhurried
rising up the sky
until it slides from view.
Whether it can find
your path or no,
release is chosen . . .
though
I still hold tight to
memories of you,
your bright string of poems.

Oleander Snow from Yucca Flat

She hears her students cry, "Come see! There's snow!"
How foolish on this broiling desert day
to think these children possibly could know

of whirling flakes. They've never watched them blow
in lacy sifts of white. Not here, I'd say!
She hears her students cry, "Come! See! There's snow!"

Their choral invitations bid her go
to see them shaking branches in their play.
(To think these children possibly could know

that oleander bushes left to grow
so tall—hide future pain in white bouquet.)
She hears her students cry, "Come. See? There's snow!"

Pink blossoms, narrow leaves begin to show
as flakes of ash fall from their overlay.
To think these children possibly could know

they play like simple guinea pigs below
atomic testing's fallout—in the way.
We still can hear their cries. "Come! See!" There's no
way these dear children possibly could know.

The Rendering

One does not love a place the less
for having suffered in it.
—Jane Austen

The black wood stove glows hot enough
to render fat from hogs raised to feed our hungry winter.
Their sacrifice is purified by this last chore,
provides grease we need for making soap.
The oblong pan atop the lid absorbs red heat,
fills with fat drawn from tawny, blistered rinds.

Smells surround us, satisfy. Stiletto winds
whistle, stab under weathered doors.
Hams salted, pink meat bottled, bacon sliced,
and now fat rendered, mean we will survive.
Like us, wolves crouched in piercing winds
gnaw every bone on butchering day.

I watch from a straight-back chair, its legs
pressed to the wall, as Daddy centers
forks for handles. *Oh!* Mama breathes,
as he lifts and turns toward the cooling shelf,
her eyes fastened on the simmering pan of grease.
Her mouth grows tight, *Oh, Lee!*

Knees tense as the shaking pan above me wavers,
crossed ankles draw in slowly as hot gold spills.
I see anguish on his face, the rain of liquid fire
as Mama grabs some homemade salve
to swathe my trembling legs, while sounds
of metal clatter on the fat-slickened floor.

Holding Room

In a plowed field at the rim
of the southern Utah desert
one of those Schnebbley brothers

found connected bones,
the skull of a young girl,
and a set of terrible blue toenails.

Hearing about it, I have nightmares
in which I stumble across a rib-cage
still wearing a backless hospital gown.

The Schnebbley boy's find
was a partial skeleton like the one
hanging in my father's office closet

by which he learned anatomy.
A kidney floats in a bottle on my dad's desk.
A jar of liquid cocaine lies in his little black bag,

for setting nose fractures. My father leaves
the lights on, the door ajar, so his patients
cannot trap him in their comedies.

The Accompanist

From the bleak glow of the pit, he watches
her, thinking of her portrait on his piano
where a lace mantilla veils her rosary
and her throat is signed, "Carmen, with love."

Tonight, she is Lucia, dying
at Lammermoor Castle, her mad cadenza
lifting precisely as cut cards over
the footlights. After the applause,

her arias walk him home. He gives himself
to her voice, his fingers strong but pale.
Palms border his backyard, whispering
ringed secrets of how trees grow.

His breathing keeps time with the metronome,
Wagner's busty women in metal brassieres
vocalizing at Valhalla. If he could convince this diva
to accompany him to his neglected room,

he would trace a cadence of darkness
over her clavicle, down to the navel,
searching for the sound of her blood, circulating,
her unexpected hunger to give up singing altogether.

Restaurant in Naples

The waiter talks of his room
above the tavern, clean
and smelling of spice. Dark
and oily as olives, he finds
me beautiful. In Athens

he braided an older woman's hair
each morning after they became
lovers. Now he wipes my table
with a fluid, polishing motion.
I could wait for his shift

to end, anticipating the spicy room.
From the trellis beside his window
he might touch roses to my hair,
the scent of his hands on my shoulders

in the cramped sheetless bed.
Instead, wondering why he left
the woman with braids, I cover
my own hair with a touristy blue scarf,
wimple-like in its cheerful

refutation. I leave him
ample gratuity for tipping me off
to the fact that celibacy
is never a coincidence.

Guest Room

Our children were conceived
    in a carved maple bed shipped
from Milwauakee on the train
    by my husband's grandmother in 1937.

Last night, celebrating thirty-five years,
    we turned back its eyelet sheets,
the floor seeming to lower beneath us,
    the bodies of all the women

my husband *could* have married
    crowding around the foot
of our bed, handing us their weary
    hearts, struggling to remember

him. I offered them my hands, fingernails
    with sunken moons. Our shadows blended
on the wall. Through the open window
    I saw glaciers, snow folded

in their laps, and wondered if they were
    breathing. This was the same
carved maple bed where, so many years ago,
    the stork left our children in the dark of night.

Sheep Ranch Near Hillspring

She never speaks to him anymore. Her tongue
is as bone-dry as an irrigation ditch in winter,
her ankles grimy as a crooked ewe's. Dribbled
wine and spots of sour milk stain her blouse,
and now his lead sheep has given up the bell.

His wife's pantlegs dip ragged against the floor
as Hunter, her old Aussie dog, howls night for night
beside their window, duetting with the baby till its
mother bundles the infant close to her nipple. Such
polar Aprils—the rancher sees mirages of mermaids

riding pond-water billows, his lambs losing the snow
battle. By June, his wife has stooped to wearing his own
clothing: tattered army fatigues and denim overalls.
Dressed as a refugee, she spurns his affection. This
woman gave birth at home, clips and shears, mixes feed

and dungs out the pens, her breasts leaking milk onto her
camouflage tee shirt, the baby unsatisfied until her coming.
He—her husband—coasts through daylight hours,
doting on his trembling, newly shorn, pink-skinned
flock, hoping to outlast the slow-witted beasts.

PATRICIA KARAMESINES

The Pear Tree

When early autumn's storm wrung from the clouds
Summer, wearing the last thundering rain thin
And sharp on the wind's rasp; when thorns
Of the first frost bloomed over the grass,
And the morning glory hung brown and bitten
On the garden fence; on those first nights
Of cold window glass and the drip of chill
Onto the plank, when I wrapped in the blanket
And the dog curled at my feet, I heard,
Above the clay clink of wind-churned chimes,
Above the wag of the unlatched screen door,
Round blows of fruit fall against the ground.

I have been here three years' windfall
Not hearing the bump of pears, but when the tree
Burst blossoms against the window, I watched
Crawl across the floor shadow from thousands
Of swaying cups lifted into the storm of pollens,
And when after petals leaves screwed from the nodes,
I looked out into green overcast: fruit had pushed
Off flower and bent down boughs as with old age,
But more mystic that blunt drop of fruit earthward
That jerked my ear like a new word.

Someone else should hear it: I could better tell
How, when the wind rattled its sticks upon the houses,
I heard a pear fall to a bruising; how it struck
Above the rip of water from passing cars' tires;
How, as I let slip with sleep my garment of senses,
A tree caught the last thread and plucked it
With a ripe pear; and how I lay awake beneath rainy
Leaves or sat for spells by the window, as one haunts
Heaven those nights her globes bear down the branch
For a single star to fall away in flame.

242   Fire in the Pasture

Glaucus

for Leslie Norris, 1921–2006

I am no monster . . . nor a fierce beast, but a god of the sea . . .
—Ovid, *Metamorphosis*

We can't say what Glaucus knew
From watching storms crush and reshape
The surge, what voices he'd heard
When the tide swelled onto the beach,
Or what he'd seen in fish guts dropped
On sand. He merely husbanded the waves,
Throwing his web over that endless face
Of expression. Not a fisherman
To prowl safe waters for dependable yield,
He went daily before the backward stepping sea.
That's how he came upon the water meadow
Where no bees dipped the flowers.
The grass had never borne a footstep.
Glaucus was its only creature. He cast
Net offshore, watched it sink away,
And with a few lines running between himself
And some place beyond clear prospect,
Waded through eye-watering glare angling off
The sea's hooked and changeful scales.

He laid his catch on the old grass,
Saw dead fish shudder, retake life, lift
Themselves upright. Dorsal, caudal fins
Manipulated air as though liquid,
And under his look, they swam overland
Back to the breathable deep.

It's hard to grasp how Glaucus thought, "The grass."
Harder still to imagine his eating it.
He must have decided during some untold history
To bid farewell forever, to leave lines and nets
Masterless upon the sand, and the swale
As he found it, at the edge of his gone world.
What should we make of the desire that took him?

We, too, have stood on the shore of the thousand-fold myth,
And still we stand, awaiting science or some parent.
What occurs instead is the muteness of vast event
And the crash of the breakers of mystery.

Thus Glaucus went beyond strands
Of the imagination, god with a raveling green beard,
Hair an undertow in itself, heroic shoulders,
Blue arms, and legs fused, each curving
Down thigh and ankle into a fluke.

But we can't envy him. If he came to us
We'd spurn him—like Scylla did—as a monstrous innocent,
The changed creature of some obscure devotion.

Introduction to the Mysteries
(or How To Read a Poem)

—for Sean

First, kiddo, disperse that obvious shadow:
to read is not to know. To read
is to listen from your quiet place
to the teasing laughter of some new voice.
Listening requires aptitude for not knowing.

If you read a poem, yourself, alone,
watch for those sudden synchronizations of,
you know, pulses, which, happening, don't prove
knowing, only meeting: two languaged souls
adrift on unfolding sea, converging at crosscurrent
symbols, flowing together then pulling past.
Isn't that romantic, toots?

When you read a poem, imagine words
anticipating arrival, turned voice-
toward you already. Step up to what song's
piping hot to be heard. But don't try to know.
Meaninglessness is that blue butterfly
on the diamond-stud pin. Such a waste!
Something in person-reading-poem-
reading-person ever escapes, like light,
into the wink of the abyss. If in reading
a poem you don't turn at the crack
of a wall yielding, that creaking noise
as the universe—all them stars—buckles,
you ain't listening, dearie, only knowing.

Even when, after chasing flights of laughter,
you meet in the boonies some poem in its skin,
remember: To see is not to know,
but rather to come upon as if in the forest
meaning playing naked in the stream.
That's where it lives, love.
Get grabby, you break its green embrace
with the current's deepening hold.

To read a poem is to stand with it
and to move, to change
in ardor of exchange, to wind with words
into a nerve bundle of world's desire.
It isn't to know, darling, it's never to know,
but only ever to follow what calls.

The Orchid Grower

Clinton F. Larson, 1919–1994

He sought to grow rare orchids up bright air
On theory they were closer to the sun.
Such trailing gardens of the blue compare
To virga with refractions overrun.
And since these curious blossoms manifest
Some edgeless artifice their vines conceal,
All fanciers must their clayey stuff divest
To see what Sol his tropic buds congeal.
His mazes trellis on the light's pure ease,
Where petals, nearly colorless from glare,
Distill all hours estranged eternities
That tease the tethered eye's myopic stare.
Such speeches of flower to heaven's plots aspire,
Bind root twixt worlds and hang exotic fire.

The Peach

Blake's angel, for all his winks and nods,
Wouldn't have it, though it hangs for having:
Drop of down and blush quavering on the rim
Of ripeness, playing at a fall.

Pendant at the tip of a branch astray
From the greater fruited spray
Where sister peaches cluster meekly
Beneath green custom, this one sweet dangle
Trespasses air my side the fence
Where sunlight fires its skin and any breeze
May dance it.

My neighbor who set the tree as start
Is a man of strict authority, armed, invested,
An officer of our active legion laws.
He knows where all the lines are drawn,
Where fences stand, where right leaves wrong,
And keeping his faith good is wise.
Although this juicy prodigal does seem
To trail a gray gulf, he may better know,
And so the peach appears to plump and glow
With consequence, a nectareous world
Ripening on a branch of orchard heaven
Under scrutiny from many angels' eyes.

Taking such creature to tongue suggests
That becoming as a god by fell choice:
Will birthing, her first cry, Desire;
Light, on which the eye opens suddenly,
That infant slit of lid permitting
The flash from good and evil springing apart
To change the eye forever; then, vision:
Probability, lively, everywhere at once,
Refiguring the garden, reforming
Every place the eye alights each time;
Gleams of possibility sparking like drops
Of dew, infinite, engorged with sudden sun

As far as the eye dares see—to the stars—
And, clinging to skin, so wet and cool,
Instant thoughts of nakedness
Blush the body and Will seeks clothing,
Her prior choicelessness seeming comfort now,
If unfitting, and inaccessible as the opened womb.

Such first physics infusing All and Now,
Poised to go at breath, I too partake. So:

Day by day shall the peach hang unmolested.
With its toys of luster it shall bob and sway
Till summer drops its sun, till it is swept
From splendor by timeliness or wind,
Or till he whose lawful peach it is
Decides its fate by his own hand.

In Spite of Her

Twirling thread around
one finger, she begins a chain

the hook is held incorrectly

with extra fine thread—always the best.
Two singles, a line of cross trebles.

Hates directions has no clue

The next row begins—
Carnation-pink, like the stunning roses
beneath her window.

Too self absorbed to garden properly—
blooms flourish in spite of her

Edging perfect. A satin ribbon ties
above the opening.

In three weeks her granddaughter
will be born—

unravels knots, curses string.

Divining a Lost Summer

I've pushed aside the papers in my tray
and culled the wilted leaves from my bouquet
set on the shelf. I've lit a candle, made
a pot of tea and scones with marmalade,
the kind you liked. The blinds are slit; a cool
north wind has melded palms into a spool
of endive colored fronds. It's quiet here.
I close my eyes; blurred images appear.
The room recedes. I sip the bitter tea
and think about a time by Paignton's sea.
Your gauze-like scent clings to the walls, despair
and giddy memories return. I swear,
I hear a gull and jetty bell's refrain.
They both dissolve like sand hills in the rain.

Draining the Cup

After she agonized about the equity
disappearing from her home, and walking away
from the city she grew up in; after she wept
at the thought of leaving white plantation shutters
that slit the morning into little ribbons
of warmth, and the fireplace mantle she had constructed
to look like a picture she found in a magazine—

after she anguished over living in a small apartment
with no garden; after she announced she was taking her piano
with her, no matter what; after she talked to lawyers
and accountants who said there was no logic
in staying—

after she moved into a pint-sized rental
by the beach, and stopped the three hour commute
each day; after she realized a dishwasher for two people
wasted more time than it was worth; after she discovered
her cats got along better in a tiny area; after she could
sleep in, and have an extra cup of tea
before eight o'clock—

after she had no flowers to clip or sidewalks
to sweep; after she spent an hour on the sand and studied
a strip of scarlet cloud that stretched
from Palos Verdes to Santa Monica; after porpoise
appeared and the sun's back-glow turned the bay
into a goblet of rose-colored waves; after she bought
a hot chocolate on the pier and proclaimed it
the best dessert in the world—

She realized how delicious it could be
when the cup is drained.

Fire in the Pasture

At Sunset by the Oak

I've come into the shadow of the oak
to feel the spine of summer leaves. I've come
to rest in realms of dampness, darkness. Stroke
familiar branches beneath twilight's thumb.
I've come to wrap long vines around my breasts
and smear wet clay upon my dress. To weep.
The nutmeg colored bark becomes a test.
I find my way, I find my way. Time sweeps
me like a leaf across a fieldstone wall,
where like some flightless young, I huddle, cold.
I've never found forgiveness in the small
of night. That human element, controlled
by drifts of tulips and the lilacs' white.
That place I cannot love you in the light.

How to Break a Northern Spell

Remember your expensive basket
of fuchsias the moose ate before sun-up
and the fat mosquitoes that hovered
around your head when the bedroom lights
went out. Recall how the kids went to school
each morning, beneath street lights
that barely lit the sidewalk. Count the hours
they wouldn't go bed in the summer
because the sun never left the sky.
Keep in mind the snowsuits
you zipped and unzipped, so the children
could pee every two hours.
Think about the dog and his muddy
kennel, car locks that froze, the Chinook
wind that blew your neighbor's balcony
into your yard. Erase the feel
of static electricity zapping your finger
every time you flicked a light switch.
Imagine the scent of a wet wool blazer.
Pack all those memories
into a tarnished little locket, rub it
like a counter-charm—dig your toes
into the California sand.

Vineyard

Yes, the zucchinis grow heavy and wicked,
and yes, a porcupine parses the orchard
one rummy apple at a time.
But the true inventory begins when two brothers
in mummy bags carve up Cassiopeia,
first with index fingers, then with closed eyes
and a buried love of their mothers, expressed as sleep.

Their uncle smoking under the eaves has traded
places with the wind. He's canvassing backyards,
the wind has turned bald but philosophical.
New roller skates and an ax in the peonies
create a cautionary tale by moonlight,
whose heroine huddles in the front room
trying to free Chopin from torn sheet music.

Beneath her, in the basement, her older sister urinates
on a plastic wand that turns
her misgivings the shade of her boyfriend's car.
To the side of the house, a tiger
salamander in a bucket holds the night
ransom. Up ahead, one peach tree, three grafts,
like agony spiking in Jesus and the two thieves.

The Father who suffered him to be nailed
climbs over the fence. Wanders his overgrown
vineyard in an underfed body, to remember
lostness. Takes a swig of syrupy Coke
left out all day, coughs once, then wipes
his mouth on the neck of a sleeping mastiff,
who dreams apocalypse in greens and terrible blues.

To the Lost One-Third

What should I call you—devil spawn, Satan's imps, lost ones? Or do you prefer Legion? Something elegant about that collective *I*, that singular *we*. And what of the Gadarene boy you possessed, who frothed and wailed, fell into fire, broke chains, cut himself with stones, etc.—was he elegant? Of course, the tale came right eventually. The possessed one regained his mansion of organs and a mind swept clean. Jesus, who began as itinerant preacher, ended as Christ, casually morphing into light and truth and hopping a ship to the next town. Even the pigs you drove off the cliff drowned quickly, and will one day resurrect, floating out of boiling waters, like lemmings on rewind. But you, Legion, you have no body to home to. What keeps us safe from you—crosses around the neck, holy water on the brow? Do the same unclean spirits haunt us for life, looking for a breach, or do you switch at will, greedy hitchhikers inventing your own route to Budapest? What is the body? It wheezes and grunts, prickles with heat, gobbles fetid air, slobbers like a dog after every passing lust, stares out windows into echelons of blue, drowns in pools of ether disguised as sleep. How can you want this cloven hoof part of me? You who remember all, but believe in nothing. What was it like before this life? Did we sing in that minestrone of waiting? Did you, did we have godly names?

Why Do You Keep Putting Animals in Your Poems?

I open windows to catch a glimpse of *grace*
on the horizon, and in they sneak, coyotes and crows,
pikas and the scholarly vole, dragging scoured skies
I can see myself in. Much cheaper than booking
a flight to the Galápagos. And they teach me.

Badgers rarely invent stories to make them sad
about their bodies. And the wrinkliest of Shar Peis
never dreams of ironing its face. My happiness
is like a flock of sparrows that scatters when a bus
drives by, then re-strings itself two blocks away,

a necklace of chirps festooning a caved-in barn.
Lemurs will bite a millipede to release narcotic
toxins, then hand the millipede to a neighbor
as if passing a joint at a concert. In a Rhode Island
nursing home, Oscar the miracle cat curls up

with residents hours before they expire, converting
death into purrs for the next world. A poem is grave
and nursery: the more creatures you bury in one place,
the more hunger bursts forth somewhere else,
like bats at Carlsbad when the brightest day turns dusk.

The night I stood on my sister's feet and learned
to waltz, a porcupine braved four lanes of asphalt
and hurtling machines to chomp our windfall apples—
two miracles of syncopation held together by a harvest
moon. As Marianne Moore taught us, an hour

at the Bronx Zoo in a tricorn hat leaves one happier
than nine months with a shrink. Comes a time
you just have to wiggle your pin feathers,
wag your ghost tail, feel your teeth grow long
for the ragged salmon throwing their bodies upstream.

To the Ode

True, you intimidate me, but when I slip you on,
like Horace's bathrobe, all things spark

to life: an ant as worthy of praise as a phoenix,
Styrofoam cup as capacious as Grecian urn.

Nothing too trivial for you—not clouds, not the bent
spoon carrying gruel to the dowager's mouth,

not spotted dogs in heat. Thanks to you, I talk
to my orange juice before I drink it, I begin

a Q and A with the rain, greed converted into awe,
an ancient Mayan city behind my sternum.

What is water, but a confessor, happy to wash away
my grit? What are train tracks but a ladder

to heaven turned on its side? What is a rotting
mouse but a country of flies buzzing with praise?

Backyard Georgics

Gone the homeland, gone the father,
        nothing left but invisible north
    to magnetize your doubts.

         *

        One clock for errands,
one for midnight trysts,
       though neither will hurry a slow train.

         *

Is a snake touched thrice one snake
        or three? What is the opposite
    of *rapture of the deep?*

         *

        A lightning strike to test
the gestalt of stillness, an apron
    of lambent stars to taste the dark.

         *

Interview or early wake?
        A birdbath at noon in which
    you glimpse your own plashy face.

         *

        Prairie is not the floor nor sky
the coffered ceiling. Even a scarecrow
    is wise beyond its straw.

         *

Playing god, my son spells
        his name in spilled juice, smashes
    any ants brave enough to drink.

         *

Teach me to clench deep,
like the honey locust in fall,
        then shake shake shake my terrible thorns.

                *

Orchard gone feral, sky dark
        as Ecclesiastes: when I sliced
        the peach, tiny moths flew out.

                *

        It takes a calendar one damp day
to declare fall, weeks of dying
        mums to second the motion.

                *

First frost: a trio of robins
        at the dryer vent bathing
        in the lacy breeze of tumbling bras.

                *

        Look down: a river of grass. Look up:
a velvet lost and found. Look inside:
        no straws to drink that dusk.

                *

Not eulogies or hearses
        but the sandwiches after, estranged
cousins chewing under one umbrella.

                *

        Little Dipper whispering *sip,*
but which unholy spring will leave us
        whole, which gods dare we drink?

                *

Woman's watch thieved by a jay—
        ah, to be lifted like that, carried
        like time across lapping waves.

The Model

Our decrepit tree house
    was only an approximation
        for what the world was like—

a childhood assembled
    with whatever was on hand—
        a constellation of nail heads

that held it all together.

Elegy for a Poet Whose Books I Didn't Think
Were Worth Re-Reading, Not Until Now

for D. D.

Say she leapt from the bleachers,
that the second poem in her first book
is called "The Law of Falling Bodies,"
the same book's fourth-to-last poem
called "For Sylvia Plath," and it would all
be true. Say every second of the day,
the world must come to an end
for someone. Say she lost hope, gained
weight after being abandoned by whomever
she loved, her children also grown
and gone. Say it was mere coincidence
she chose Good Friday to make the leap
from this world into whatever world
comes next—"The Transmigration of Souls"
& "Brides of Christ" also from that book
published more than two decades back
where death's seed had possibly
already been sown, a book that got me
less than a dollar when I sold it back,
not thinking I'd ever need to open it
again, not until she drove her car
to the stadium parking lot at my
alma mater and simply disappeared
without anyone taking notice—her body
"perfected" when the field-hockey girls
stumbled upon it after practice, likely
to have never read a single line
she ever wrote, this copy in my hand
a discard from the Cook Memorial Library
in Libertyville, Illinois, which I secured
for the lowest price online—this clothbound
unsigned first edition with all the "usual"
markings—the list of Due-Date stamps
shorter than anyone would have liked—

Sunnyside Road

Six stone lions standing guard
over bushes heavy with summer
roses the size of newborn heads
as school lets out for good, me
in your bed, your head clogged
with phlegm, you having gotten
drunk three nights out of seven
every week while I was gone
so you wouldn't have to feel
the trashed-out beauty of this
place we walked in early June
as I now retrace those steps
that led us to Sri Rathiga where
the waiter seats me right beside
where Krishna's and his wife's
ecstatic dance inlaid in wood
hung above our table filling up
with those soft green peppers
not to be found anywhere else
in Ilford, and it's true, I think,
everything you said that night
when we became a we, all that
talk about how *unreal* we were—
a holiday from reality was how
you put it. Well now I'm back
for the lunch thali, the pale band
of skin around my right ring
finger almost indistinguishable
from the day I put its golden
weight on thirteen years ago
(my partner saying, *you'll have
to take it off yourself—I'll never
remove it*) as the waiter asks
if I'm on holiday, and I say, *yes
here again*, and if I do not say,
this is where I fell in love, this is

the place where I knew I'd be
changing my life!, all the while
thinking, *won't this waiter leave*
me well enough alone? Once
I dined with my Beloved here
and now without—is there any
difference? The lassis are thin
as ever, the sauces too salty—
all the other tables empty now,
the music being piped into this
room something I have never
heard before—all of it mixed
with sudden bursts of applause.

Next Day

Between the cycles of wash and rinse, a song
about to be sung, all ears lulled by a radio
while toddlers teeth on disposable pens,
while lovers spill speed across the stones
of a glassed-in vivarium, lepidoptera at rest,
in flight, in dreams, each caught in a storm
of juvenile chatroom cyber smut soaking up
chronic carpal tunnel pixel by pixel, hypnotic
pre-dawn infomercial drone in exchange for
flat TV and digitized sound, our solitudes
wired into subterranean optic lines, decrypted
surge-protected codes cruising anonymous
glass abuzz with neon glow and embryonic
lexia languishing on a music stand, marginal
notes scribbled-out below the staff, below
the institutional clock face masking hours
in that brownout run ariot, your appetite
camouflaged in grunt fatigues dirtied-up
at the knees, a song about to be sung, daisy-
chained anxieties now horse-drawn through
a gas-lit park where the dread of connubial
bliss and miniscule tectonic shifts delivered
a tremor through the family skating rink—

Genesis 29:20

You were famished, ready
for whatever I'd put in front of you—

noodles steaming on the table
when you removed your coat and said

Hang this! Not a single empty hanger
in my closet so I slung your coat

over one of my own. A meal is all
we ever shared—your body I know

better than your husband ever will
who never had to wait and serve

seven years the way Jacob did
for Rachel—*and they seemed*

unto him but a few days for the love
he had to her—only to be

given Leah, the older sister.
How Jacob toiled for an additional

seven years to claim what was finally
his. You sat in the same chair

where my wife often sits in her robe
or nothing at all, night after night,

year after year, which made me think
of Jacob, and the ecstasy

he was willing to endure.

NATASHA LOEWEN

Reunion: Poetry Section, A–D

I never imagined the next time I saw you would be here
in this small-brand book store,
reminiscent of that littler one
where you opened to me a new collection
from Carol Ann Duffy
and I read her poem written as Anne Hathaway,
too embarrassed to say aloud I was not following
because I forgot that this was also the name
of Shakespeare's wife.
I was, of course, thinking of the big-toothed actress,
as you may have guessed but were too kind to ask aloud.

Many years have passed but I recognize you:
hyphenations, capitalized first lines,
Greek references.
Pulling you closer, I search for evidences of me
while a year's worth of Mozart plays up my heart.
This is not idle browsing. This is a reunion.

Perhaps I could too appear here,
were I more talented, brilliant . . .
Paperbacked,
smooth waxed skin,
our names so close together.

We might be pressed together,
my back to your front,
alphabetically, trading whispers in the night
when everyone is gone but the store cat,
when all is locked up, like our meanings,
bound in metaphors and well-placed commas.
Until some soul
plucks one of us away from the other,
or imagine if she purchased us together:
Into a plastic bag, turned about,
my spine to your rough-edged breast, front-facing,
and seeing you then,
a first edition to be widely coveted one day on eBay, I'd say,
"Hey, baby. Nice typeface."

twenty-first century mormon poets

She Was Only Seven

A tired guard,
the listing post will not tell.
Martha Stewart snow glitter
shrouds the blooded ground.
Shrugging, the tallest tree
with its open umbrella bones
is a moral relativist,
like the worst of trees.
When the only God here
is the single eye
of a flood light,
the paint-chipped plywood shed,
its inner workings of
shears and shovels,
provides a shady corner
for Hide and Seek,
dee-double dare,
Show and Don't Tell.

The Marriage Bed II: Role Reversals

I have sometimes swapped us
in my mind,
you, Fiddler on the Roof,
an orange traffic pylon,
a hammer for a nail,
me, a cracked china plate,
gold gilded, barely utilitarian.

Places traded, I am blessed with
the ease of have-tos
while you are burdened with choice.
My discipline is gifted by schedule,
monetary reward, immediate results.
You sit at home with expectation
upon you, fallen from the ceiling,
magic-making, eternal consequences.
Dream it into existence, I guess.
shrug

Bearing your softness,
the curve of your abdomen,
my hand would cup you there,
cradling the birth place of my life,
and squeezing you gentle there
a moan would slip out
but not thinking I get to touch the million
bites of trivia of you-ness, thinking of
myself
my face burrowed in your hair, inciting a
gasp of sudden desperation;
I would use my knees to spread your wings,
pin their powder,
admire your beauty just for me,
captured, labeled,
plunder you,
know your squishy warmth,
leave you my mess to clean up.

But I mix up bitter role reversals
with how I would have fixed things if I were you,
because, the fact is,
from the first night,
you kept to your edge of the bed,

flat-backed and oyster-worlded,
anti-climatic after so much pining,
you ignored my whimper.
I breathed in the poison that would take
nearly twelve years to kill me,
my own hand loving the small,
delicious mound of belly,
whispering soul lullabies to sleep,
arising sun-fresh smiled,
inventing companionship.

The Art of Missing

So as not to think of you,
I distract myself with the snow
smushed in grey cork-patterned blankets
on the slanted windows above,
black-lined edges, Wilton food coloring
mixed in as it fell to landing.
Blue peaks through, and clouds
travelling quickly to an important appointment.

The sun thrown on the orange bricked wall,
the shadow made by glass-flattened snow,
has made an atlas upon the grid—
latitudinal and longitudinal lines
pin pointing fifty places I'd like to take you,
places warmish.

Outside, millions of twinkling translucent fireflies,
a milimeter or two across, no two alike.
The sun backlights a Vegas-worthy dance show,
shaking their breasts, feathered heads,
they are sequined, beaded and brash.
Everyone not you looks away, in conversation.

Someone has made a snow angel. The foot prints
snake over, carefully exiting again from their entrance point.
Do you love the person who made that snow angel
like I do?
Yes, you do. I know you. You are full of love for the world.

But I will not think of that.

The Making of Eve

In the sleepiest part of night
all the insomniac fairies
paint the freckles upon her face and shoulders,
a blend of sunshine, gumption, melanin.
Whispering more Jane Austen
than is good for her into her ear,
they paint her hair with strawberries.

She will stand beneath an apple tree
three months from now,
a journal in her hand
of all she thinks she believes and is,
the tall grass shifting to her,
the sun washing sepias,
as the young man who loves her takes her photo,
tenderly repeating her name to himself.
She will smile all her best smiles.

On the drive home
she will glance through the photos.
She will find only frames of wrist,
collarbone,
a flash of auburn,
one blue eye.

Salt Lake City Cemetery, Jewish Section

Diaspora/diaspora

Ours in theirs,
Or theirs in ours?

Together driven past
Earth's small ends,
One to make a new beginning, the
Other on to new extremes.

What can we offer beyond our love,
    Cool groves above the Magick Lake,
        Graves among our prophets' graves?

Cohn Levy Siegel Shvarts
Our kindred—and reminder of God's bleak adoration,
The fate He chooses for the Chosen
This exquisite proving of His souls
Who dry like tea on distant stone and
Disappear forever.

Oz Chronicle #2

When Jesus stole a Buick
He had long flaxen hair and
A face from Stockholm
And smelled like Brut on a hot summer day.
He laughed and sang and drove west
Fast
Like the end of the world

Halfway across Nevada he'd
Filled his car with hitchhikers and at 3AM
Said, "Go to sleep and leave the driving to me."
At 4AM Jesus dozed off and missed a curve—
Damn near rolled that Buick but
Woke up
Just in time thank God

He stood in the desert
Our avatar
Slapping mosquitoes
Looking back over the path the Buick tore
Through the sage
Shaking his sweet head in the moonlight
All amazed.
A trucker with a heavy chain dragged us back on the highway
Narrow
If not straight

When Jesus got to Winnemucca
He bought everybody a big
Breakfast at Denny's.
"A toast," he said, raising his black coffee
Steaming
"To the road and chance. Nothin' like it!"

He left us there and drove back to Utah with
The windows down
Playing Asa's "Jailer" at top volume and

Bouncing on his seat in
A trance of pure joy

Before he pulled away he said,
"I hope you like California.
We've got a few issues to
Sort in paradise
Then I'll see you on the beach"

Oz Chronicle #3

1

Graham Greene's
Journey Without Maps
Got a lot of mileage that day.
I bought it used at The Dusty Bookshelf
In Lawrence and
Read it on the plane from Kansas City to
Salt Lake

2

The Jihadis reclined—earphones, white pillows—
One on either side of the aisle
Eyes closed on Frontier Flight 828
Dreaming of suicide & virgins
I supposed

I had gotten on with Graham and
Damn near walked off again
Having no desire
To be part of a dive-bombing
Over Denver

3

Yes
I saw a wicked karma up there
And I'll tell you this:
The Lord is not pleased with margueritas
At 39,000 feet

4

But somewhere between Topeka
And the Rocky Mountains I let it go.

"The other map," wrote Greene, "is issued by
the United States War Department. There is a
dashing quality about it; it shows a vigorous imagination.
Where the English map is content to leave a blank space,
the American in large letters fills it in with the word
'Cannibals.'"

5

I LOVE
A man who reads Graham Greene
She said (hands on hips).
Where did *YOU* come from?

Kansas, I said. About two hours ago.
I'm married.

Here you can have more than one,
She said and laughed. She touched the book
Then turned and bounced into the Utah night
Looking back once and smiling
Sweet thing

6

Let's face it:
Civilization screws with your head.
The phone/the tube/the car/the plane/Islamabad
Even a book from Lawrence some girl in
Salt Lake City finds irresistible
For no reason I could tell unless it was the
Warm evening in a coffee shop on 4th South or
The crowd, the jazz, the streetcars, the stars
You could barely see.

It's too much.
Really
It is.

twenty-first century mormon poets   277

Oz Chronicle #4

1

Shinjuku Station,
Am I dreaming?

But in my graceless voyage there
Is grace somehow
And what I don't believe
Is true

2

Bamboo runs along this track,
A green explosion.

And it is clear that
Nature knew the way
From countryside to city.

It's all connected to Shinjuku Station where
Trains howl
And a million eyes are closed

3

A man wears a T-shirt that says
"Shit 30" except the 3 is backward.
What does that mean
In Japan? Who can read it?
The man smiles
Pleased with something
Only he can hear

4

And those who rise from nothing
Like Capote and Disraeli
Mean the world to me, even in Shinjuku
Which is far from everything
I know

5

Am I someone
Who makes that world go round?
Will I still love god
When I am unafraid?
These questions point nowhere
Yet are my guiding stars

6

My son stands near me
On the platform of Shinjuku
Yet is far away far away far away
In a place I've seen and tried to tell
Where love is lost and wounds
Heal slowly. He did not hear.
What else can I offer?

7

Shinjuku
The word like water
Cool and blue, flowing
Into that ocean of pain
Long after the electric in my
Head has died and the
Bamboo and my son and the trains.

Reflections on Hebrews 10:31

Far more fearful to leap from them,
for the hands of the living God are too strong
to hold us against our wills.

From that leap we fall forever until we catch
on some forsakenness,
and look down and sense below us all
his hands are stretched out still.

I also confess the fear
of falling into those same hands,
for the leap of faith is not into a void,
but from it, that sterile, static point
of godless fear from which we fear to jump.

But faith, there is no sting or breaking in hitting the hands
of the living God, no matter how artless our fall,
for we always splash down in the center of either hand
into a small pool, warm as blood.

Casual Ministry

We could have dew lists
rather than do-lists,
let responsibilities
fall upon our minds coolly
morning by morning,
discrete disappearing
as day continues,
what we must do not distinct
from what we do.

Why you should not bite your tongue
(didactic poem #2)

Do you think biting the tongue enough
will clove it into Pentecostal ignition and you
will speak everyone's language just right?
(If you believe such self-mortification,
you have one hair shirt for every day of the week.)

Or do you think this unruly member must be canined,
ripped apart as by a concentration camp dog?
(If you believe that you shave your head
or other people's heads entirely.)

No, you reject either view,
for nothing flourishes by violence,
pain is poor restraint,
and you know the woman who starved
because she was always biting her tongue and couldn't eat.

It comes to this:
angels will to dance on the tip of your tongue
and your own words want to bounce just once
then dive into others without waves.

In Memoriam G.R.G.

Our guilt is that we will never be worthy of other people's suffering, and fail to be worthy comforters. Called to sit, witness, and enjoy with due humility what others cannot, it is in some respects easier to lose than to retain. How shall we mourn with the mourning? When the elation of embrace is as strong as the heft of release, when we love the living as strongly as we love the dead, when we have nostalgia for now and a longing for here, we will have almost transposed grief to praise, we will have perfected mourning.

Earth Writing

Eastern states mosaic the map.
Moving west, the states are more like patio tiles.
it looks like the cartographers tired
on drawing West,
the way second graders
begin a story with tidy scrawl
and write bigger and bigger:
fat *D*'s, broad *U*'s, and be done.

Or like people who save places,
spreading quilts on the green
for friends coming late to the concert.

When you claim nothing,
your hunger is infinite.
Getting little,
you demand much.
Lines have to be drawn
so you have at least three trees,
one thunderhead,
and part of a creek—
so those rocks and that mountain
don't consume the county—
and when the wind picks up your soul
it remains in state.

Road to Carthage Sonnet

Two cultures, both imbibed with liberty
in Hancock County, where we lay our scene,
as ancient trouble meets democracy
and moral strife makes mortal hearts unclean.
From forth the frenzied fury of their foes
a pair of plaguéd prophets give their life;
to liberate their friends they juxtapose
their stringent faith against fierce civil strife.
The prudent passage of th' anointed youth,
Ford's acquiescence to the mobsters' rage
—he, by seeking peace, perverted truth—
will be our homage to the classic stage.
Commencing now with frontier acrimony;
Concluding when they seal their testimony.

Joseph's Soliloquy

Now here I am at thirty-eight years torn
between the Mississippi's shifting shores.
No longer young, I've not the youthful dread
of unknown pathways that dead-end to black.
The rudder of my life's not steered by fate;
God's Will shall set my bearing and my port.
Life-long it's been my lot to swim upstream
against the current mulishness of men,
where I must daily dodge the crafty snares
of those self-righteous in their motéd eyes.
I would to God my struggles here were o'er.
To live unbothered by the hordes of hell,
to play a solitary farmer's role,
would be, of myriad lives, most consummate.
To work the mellow fields by morning sun
and tinker with machines in afternoon,
read Homer, Virgil by the waning moon—
Perhaps there is a place out West,
where none may stir my peace.
I'm thirty-eight.
I've stood the seven trials of Abraham:
the loss of home, the call to holy war,
the sacrifice of all, the turn-coat friends,
the loss of love—the Hagars in my bed,
the loss of children, then finally from the Lord,
my sons to soothe our quest for progeny.
May God in Heaven bless my stalwart sons
to gaze beyond the twilight dream and see
how Zion is redeemed from foul men's minds.
I've set the groundwork with an uncut stone
that teeters on the mountain top, then rolls
blood terrible onto the valley floor.
But thirty-eight is less than half the course
to five and eighty years of troubled life
when, by God's promise, I may see his face
and supplicate his home. Lord, give me rest!

Fire in the Pasture

And if not rest, then give me Samson's strength
against the pillars of the Philistines.
Or give me wisdom like King Solomon,
until we crown the spire of His House,
but withhold from me his fanciful desires.
Just give me raven's meal and Eli's coat
before I mount the chariot of fire;
whose spark may detonate the fuséd curse—
the tinder of this modern Babylon.
Or not.
For none of these appointments is my fate.
Mine is no fiery pyre like Joan of Arc
where weak-kneed multitudes regret their sins
before red embers of their deeds grow gray.
Methinks that I, like countless lion meal,
shall face the faceless mob of modern Rome.
for I'm as guilty as a Spartacus.
I led the insurrection of the slaves
as one who fought to set the captives free
against the keepers of the ancient myth:
the doctors, lawyers, and the Pharisees.

Stephen Markham's Complaint

When, in the spring of eighteen thirty-nine,
we brought the saddled steeds that galloped from
Missouri's jails, I cursed the evil mob
that held you brethren winter-long beneath
the cold, dark, musty ground of Liberty.
"Curse not," you said, "it was a test that God
required to give us all experience."

Experience—a most unwelcome gift;
as if, when ravaged by the test of time,
the present phrasing of misfortune's scenes
are shriveled in the synapses of the soul
and only raw remembrance remains;
we'll lucidly consider flaws and faults,
and deem them caused by nature or by youth,
and vow that "next time 'round," we'll act with sense
which, first time 'round, we lacked because we loved?

A liberal lord is our experience!
Where greater portion brings a grosser pain;
where foul afflictions and tireless tribulation
give wider wisdom, singular resolve.

Impassible

'Twas the week between Christmas and New Years
that brought the year twenty-eleven
when the snowplows balked, and the deputy talked,
and I finally gave up on heaven.

When I started to work Wednesday morning
the snow was a-falling sideways.
Then my old pick-up sank into a snow bank.
and I knew it'd be one of those days.

'Twas sunset when the blizzard quit howling,
and I broke out and got the cows fed.
I slept sound till dawn, then I let out a yawn,
and I hooked up the tractor and blade.

First I tackled the hill where the snow drifts
had blocked the road into town.
Then I plowed some more, toward the Reservoir,
when my tractor suddenly sank down.

It's not easy to sink a Deere tractor
with 4-wheel and axles that locked.
So I swore in my wrath, and kicked up a path,
then I fiddled with the forks and I rocked

them forward awhile till it broke loose.
I drove back, and for jiminy sake
I pulled out a full den of drunk fishermen
Who were headed to fish on the lake.

After I pulled out the third mired pick-up,
I piled up some four feet of snow
as thick as cold lard 'cross the cattle-guard
and I put up a sign that said, "NO!"

In church Sunday morning I had hope
that my good deed should earn me salvation;
but I was appalled when the Deputy called
and threatened to write a citation.

With so much at stake, I sped home to the gate,
but the snow on the hill was too soft,
my front tire caught the bank, in the drift my rig sank,
leaving me to walk down to the cop.

"You cannot block the road for their safety,"
he said, "Not even I have a say;
If you'll tear down the mounds, I not have any grounds
to write you a ticket today.

Dressed in my Sunday duds, I told him
'twas Christian to save them some grief.
But he said he had called the Commissioners all,
and cleared it with the County Road Chief.

"These people just want to go fishing.
I can't let you block the road.
It's their own sorry luck if the fishers get stuck
as long as *you* do what you're told!"

I said, "When they get stuck, I'll help 'em.
Last night was eleven below.
But I can't spend all day helping anglers who say
they have planted their rigs in the snow."

"You have no obligation to help fools.
The snow is an Act of God,"
said the county deputy without hint of charity
and whose rules weren't the ones I was taught.

The John Deere helped me tear down the snow mound
as I ate my full helping of crow.
Then I revved it up big to pull out my rig
that had buried itself in the snow.

But pulling it out roughed the snow up;
and the snowplows were four days past late.
There was little doubt, no one could drive out
if I didn't blade a path to the gate.

I had told him I was just trying to help folks
but he laid down his Government Rules.
Of course *he* was parked still at the base of the hill
and I wasn't obliged to help fools.

Fire in the Pasture

'Twas Sunday the day after New Years
in the year of twenty-eleven
When my tractor blade balked, and the deputy walked,
and I finally gave up on heaven.

Eleionomae

On a lip of her bent-branch bank
he dips into dark-watered sleep,
grows stupid and saw-voiced with dreams.
He, a dark cap of curls in the still, freestanding reeds.

In her own oilshining ocher hair she weaves
soft-stemmed weeds of gold and green. Deep
dragonfly eyes hover with helicopter wings
about his heavy head and neck.

Out to her aurous amber arms, he turns,
hands that once held Hercules
tremble in her spray-slick touch.

And she, lips spread in ancient, aqueous smile
lifts her lambent limbs and shakes
quicksilver strands of water
from her hair in crystal pleats.

Elias

In the heavy hush of this blue shadow the smoke
of odor rises, long-fingered and green

wet with spent worries, a spoil of tuber bodies
clasping their thin stems together, breathing

vegetable spice, slender and savory into the
thick bouillon of a blue sky, a cauldron of calefaction

doubling and troubling a sorrowful and sweltering mind.

Still,
underneath this juniper tree,
I lift my cheeks aflame with summer sin and feel
the faintest cooling flurry
of a leaven-laden
angel's wings.

Soft Bastards

I know now
why I
love Latin:
we
are both such
soft bastards.

Gilded by God-
speaking old men
who have adorned and admonished
us that what we wear
is more than what we are:

a cathedral-high palate
over a curving gold tongue—

and purple folds
of papal robes
wrapped weightily around
a pagan's heart.

The Short Books

Now, Micah lives near Nahum
in the Bible's closing pages.
Micah is an optimist,
while Nahum speaks in rages.

Micah sometimes wishes
he lived near Lamentation.
It even could be better if
he moved to Revelation.

Habakkuk and Haggai
and Zephaniah, too,
have said that if he leaves them
they're going with him too.

So if someday you find the books
are all in disarray,
open up to Nahum;
Read the things he'll say.
He'll roil with ringing rhetoric,
he'll every point belabor.
And I think that I'm with Micah:

He'd make a very lousy neighbor.

Jacob, to Esau

Brother Esau, I can tell you now
    no angel has a sense of humor;
    just a light-licked sense of small
    roses unfurling from toothlike buds,
    lizards skittering clawfirst over baking stone.
        At this, he may smile, as at a toddler's stuttering words.
You will not doubt my chin curled around his holy biceps
      and felt at home, so often had it locked
      around your red and hairy muscle
      as a child, as a youth, as a frightened and furious man.
        Strength was, I always thought, your true, unpurchaseable birthright.
You would not
    I believe
        have buckled in the searing hasp
          the holocaust
          the glare with human hands
          the body and bone of light.
You would not have unraveled in the joints and limbs
        when his knowing fingers stroked your iron thigh.
    But I was ever, ever the sham of you; and my only hope a wriggling slide away.
Of me, our father might have said once *Truth leaves no handhold for conniving fingers.*
    To which I add this wisdom: *When they wrestle*
                angels do not laugh
                the frightening, familiar
                well-loved laugh of my brother Esau.

Pop Art Songs

1. Cartoons

Here I come to save the day! I would sing
With a pillowcase tied behind my neck.
I was in need of champions back then,
Mighty Mouse first then the mere pretenders,
Underdog, Bullwinkle, Gumby, Pokey.
Heroes sang falsettoed anthems in tights,
Masked (for obvious reasons),
Wanting to be as beloved as
Mickey Mouse was without the means.

Ten years flying around chasing cartoons
Like a million kids, who required them less.
On the day we moved, I buried Gumby
In the backyard six inches deep in muck.
I made a map—since lost—said I'd return
Someday and did today, thirty years on
Having flown 2,000 miles from my place
In Gotham City. But he was not there.
He disintegrated presumably.

2. Meatloaf

In those days its ingredients were
For the most part those evening meals
We had abandoned.

Back then, suddenly liberated from high chairs,
We were out to rustle up trouble.
We herded danger; we chewed on the new.
We saw no reason for meatloaf.

There was much we missed in those days
Before we learned to eat food we hated
And say please for things we didn't want.

3. Mr. Bubble

On languorous afternoons with nothing at all to do
I ran away from home by hiding in the bathtub.
I ignored what they yelled:
"Unlock the door, you cry baby."
I became bigger without them near.
I found strength in suds.
Even if I always felt a little itch,
A sticky spotlessness afterward,
I believed in Mr. Bubble,
That he could rise between my pinkie toes
And float from bathwater
Like a fragile balloon
Up and up and up
To paradise.

4. TV

Do you remember the episode from Lost in Space
When June Lockhart does the laundry?
She throws soiled spacesuits into the washer,
And seconds later removed shrink-wrapped bundles,
All as the planet is about to explode.
At my house we didn't watch television news
So don't ask me about Vietnam.
But I do know all about Gomer Pyle,
The Munsters and That Girl.
I missed the video moment when Jackie Kennedy
Crawled over slumping John,
And I slept through the broadcast of silver astronauts
Bouncing atop the moon,
But Darrin and Samantha Stephens lived at
1164 Morning Glory Circle
In every episode of Bewitched but one.
I think that says something.

5. Barbie Love

We might have married Barbie dolls.
Leggy, svelte, with lithe, hard hips.
Their hair cascades in undulant curls
To smooth waists the diameter of a pencil.

Barbie never talks back. She smiles and undresses so easily,
One strong yank does it.
And there she stands with nose and breasts upturned,
Waiting to do whatever it is you want:

She is in your hands.
You can bend her backwards, lead her by the hair,
Make her head turn all the way around
To follow you where you go!

But you have to be careful.
These Barbies that we wanted for an evening,
Or maybe longer, can poke out an eye.
And if you pull a leg too much

Or twist the arm, something inside the nothing snaps
And the head falls off.

Internship at a Large Firm

I remember the way they went after their ice cream cones,
licking away like little girls, pink tongues
slathered in cream, relishing, savoring,
shaping the 49-cent desserts
like grand artistes. Silky ties,

salt and pepper comb-overs,
the respectable swell of the dun-lop
(bellies which had done-lopped over their belts).
I thought they'd be biters, that's all,
Bud Light kind of guys,

working late kind of guys.
I'd seen them when the market opened,
on the phone with New York,
San Francisco, selling securities
to the big boys in Dallas, Denver,

ties loosened, palming phones,
saying those sons of bitches in Boston,
they'll get theirs, wink, wink.
And yet how gentle they were with the chocolate-vanilla,
how softly their fingers gripped

those paper cones, how sincerely the tongue carved
that soft, non-dairy cream.

My Daughter's Favorite Bedtime Story

Go, Dog. Go! by P.D. Eastman, a story
about dogs: big and little, red, blue,
yellow, and green dogs that skate,
ski, swan dive from impossible
three-story rowboats. My daughter says
"Be careful" to the page with two dogs at play
on top of a blimp high above New York.
There's no easy way down,
and though my daughter's only two,
it bothers her the story never tells
what happens. We both like the picture
of three dogs in a boat at night
having a party. Mid-ocean, midnight,
the black water smooth as sleep,
or maybe death, but she'd never think of that,
would she? Does she see in the sky
a smile of teeth for a moon? I wondered once,
with my daughter's hair like spun glass
floating on the pillow next to mine,
if it's how God feels, watching the pages,
knowing the end and the beginning,
having already read it a hundred times,
or more. Still, my daughter can't wait
for the ending—the great dog party
—on the grassy top of the giant tree.
Dogs from every page together at the last,
eating big triangular slices of pink
frosted cake, jumping on trampolines.

It's all over then, the boats and blimps
and cars and parties vanished like waves
rolled out flat one after another, pages
against the shore. Then comes that moment
when all that's left—she's learned already—
is to turn back, back to the beginning.

Working a Turkey Pen

I'd take a few practice swings,
like golf.

Walking a pen of toms,
hunting the diseased

like the Gestapo—
the grain of the wood, the turkey face,

the sun—
a solid hit felt good

and the board wouldn't vibrate.
This is factual and more or less a narrative,

but I wonder—
I had to kill

the sick before contagion spread.
The last thing I wanted

was possibilities—
contamination, death.

What comes after
is always more interesting,

like reflex—the bird's, my own—
like licking my finger

to wash the dry spots
from my shoes, jeans, fingernails.

To Rosie, Not Yet Three

Funny thing
asking—
Are you poopy?

—and meaning it
so sincerely, no sarcasm

or mockery,
just earnest desire

to know
if there's a load

in your shorts.
And you, crouched

beneath the baby grand,
telling me, no,

when the stink
is as thick as this August air,

lying to my face,
as sweet

as an elevator love song.

After This Life

You will come back as a tree.
A thick, generous tree,

limbs wide
to hang a swing from.

It will be summer

but not heaven.
All day you'll dig

for the deep rivers
beneath you

surging in the dark.

You'll have no tongue,
no mouth to drink

or speak from,
lips to smile.

Only root and longing,

an empty swing,
and the wind

like an animal breathing.

Marie Curie, Dying

She loved her husband mostly
in the evenings,
sun lighting their backs,
when his shadow
was long as laboratories.

They argued over tea,
clenching their cups. She shivered
with the sweep of his voice.
He left faint fingerprints, like fireflies,
on his notebooks, the china, her face.

She liked to lie awake beside him,
arms looping his luminous bulk,
breathing in his light—
unearthly as eels, but
not radiant enough to read by.

He wrapped himself in overcoats,
umbrellas—they both did—this was
Paris—but he was brilliant; he was
dazzling; even the rain
steamed off him, and everyone stared.

As the years passed he blazed
up like cloudfire in a storm;
his eyes scorched and hissed
into her pale skin,
and she tried to catch his light

in jars and beakers, bottling
it, saving it against the winter,
but it seeped from under the lids
and flooded the cramped cellar, surging
and curling while she batted it, frantic.

He kept his gaze fixed above
the drab streets. One wet April
he stepped off a curb like a heedless comet

and was crushed beneath sudden wheels. Light
leaked like blood from his startled limbs.

She watched dazed in the thunder
as he died beneath flashing
currents, calling, he and she,
both calling and howling
until their raw throats glowed,

and she swallowed the last sparks
from his electric fingers,
gulped the lightning, watched
the fading and dying
of the preposterous light from his eyes.

In time the saved glow invaded her blood,
and she sweat lightly in phosphorescent fevers,
grew quiet, started wandering nights,
eyes open and careful
in the flame of her own conceived radiance.

Translations

Between the tears and bears and scribbled walls
I can find little time to shout (as I
would have to shout, or interrupt myself
to find the shoe; acknowledge comments; try

to put the lid back on) to you the way
a yellow curl of smoke washed the moon green
and how I wished to wake you in the dark
but watched you sleep instead, eyes quick with dreams.

All day I thrash in oceans full of words,
too slow to catch the drops before they're gone.
At night, the dreams that flash behind my eyes
are softer than they were, and fade with dawn.

There is so little time for poetry.
We will grow old, I know, and it will keep.
But read it, if you can; the way I stretch
myself against you even in my sleep.

The way I turn at your step on the stairs:
How anything I once gave up has thinned,
shifted; reappeared changed and whole, to wrap
its shape around the two of us like skin.

Eve's Tigers

During those first nights
she lay awake, cat-like,
watching shadows move

between dark trees.
Tigers, he had named them,
but it was to her they came

in the quietest times
before the dawn.
Some last memory

of a friendship perhaps,
of clear pools, sun-drenched,
beneath acres of green.

Eyes open, she saw them,
circling, her husband clean
and guileless in sleep,

protected by his own exhaustion.
And always the sun rose
bright on empty clearings,

and in the light of day the trees
were silent, and there was no need
for any speech but Adam's,

and her own. No matter, then,
if the heavy nights stretched
like a veil across her,

if the whispering tigers
came again and again
to question her dreams.

After Eden

Understand this, if nothing else: that she
had only known him darkly, fragmented
like shadow under leaves. That she was free.

That she had only seen his sleep unsaid
in flecks between his eyelids; dark as storm
between the lightning; thin and strong as thread.

Perhaps at night the sighing owls swarm
eagerly round him; perhaps in his heat
the trees reshape their bodies to his form

and curl their fragile roots around his feet.
Perhaps he falls like hailstones through trees,
or crashes frightened through his dreams, the beat

and boil of blood rushing like rain to freeze
inside his head. Under his eyes there could
be crossings still subsiding as they breathe

the breath of one man only.
                          Know this: good
felt natural to her. Some few things she knew:
his hands were cold as silver. When he stood

like moonlight in a clearing, he was blue
as angels, tall as gardens, faint as stones.
You must believe this: that her ribs still drew

their light from his. As if a mountain groaned
and rose beneath her in one morning, this
unusual, lifting sun inside her bones.

Sheep

The night was not still;
even at dusk none of us
were easy; even in the moonlight
no one was calm. It was nearly
quiet. Instead, there was rustling.
The sound of crowded
air, of things just-above and just-
beneath. Of waiting. And then

we heard the daybreak,
noise like sunshine, gold
as meadow flowers.
We shifted closer, wondering,
and watched the dark sky light
with sound. *Birds,*
we whispered, but above us
the trees too were watching.
When the familiar night fell
we breathed again, bent
our heads to the grass,
gulped the comfortable air.
And yes, we are content

to graze, sleep, spend
our deliberate hours,
feel ourselves heavy with young.
Still, some nights we look up
without knowing why, hoping
for a signal none of us can quite
remember, a direction that has somehow
escaped us, although there was a moment
we understood it; a moment
that held more than trees, grass, sky.

Don't Tell Me What, Todd:

A Poet to Her Muse

Nine ladies in gossamer for the Greeks, but for me:
you. Sure, the first muses likely bathed once a week,
had crooked teeth, etcetera. But they were cogent,
at least, and spoke sweeter than you've ever spoken
to me.

Todd, waking me nightly from sleep as you stumble
out the local bar, wet bearded; you're shouting funk
down the street—plots for world peace in free
verse, leaky similes—funk I'm sure to think
resembles nothing coherent come sunrise.

Come sunrise I'll be phoning you again through my
dreams, telling you of all I could do without your
chatterings, and yet fearing, beneath everything I
said, if you left there'd be no whispering in the
mornings, no one to rattle me with love.

Always the Night Sky

No god but sun and the lightning. When the first humans finally caught a brush fire they fed it for winter months. They thought it like life: when the breath stopped, it could not be revived. The world over, one smoldering light.

They had to create the gods before the gods would teach creation. Then from tallow, twine, and fire-flies: candles, oil lamps. From Delphi, torches flooded the known world, fastened to chariots. Asteria spread herself outward, downward. Earth patterned after Helius.

Today: fire pits, wicks, bulbs. Across the globe, constellations grounded, forged to outnumber, launch, the stars. And from our satellites, tracing earth's tungsten, raining film—all this footage, lighting into space.

Creationism: Five Theories

1

White. Every documented fact has started with a blinking black line in the top-left corner of a one-inch-margin box.

2

I believe I was born blinking. I believe I was born Siamese—I mean, my mother's brain and mine are inside of me.

3

Then earth came clean, rubbing Adam's dream from my ribs—she grew gills and fins—some backwards evolving beauty earth is.

4

She shrinks herself from eel to amoeba, wavers her flagella, swims away. God rides on her back. Eden slithers. Black.

5

There are bird bones in the clouds. How they fly too. Ribs as wings. Words stream: how we come too.

Prayer Cap

Krishna pinned the Indian Ocean convex
above Great Britain. Earth's sacred kippah.
A brave display of darks and greys;
Today there is one cloud and no sky.
An omen? Hint of Maitreya?
Then praise this day without the sun;
her needed nap to wake us from
the routine of rise, the pulse of set.
This generation, too walled-in to ever rest.
Petals of ocean drip as Krishna
slips life to us. We rouse when
that stratus cloud wrings and wets
our desiccated tongues—now sending
soothing phrases soaring up to God.

Benediction

Tom Dólejan and his drunken prophet wife, Maria, put the dog and cat in the truck. It is raining, just as she said it would, as they pull out onto the highway, heading west.

Water slips down roofs, and people pour outside, hands cupped, to witness what is just as she'd said—an oily speck of light in every raindrop, illuminating roof tops and telephone wires, spotting the city in a sloshing constellation. Tom holds Maria's hand in her trance, and asks if they'll get back to the city. The streets are filling fast, wipers and brake lights.

Too many, she says, too many threads to cut, sins to count. The Fates backed out long ago, let the spools loose, crowding the room, waiting for God to toss a match to the earth.

And now light gilds rain. Gold drains gutters. Evening mutters, electric waters. Blind spots sputter, sap drips from billboards. And before Tom and Maria Dólejan leave the city, they stop to take in the scene. Tom and the dog step down from the truck as angels romp in the streets, angels bearing a beautiful heat.

Away From Me, Toward Water

She walked, scooping bird-seed
from the mouth of a paper sack, as if

>   plucking cherry blossoms
>   collecting first-haircut curls
>   spreading crumbs through thickets.

She said no words, flicking millet across the grass,
distant churches perched on her head, speaking losses:

>   twelve months I wouldn't live
>   a toddler I would never meet
>   places I wouldn't be, hold, or behold.

She hardly lifted her bare, pond-bound feet
shuffling through birds as they flocked to her

>   like lovers
>   like leeches
>   like children.

Whitewater

Rafting done right cleanses
the body—blood, sweat, and piss
leaving you for the ocean.
Poseidon is a puddle-pusher
compared to the Staircase.

Heed the river. He is much
older than the men he eats.

Class 3s are for kids, boarding
    other vessels, oars ablaze. Splitting
        the chute in a Class 4 eliminates
            guide-dumping tail-whips. One foot
                the wrong way when entering a Class 5
                    will shove you sideways up the haystack,
                        shoot the man riding the bull ninety degrees,
                          taco your boat, and devour the entire crew.

A lifejacket won't save you
if you've got a broken neck.
Get your feet downriver,

                  push
                     off
                the
                    rocks.

                        If you're under,
                          note the bubbles before swimming:

                              Charon is the wrong way up.

Rafting done wrong spits
you out sixty yards downstream,
bobbing face down in an eddy,

                      one with the water.

Le Metro

I don't know the French verb for 'to reek,'
but it's probably monosyllabic, starting with **F**.
Standing on a train under the Eiffel Tower I forsake
protecting my wallet to squeeze my nostrils shut.

European girls—all fashion and eye contact—weave
me in and out of the piss-plus-raw-eggs stench
that has me ready to cry. They come and go, taking
their imaginary risqué lingerie with them.

One mademoiselle alights on the seat next to me.
First thought: pull the tourist card, fake idiotic French,
and get a smile out of her. Second: this fetor
gives me insight into the life of a Greek soldier.

The Trojan horse must have been something
like this: glazed bodies crammed into an airless shell
simmering in manly perspiration, wondering whether
Aniketos' farts make the journey better or worse, trapped

with only a promise of fresh air at the end if I stay
quiet. The train slowed and she stood to exit. I down-
upped her legs and stilettos, deciding she'd make a fantastic maid.
Screeching brakes ended our unstarted guerre des sexes.

She glanced back and I felt the door *whoosh*.
It sounded like this: *whoosh*. It *whoosh*ed.

Morning Storm

A quiet blue bird
Stuck in the crib

Ryan pokes his brother
Down the hall

Sound of sisters cereal in the kitchen
Mom and Dad sleeping snoring

The lopsided evergreen dances silent outside glass

Mom and Dad sleeping snoring
Sound of sisters cereal in the kitchen

Down the hall
Ryan pokes his brother

Stuck in the crib
A quiet blue bird

Three Months After the Last Time

I saw her, I realized I had forgotten to ask
how sesame seeds stick to the bun.
She worked in a bread factory, not a bakery.

But I didn't ask; never spoke to her; wasted
weeks of every-other-day opportunities to smile,
break the ice, speak, sit on her side of the room.

Perhaps she knew other things: why donut holes
are bigger than holes in donuts, how yeast touches
dough differently before the stirring starts,

whether the often-overlooked loaf ends
prefer being the bread's "butt" or its "heel."
For all I know she knew everything; could have

cracked my mind like an egg on a counter corner
and dropped me into a batch of powdery things—
things as they are and as they might become.

I could probably pluck her name from a page
and see if it was cooked to taste. Years from now
maybe I'll wake up at 4am and blurt it out,

but only maybe. The buildings between us shiver
sometimes. I still wonder if she daydreams about class,
if my dead-end jobs fascinated her, if she too passes nights

sitting on carpeted steps writing poems about me.

Coring the Apple

Instead of the thorn,
Hast thou found honey?

I would like to ask Eve someday
What she saw in the apple.

Before she chose
The fire-stung glory of mortality,
Did she pause for even the space of a breath,
Tremble at the bruise of pain, the sharpness of the briar?
Perhaps she sensed the hope nestled star-like
In the core of the fruit,
And so risked all she was for the quickening—
The promise of the seed dreaming deep in the loam.

I would like to ask Eve someday
What she saw in me.

Umbralucent

The snow is on fire with moonlight,
Trees casting blue shadows like smoke.
Midnight splits a maple,
Branches leaning windward while
A lunar-kindled silhouette
Traces calligraphy
Over the stark clarity
Of white below
Until I cannot tell which form
Was first—
Which belongs to heaven, and which mirrors earth?

Cinderfolio

There are such queens in the scrub!
Shy sovereigns waiting for the royal red,
Autumn's trumpet to announce them
That they may air out their citrine
Silks and garnet fans to dance
With sleek, bare-branch abandon,
Shivering dreams off their boughs
In a blush of paper embers.

Aphelion

I listen for the cold
Snap of branches
Beaded in hydrogen jewels,
The rustle of souls
As leaves take to the sky—
Frost pearling silence
Like stars
Coming home.

The Fallen Gardener's Ode:
Cirrus Wishes

I have seen the ribcage of Heaven
Hanging in bones of mist,
Falling in fleshed out tears
Of rain and ice.
Here, then gone—
Like a breath too soon exhaled.
Only corporeal earth tells the passing
In blushes of color.
I have cried for picking a dandelion.
Bright-faced warrior, green-spiked leaves
Brave and strong against the world,
My dirt-grubbed snapping fingers
Grasping hard at its life.
Soon, even beautiful defiance breaks in
Bleeding milk sap cleaner than pearls.
Amazing, if I leave the stem untouched
This same microdot sun child
Blows into a thousand silver wishes
If only left alone, to grow.
Maybe that's why I persist—
To grow a thousand feathered wings
Among dandelions and cirrus clouds
To live and bleed and die—
Yet, there lies a state of grace
Between the breaths of me, here and now.
Let my meaning speak in flower-whorls:
Search the petals of the peony—
There are stars in the folds even I can find.

Postcard

In my hands it feels small and thin,
almost like holding you.
I swallow your words like a prodigal
counting again the weeks you've been away.

The picture is Beatrix Potter's sitting room,
her table rounded by three Victorian chairs,
proper and high-backed, stiff, a bit frigid even;
her walls hung with plates and art:

her things: conscious things: like you deciding
which card and when, which sweet murmurings,
how to bend closer to paradise;
the intricate measurings of love.

I too decide, thinking that fine place
between sentiment and sentimentality.
I fill the miles with memory—
the way you correct hair that falls

into your forehead; the way your hand
comes toward me like a scared child,
but warm, our skin remembering;
an afternoon when we watched blackbirds

dance and weave in the cattails,
the sadness of their wavering chorus,
the small gift of their yellow heads,
the intricacies of their community.

Mired in this dull ache
I think how simple separation seems,
how many times I've leaned toward you
like Donne's compass seeking a circle.

And how in the airport a few days from now
we will move toward each other
in the sweet dance of clumsiness—
those first moments back together.

Above the Aspen

1.

When the cerulean sky
took me back,
saying, yes, my son,

I entered her like I had left,
a body without blood or bones,
a weightless spirit, ready and nervous.

Tree souls: light and like-bodied essences,
courses and courses in song,
in dance. Swaying slim trees
white-silver-gray.

No sun, a place making its own light,
no clouds. And birds, white
and untroubled, in the constant
soar of bird.

2.

How easy I begin to forget.
How easy.

3.

I am pure music.
I am bird of paradise.
I am painted buntings.

My flitting from limb to limb
is a song of sweet notes—
cheeps and *cheets*.

I flash and whir,
perfect bodied.

My name is a song
a slight breeze says.

4.

Ophir's ships float off shore,
in something like the sea,
but no waves, no water;
they ride low, laden with gold,
jewels, and ivory tusks.

5.

I want to touch the trees,
their white bodies like skin
I remember,
inner thigh, inner arm, stomach,
breasts, and secret passages.

To walk through them
in my old body, late afternoon light,
to see trumpeter swans,
vain and black masked,
oaring the sky above me and the trees,
slow sweep of wings and feather-tip,
a V big as a county;
geese honk and flight;
and the quick spurt of mallards
rising off water.

Light filters through the trees
like water I want to touch,
dipping my hand and arm
to the shoulder. And leaves
quaking.

Colors I have worn.

6.

In the high order of stars
diagrams of constellations,
omphalos, the cosmic center,
gate and gatekeeper to God's land.

I stand at the four stars
like a cross, arms out,
reaching for what I think
is mine.

I awake.

Welder: Falling

. . . how everything turns away
—Auden

When he steps back
from the red heat
and raises his face shield,
his wings melt
and he splashes into air, flailing,
seven stories up, the tip
of his fire swinging in a blue arc.
His helmet catches a wave of air;
he reaches for the rope
and saves his fall,
the lunge yanking him
spasmodically, again, and
against the new building's brick.
His hat cracks the gravel below.
"That's a damn fine truck:"
says a man near the fence.
Three guys sit on sawhorses,
eating lunch. A long-armed forklift
beeps backwards, its load
shifting on uneven ground.

I Believe

I believe in dirt. And the anthill's leaf carriers,
the trail they cut into geography, the way
a sick ant leaves the nest, voluntarily,
in order to die alone.

And the sun falling towards its horizon, a candle
sitting on a sill, the night birds rising in shrill notes
and wing beat. The size of a gnat's mind,
its foot barb, the mite crawling up its leg.

I believe Adam when he said it wasn't easy
naming the animals, living with Eve; rotting fruit,
what to make for dinner, wearing the same smelly
skin to work each day. Only one woman to look at.

And God. I believe him when he said enough,
the delight in rejection, the short-lived rest
of the seventh day, Eve swooning before the snake,
Adam's jealousy, the unbeaten path out of Eden.

Above Henry's Lake: Mid-November

As if the bird-god knew a sign would remind me of belief—
he sent an omen—not an eagle with a white goose
hooked and bleeding in its talons—
but a neighborhood of Waxwings.

They did not swoop down in a clap of thunder,
or materialize in the shattered edge of lightning:
they appeared from nowhere: a vision, an incantation
of fifty or sixty small fawned bodies

rising and falling in unison like a startled gasp,
or a balloon let loose of air, a shook carpet, a puff of dust,
like a giant heart *whuwhumping*, each combined undulation,
each acrobatic somersault a new metaphor.

A picture show from the early days—no sound
but the whir of wings, a small, careful practice
of group flight aerodynamics, of a god dipping
those sixty tails in yellow paint, just so. A brush stroke

on the sky's blue canvas; a small play of ballerinas—
on a moment landing in Junipers, then off
like startled minnows. No sound but the sound
of synesthesia, of swirl and swing, of life lived high and fast.

No sound. But the bird-god conducted
each movement and his wand sprayed the birds
in a different pattern of choked spasms, of pulsation,
lifting and rising a *passi lenti* in the breath-held show

of blue and snow and Juniper, a small moment of watching
without effort, a brief mood of intense happiness,
a gift I keep opening and opening—
the unwrapping a rhythm like circadia.

City Dog

The day I die I hope this old yellow dog
will slip from my fist like string through a bead

and jog west, tongue out, dim eyes leaping
to the distant green and granite face

of the mountain that presided over my youth.
This final errand: to shed over seven states,

through days of unslacking hardwoods
and humid miles of corn, the great weight

of living within the blackened brick walls
of this restless city, and to grow unworn again,

to return as the last bright spark of my prodigal heart
to the bowing lupine and flickering aspen forest

where my broad father, and his before him,
gave his bones back to the everlasting earth.

The Wild Turkey

Maybe you learned to hope,
Junior Meeks, from that ancient wild turkey
who found you leaning in a stupor
against the woodpile, picking laundry
from the line. He unblended from the underbrush

before your eyes and swelled
across the back lawn like the final
word on things. That old bird, his yellow
sticks and heavy tattered fan, the huge
red drop of his gobbet—

my, he was something,
come the long journey
across the woods to discover you
staggering boxer shorts, your smokes, the usual
eyeopener at the patio table,

come like some Columbus casting out mysteries:
the beads of his eyes, the wondrous
steel of his presence, his dark body like a window
to which you raised your eyes
because the world had just changed.

But then, as you stumbled out
to greet him, to fall on your face
and praise him for the angel of God
he was, his wings coughed him
up off the lawn and into the woods again—

a clumsy impossible flight
like that of the heavy honeybee or, more accurately,
as if you yourself had unstooped, stretched
the crooked sticks of your arms,
and leapt into the sky.

Poem to a New Wife

Maybe you don't know
but a man has more than blood
ticking in his machine:

he has fear. With women
it is not the same. Just yesterday
the stuck lid of the pickle jar

stayed stuck in his grip,
but the jar, the very jar itself,
shattered. The sandstone at his jaw,

the mute might in his back and shoulders—
this is not quick wren of a boy
who spoke your name from the lilacs

of your seventeenth birthday.
He wonders what next
will crumble in his fists.

And so, when he circles you in love
and your ribs strain like timbers,
do not cry out.

Instead, pull his face
to your neck, feel the wool
of his breath at your throat

and speak to him in murmurs
of the highways you see rising
from his palms, the cities from his bones.

The Road to Vegas

Maybe we'll make Vegas
by sundown and see the city go up
in lights. It doesn't matter

though, because even a twenty seven dollar
room couldn't bend the rebar
of your bones around mine, or please you

into forgetting that I have gone
twenty-seven days without work
because I can't get my mind straight.

I have tried to explain my head
is like that old adobe house
on the Draper bench whose roof

burned off years ago—I've been up
there at night and that place
is full of stars and wind and squawbush,

nobody picks the walnuts there,
and they pop under your feet like seashells—
if only you would

rent a room and fold your arms
around the laced fingers of my ribs,
and bury me in the soil of your body

I could make it
this time. I could turn the canvas
of my back to the sun and paint

highways across this desert,
I could lay hard tens at every table
and gamble us out of this hole.

To Remember is to Live

That morning a wet sky leaned
hard into the East River.

I was not well,
wearing my brother's castoff great coat
with the collar twisted up,

and as I shouldered my way
to the red and white Roosevelt Island tram
that would swing into the heavy wind
and carry me up and away to Manhattan,

I saw a huge white swan swimming mightily
against the charcoal tide—
not one of the shabby yellowed creatures
bobbing in the Conservatory pond,

but a brilliant wild bird
laboring in the outrunning water
beneath the Queensborough Bridge.

Already so much of my short life
is lost to memory, but that moment
I remember like a single breath
amid a lifetime of breathing,

a wild white swan struggling
against an East River
rushing to lose itself in the sea.

Sage

Its small twisted white trunk
springs naked from the red
soil, barkless and raw,
reluctant to erupt into the dry canyon air
its sinewy branches clinging to the ground
split and ragged
as if they were stomped into
place by the booted
foot of a careless giant before
springing up thick and fragrant.
Leaves, tiny and dull, hoard
what moisture its roots manage
to coax from the ground.

He was a man of the sage
vulnerable and rooted in place
timeless he watched and waited.

Rain came but seldom
and when it did, it tended to wash
away his supports rather than refresh
but that was the way of it
always the way of it.

Winter Gifts

Why do the dark-eyed juncos
stay?

In the gelid inversion
low clouds
give little reason to sing

Why linger here?

They flit about as if it were
not near winter solstice, not chill,

as if the dawn were not empty
of warmth

Why board in such stark haunts?

The seeds are few and insects fewer

The calculus of their presence brokers
a secret only a god would know

The Slaying of the Trickster God

Prologue

When two universes collide
one is destroyed, or
is it
masked?
hidden
in the wind,
preserved,
like a seed to come
forth later?
The other however
folds in on itself,
slowly,
a topological twisting,
until it engulfs itself and
is gone.
Coyote-Man, it seems, never
learned how to deal
with motorized vehicles.
They escaped his desert
logic.
Hasje-altye—Talking God—
never prepared him for
the intrusion.
The invasion.
But who's to blame?
Who would have believed that
metal
and carbon
seduced from the earth
could be
combined to bring
forth such a monster—
such an engulfer?

I

"If you see a coyote stop and
I'll shoot it."
My brother unholstered
the .357 and checked the loading.

"Russ it's Sunday. You can't
shoot on Sunday."

He put the gun back under the seat.
"Oh yeah, I forgot."

Lightning flashed
across the night, across the
desert, leaving only dark lines
tracing over the distant landscape
the path of ancient
water courses. Only
the smell of rain,
escaped the clouds
lowly
hugging the sides of the La Sals
miles to the southeast. The stars and moon
disappeared in the flash, but reclaimed their
domain after the ephemeral
rupture of night.

When the trickster
creature of
myth and night
raced in front of the Torino
there wasn't even time
to remove my foot from the gas.

It was broken in two.
Lanky front legs tried to drag
from the macadam
the deadened mass that
once served so well
to propel it in merry predation.
It snarled fiercely as we watched
a few feet away—its eyes raging,

its hatred unmasked. Despite
the Sabbath Russ fired the
.357 twice—
a bang and a whimper (like both
scenarios for the end of the world),
and a different symmetry was restored
to the broken halves.

II

Returning from clearing
the forest of unworthy
trees, chain saws bouncing
in the back of an obnoxious
Forest Service
truck.

Two coyotes played in the
meadow.
friends?
lovers?

Mark aimed the truck
and fired across
the meadow and
we hit the fleeing ball of fur
at over 60 mph.
He almost flipped the truck
as he jerked the wheel a
final time to make the kill.

John and Mark,
authors of no gospel,
whooped and hollered as they cut
off the tail for a souvenir.
I leaned against the truck
darkly
and wondered if the other
was sad to be alone
or grateful to be the
one left running.

Love Floats Pale and White

A twisted knot of complexity,
floated half-way up the large
test-tube. Nestled somewhere
in that mass of blood vessels
and grey matter rested the love
for her son.

The worried faces filed hesitantly
into the room each spanked with
a concerned smile masking uncertainty.
This was the moment—the surgeon had
given no guarantee of anything. Fear
turned into relief as her eyes and countenance
recognized each face and she whispered
their names: her husband Jimmy,
her oldest daughter Chandra and her
husband Michel and their new baby Brittany,
her three other girls, Becka, Tera, and Rachel,
but who was this she asked, "Is this
one of your friends Rachel?" She
said to the shy young boy,
"Mom its me," said Kendel.
"Oh yes," she lied and hugged
him carefully so as not to torque her
head fixed clinically to the bed. She
hugged him with the warmth
she might spare on a casual
acquaintance's declawed cat.

Months passed. He was there, sloshing
around her memories like a sidelined thing.
A stranger who stood by, even if he
was the subject of the memory, like a
post or a stone remembered.

She read her journal, it had
been a grim pregnancy, she
was older for this last one, but the

boy, she *had* loved him, she really
had loved him once. She wrote of
nursing him one night late and weeping

because he was so beautiful. She knew,
knew that he had chosen her to be
his mother and she loved him for it
purely, completely, undeniably. It was all
there, logged in blue pen, carefully inscribed
moments after setting him back in
the soft blankets of his crib. She thought
she could even remember the event, but
now not only had the love vanished, but
her capacity to love this boy had disappeared.
She pretended for his sake, she knew how
to be civil and kind, that was part of
who she was as well. But she felt nothing.
Less even than she felt for the
primary children she taught.
Oddly she remembered
each one of their names and
genuinely cared for each of them.
All but her son.

She kept it in her sock drawer,
the tumor and the modicum of
complex tissue which contained
the love she knew had to be
coded there. She would
take it out from time to time when
she was putting away laundry or looking for
buried nail clippers. She would hold it
pinched between her fingers and holding
it to the light swirl it a little
to give it some dimensionality as it spun
in the liquid. The brown mottled
cork stoppering the tube had darkened
almost to black
against the edges of the glass
and the lumpy thing inside
turned pale and white like a ghost.

Fire in the Pasture

Did her spirit love
her son she wondered suddenly?
Would she get back this piece
in the resurrection? It didn't seem to
matter really. She was just curious.

JONATHON PENNY

The Soil's the Earth's Best Mother

The soil's the earth's best mother;
Old songs its virile seed
Planted by wind and weather,
Each grown by craft and need.

The soil's the earth's best mother:
Each plant a green refrain
Written by a poet father,
And harvested again.

Confession, After Battle

I'm sorry that I killed your son
I did not know he was your son
I only knew he was my enemy

I'm sorry that I killed your husband
I did not know he was your husband
I only knew he was my enemy

I'm sorry that I killed your father
I did not know he was your father
I only knew he was my enemy

I'm sorry that I killed your brother
I did not know he was your brother
I only knew he was my enemy

I'm sorry that I killed my enemy
I did not know that he was not my enemy

Small Comfort

How comforting to have something to look at while you pray—

A little Buddha, perhaps,
With fish swimming at its feet in a stone bowl or basin.
I grow tired of trying to see God's face, sometimes, in my own eyelids,
I confess it.

How comforting to have someone to talk with about sin—

The little ones, I mean,
That I reserve for silent prayer in my small shame.
I've come to fear my penitence is poorer, still, than my poor, misguided deeds:
A broken offering.

How comforting to have something to offer on a stone—

A table set for sacrifice,
An altar and a pedestal that burn the fear and darkness
From my sight and from my heart—a burden I could carry there
And leave behind.

An Open letter to Joseph Smith, Charlatan

Unruly boy,

how dare you trim the lamp down to the quick!?
What right had you to tamper with the wick
and blow the flame a bolder, brighter life
than we, its self-named guardians, preferred?

This is no toy:

this mighty, this empowering, governing word
to be blown and blasted, borne in bone, and (Heavens!) heard!
We'd careful kept its rusted notes and valves
to play our several orchestrated tunes;

your new age oil

unhinged our hold upon the book, presumed
to bring our sacred ruins near to rune.
You would dispense a covenant to plain folk;
save some space for Theology at least!

But you—oh coy!—

would make all women queens! and all men priests!
and perpetrate a scourge of prophecies!
would rather go and see God face to face!
alone, with none the wiser there to mediate!

Go to, Mal Foy!

Converse with angels! Open wide the gate!
Translate your sacred books! Come! Castigate
A generation serpentine, corrupt!
Fold centuries upon themselves and see,

unlettered boy,

what comes of all your books, your parlor trickery,
of your hat-gazing, treasure-seeking, multi-wivery,
your Zion's Camp, your Nauvoo, of your still-born temple mount,
your New Jerusalem, Apocalypse, your martyr's wounds,

twenty-first century mormon poets

and of your cult, your kin, your craze and then of you:
a name not had at all, unpublished fame, obscurity.

This do we, the undersigned, confirm as prophecy
Eternal and unchangeable, in faith, confidently,

Thorns and Thistles and Briars
(An Easter Poem)

This is a rather wretched place,
All things considered:
More paradox than paradise;

A poky little patch of dust and scrub
Now parched, now drowned,
Shaken and, as often, stirred;

A heaven gone to ground,
Ground gone to seed,
Thorn- and thistle-crowned

And for the very birds—
The dove, the hardy thrush,
The brown chat with his melancholy word.

It's an abated wish,
This dense and dropping orb,
A momentary, dark, full-throated hush;

A nascent sun, an infant star,
This crib of Adam-Christ:
Worth falling and worth rising for.

A Shaker Sister's Hymnal

Come Life, Shaker Life

The frost grows fierce upon the pane, crystals cluster in tight geometry. Inside my glove my fingers freeze. I gasp the cold until I am dumb: until my eyes are arctic marbles rolling blue and plumb in their sockets: until my leaden tongue sinks in my mouth.

The moon cracks above my head. It is the aspen wood-shaven splinter by which I see. I work beauty on the windows of sleeping Sisters. With sticks I scrawl trees and leaves, ferns and bees, stars and stalactites.

I work all night, my mind a-glitter with unearthly sight. Ice crystals splay into arches and doorways, turrets and towers, bridges and bowers. I have come at last to God's garden gate.

An oil lamp inside seems the warm glow of heaven. It beckons me on in my wild, flower tracings. And above I see the winged angels racing, on stars interlacing, their wings afire as they fling themselves against the sky.

***

My spine freezes. I draw the salty crescents large, with small, furry stars. They imbibe the moon's hard, white glow.

Inside my boots my toes are numb, I am unable to step once the mural is done. As I stumble to bed the horizon brings the revelation of day, a prophecy of bread:

I will work with my bones. I will grind the wheat. I will build and atone; bread alone will I eat. On each stone

I will write "Hallowed be Thy name." I will not seek earthly fortune or gain.

***

I Want to Gather Down

The winter bleeds, and freezes, and all with it. Godspeed could not overtake it. In all God's goodness, could he not give us endless springs, chased with rain? Towers of foxgloves for bees to roam?

Still, there are little gifts. In the sunlit kitchen I knead and knead in the kinetic posture my knuckles make. I inhale the yeast and red cracked wheat; their scents mingle, becoming heavenly meat.

I share this meat with all I see—farmers hauling loads of grain, beggars dressed in threadbare robes, children on a lumbering wain—hags, thieves, harlots, rogues.

***

With the sun overhead, I pick weeds of pain. They grow profusely in the kitchen garden. They suffocate seeds with their greedy brown roots and sap the sunlight from other fruits.

Yet, apples prosper in the orchard. I walk among this world of trees. Ladders stand stark in the morning mist, awaiting the eventual hum of bees. Dewdrops glisten on the apples' skin; all reflect the glow within.

I lift my firkin and ascend a ladder, the crooked ladder by the pond. The wooden rungs ring and echo; the earth resounds with heaven's beat. But as I climb, my firkin grows weighty. I can no longer lift my feet.

My woolen dress hangs heavily. I am but a bony rack for clothes. My heart is hard and full of dread. My feet are rooted in the earth. My heart is rooted in the body of my birth. I feel the tug of heavenly traces but cannot move.

***

The Burning Day

The Sabbath dawns with quiet fire. I inhale its pale, blue light. Angels press in around my bed, their gowns glowing amber bright.

By degrees, the sun increases. I rise and walk through burnished halls.

Piles of light cram into corners and jam my chamber door. I lift my limbs into a porcelain tub. The sun's hot rub ribs my skin into brilliant, scaly furrows.

***

Outside, leaves are lit on tree-like pyres. Windowpanes ripple and fold under bold, bright heat. The floorboards warp—wood flares and tears itself into dusty curls.

I gather these ashes in my palm; they flicker gray and golden red.

I feel an incorporeal flame within. It burns outward, consuming eyes, hair, flesh, and skin. My mind melts. It has become a globe of purest glass, annealed with wisdom by godly blast.

***

Who Will Bow and Bend like the Willow

As I walk to meeting across the grass, angels alight on windows and eaves. They are hymning and praising and comforting the bereaved.

Behind me I feel the airy shuffle, hear the woolen ruffle, sense the white presence of vanished Brothers and Sisters.

With an echoing crack I stumble on the granite meetinghouse stoop.

***

Under the cerulean ceiling we stand, like spires, until a single voice rings out the hollow *lo-lodle-lodle-lodle-lo-lodle-lo*.

Now the spires start to move. We stomp our soles with ringing clomp as we slowly pace in circular pairs.

The floor quakes as the room shakes. I labor and clap, march and sing. I hear the beat of angels' wings.

I traverse the verse of every song. Swept along by movement and voice, I whirl and bend in vision's currents, strong.

***

Pleasant Walk

The room revolves as the sky dissolves; my bodily sense has long been spent. A new landscape appears—a veil is rent—and I see a world beyond the ken of human eyes.

A towering mulberry tree appears; its leaves are cross-wise intertwined. Beneath the tree a table stands, with exotic fruit, delicate wine. I sit at the table and drink until it spills from my lips.

Straightway I see a dwelling place, peerless in its form and grace. Within, angels give me garments new and present me with fine trinkets—colored balls and jeweled boxes—not a few.

Here spirits dance in union sweet. Between them I see a staircase rise. It spirals and spirals toward unseen skies. A rushing wind flies from its heights and sweeps me, breathless, to its clime.

The universal star shines above; its amber light suffuses sight. My feet are led from step to step. Below me dwellings constellate, forming a geometric homestead.

A gold gate gleams ahead; Sisters and Eldresses await me there. With joyous shouts they urge me on, guiding me with eager care. I stretch and reach to touch their hands but cannot shake my earthly bands.

Sudden mists cloud my eyes, and I fall—through the hands of the dead.

***

I'm on My Way to Zion

The autumn sky dies in purple silk, while the moon wanes scarlet, saffron, and pearl. A clock is ticking on the wall, like the ringing echo of soft footfalls.

My painted floor is grooved and worn from nights of marching, treading thorns. Yet lines of copper nails still shine—small stars planted in the pinewood.

Why the Virgin Hangs in My Bedroom

Of all the sad saints,
she seems Most Likely to Succeed.
No ashen burlap, no
kneeling, no palms stuck together or
eyes stitched with threads
hung from stars, pulling
while earth rumbles on its axis,
the one her son installed.
Sitting on my bed
to take off my shoes,
I like the way the artificial light falls
on her crown. It reminds me of ribbons,
gold, pink, turquoise
must be the colors of heaven
south of the Border—
colors leading to lushness, to sour markets and
mango trees, a dry iguana sleeping under a fender,
to dusty pig roads, to school buses:
chariots for her portrait—
framing her perpetual stance,
sometimes plastic, sometimes seashells
but always erect
before gods and men. And sometimes,
in Caribbean nations, she smiles
ever so slightly—because
the water reminds her of the Mediterranean.

Look, how wide she throws her arms!
Surrounded by kid angels,
by banners of jewels, she puts her
ear to the trumpet and laughs.
To say that she can't hear
would be a mistake.

True Love

Somewhere in northern Nevada,
maybe eastern Oregon, where
nothing has a name—travelers
make up their own and the few that stay on
would rather forget—where the sky ends,
prairie dogs dance with truck tires and
the scrubland rolls away like an ocean swell,
that's where I figured it out—

We were pointed toward Winnemucca when
that new daughter of ours pooped up her back.
I came out of the greasy roadhouse with a giant
    Coke.
She was lying on the trunk, naked, crooked
    limbs
scratching the air like an upturned beetle
while you cleaned and dressed her.
She was your daughter then, and I remembered
the time, cradled in blood-water,
piecing her together like a ball of tin foil.
And I was your son, knowing you
only from the outside,
and from books.
I saw you striding across paintings
and through silver screens. Mother.
Goddess. Grant me
my only sin: to have wanted you for myself.

I knew then that I am an empty man,
my body a cage,
organs hanging from strings like a lurid mobile.
When I saw you that day, somewhere,
a string broke; things started to sway
dangerously until they were all tangled up.
    A marionette
left in a box and shaken up. Here a liver
wrapped around a spleen, hanging under a lung

beating against a kidney—and
I couldn't do anything but
drive on, just holding myself
together, breathing like a man in a body cast
    with you
swirling around me and in me, teasing me with
utter annihilation.

hymn to a thing that I knew and still know to some degree

A girdle and a griddle and a boy, a bubble gum boy
with his sticky and his merging. A brother and a friend
in a truck in a bed, and oranges and pumpkins and Oreos
and a bicyclist and all things fast and red. A man, a cigar
and the cigar's cigarette and a stain, a hand and coffee
in a bottle and a baby and the smell, the mud and the slip
in a town, in a jungle, in an ocean, in a box, and you
and me, a part of me, and then some more of me but not all
and some uncles, and some cousins, and aunts four to one
for change, we're changing, and some Coke, a cockroach,
and something frozen, and a threat, and witchcraft, even
some spiders and worms and skin, and a hang, bananas,
a shower, ripeness, and cooking and calling and trotting,
yes I said trotting, dripping, part flowing, converging
three spirals, a vortex, four suctions, five or six big bangs
and a largeness, a whizzing, an uncomfortable silence, and
finally, finally something I can squeeze into nicely.

Things I said to God before you were born

Hurry. In the melon glow of my wife's skin,
Winded, salt-gulp lay me down in the butcher's chair,
Open me up, soul-bones flayed and ready to begin.

I've laid low, cradling my sins. Today,
Feet shucking leaves off the porch, I learned a prayer:
Hurry. In the melon glow of my wife's skin

I heard you, swimming circles, feet like fins
In gritty water, in cold September smoke—
Open me up, soul-bones flayed and ready to begin.

Snow peaks poke the cloud-ribbed sky like pins
That prick the heavens—this could be the day so
Hurry in. The melon glow of my wife's skin,

Burnish now your blade, your surgeon's grin.
Hold my arms and trust these upturned palms,
Open me up, soul-bones flayed and ready to begin.

Under your precision, flesh is tin.
Find the heart's black rope to be uncoiled.
Hurry, in the melon glow of my wife's skin,
Open me up, soul-bones flayed and ready to begin.

To Stevens' Snow Man

Will you teach me a mind of winter?
I hear misery in the wind
expelled, floating hot between
the icy eaves and blue crusted earth.

January frightens me sometimes
with its otherworldly sun when I wake
the trees have grown hats,

rosy garden gnomes crack
their knuckles on the cold mud
and smile big waffle-smiles.
Four more months, they chant,

of Samhain's wild dark.
In winter nothing really slows down.
The spindly world still runs

hard, naked and unkempt underneath
a glittering powder coat,
the spirits of wood and dirt
conjuring their just-add-water posterity.

But myself, Nothing, I can't
hear the sound of the land
in the still silence of snow

without remembering how
this earth is getting smaller
as I watch from the window
of some strange, steely ship.

ELISA PULIDO

Dog Walking at Night in a New Neighborhood

I open the door, only to discover
this place, too, gets dark at night. And, as I
have not yet made the acquaintance
of the street's bushes, and since they balloon
blackly either side of the road like rumors,
I walk Max down the center of the street.
Across town, church bells peal from the cathedral
of San Juan, and just as I decide to brave
the sidewalk through the valley of shadows,
a fire truck, siren-less, but with lights flashing,
rolls up the street, which can only mean
that judgment has come to one of my new neighbors.

I walk the other way, through an unseasonable scent
of phlox, which rises from an invisible bed
and think about the bodies of saints, which
supposedly smell like roses even in death.
I imagine these particular neighbors
with their unseasonably fragrant phlox
must be saintly people, and just as I determine
to make their acquaintance, I'm warned by the runoff
of night watering as it slips through a drain
in the curb and showers underground.
Undoubtedly, this neighborhood, too, has its underbelly.

Down the street a blue fairy skitters towards us.
At close range she morphs into a battery-operated light
dangling from the collar of a large boxer,
who snarls and strains at his leash in an effort
to confront Max. A hooded figure pulls him past.

I walk on, still pondering this latest lesson,
when the world's stateliest street lamp—
a fluted column topped with a translucent urn—
allows us into its circle. I pause
and gaze upward, into its benediction,
then turn towards home. Above us,
the moon has been bitten off by thirds,

the last third still clinging to the night.
What can it mean that tonight of all nights,
I should experience a two-thirds loss in the moon?
I have no answer.

At the front door, while fumbling
with unfamiliar keys, I notice the Schonfelds
have left their *mezuzah* nailed to the frame.
So *this* was a house in Israel.
Me, too, Lord, watch me, too. When I sit at home,
when I walk along the way,
when I lie down and when I rise up.

On the Mormon Trail, June 1848

She needs a moment alone, away
from the children, the husband, canvassed wagons,

oxen. Without a good-bye, she vanishes
into wind-waved prairie. Three days the company

searches every bluff, rise, hole. Could have been a brave,
who admired her blonde braid, her pale brow.

Maybe a broken leg. A quiet wolf. Perhaps
she waded out to where tall grass grows overhead,

and lost the horizon. Without chart or compass,
with no knowledge of the stars, she stumbles on the edge

of the known world, slips over its side. Her husband
fears she has been bitten by a snake, fears she has fallen

into the netherworld of the plains.
He would make any bargain and never look back.

For years he sings of her—wandering,
circled by coyotes, treading tall grass.

Herman and Laurie in Retrospect

1. 1995

Laurie is seventy, has broken her hip.
In the hospital she dreams she is lying on the floor of San Bernardino's train station.

Her father steps off a train in his square-toed boots.
Mosquitoes circle his head, the way they did summers on the Daloney place.

He gathers Laurie into his arms as easily as he did newborn calves on Wyoming's frozen range and offers to take her away.

2. 1980

Laurie folds laundry on her kitchen table.
Herman, her father, is ninety-three, is visiting, sitting at the table.

He tells Laurie he and his brothers had to share a single pair of dress shoes.
Sometimes they'd go to church dances.

One brother would wear the shoes into the church, while the other two sat in their socks on a fence, and waited a turn.

Now his wife is gone, Herman tells his own stories.

3. 1970

It's December.
Herman and his wife have taken the train to San Bernardino from Cokeville.

Herman is eighty-three.
He sits in the sunshine on a plastic lawn chair in front of Laurie's pink-stucco home and imagines what he might be missing.

Ice glazing the steps of his front porch.
A row of four-foot icicles.

Through an open window, Herman can hear Minerva telling how one winter, he swam a herd of cattle across the Snake River on horseback.

She says his clothes iced over by the time he trailed that herd into Pocatello.
She says he went into a local saloon and stood by a pot-bellied stove, while melt-off from his jacket and trousers, boots and gloves, puddled on the plank floor.

4. 1942

Skirts, blouses, bobby socks, and a radio—everything a college coed will need has been packed into a pale green Mercury.

It is the end of August, 1942.
Laurie and her friends are off to college.

As they drive away from the ranch house, Laurie slides down in her seat so she can't see her father growing smaller.

Herman watches the car cross the tracks, pass the drugstore, the post office, and the Bear River Mercantile.

He watches until the car disappears somewhere past Cozzen's Grocery.

He wonders which day the first snow will fall, thinks about heifers birthing next-year's calves in the ice of early spring.

Herman turns, says to Minerva:
Seems like we never had a daughter.

5. 1934

It's early September.

There has already been a frost.

Herman and Laurie drive across sage-covered coke fields to Yamamura's in Kemmerer, where Laurie tries on school shoes.

She'll be in the third grade.
Herman buys her a pair of brown leather oxfords—the most expensive in the store.

They pinch her toes, dig under her ankles.
She can't bring herself to tell him.

6. 1927

Mosquitoes hide from sun, hunt for mates, arabesque above half-filled irrigation ditches running alongside a gravel lane.

Horses and an empty hayrack jounce toward a freshly-mown field.
It is noon, and the rack is hungry.

When it reaches the field, Herman will pitch damp hay onto the rack's empty plate.
Laurie is two, is sitting bare-legged on the bumping rack.

She tries to stand.
Herman steadies her with his ranch-rough hands.

Put a foot here, he says, and one there.
Hold your arms like this.

Revelation

I am ten, sitting on your sofa.
I watch as you paint and talk.
Your voice is a swallow,
which sometimes loops through the Andes,

spins over the terraced slopes
of Machu Pichu, then dips suddenly
to the bucket of pig slop by the kitchen sink,
or hovers over Little Bryant's shot-off toe.

It is August. You recite Revelations.
Grandchildren bang through the back door,
interrupt the four horsemen of the Apocalypse.
They ask for glasses of milk, take you away from

the canvas you have tacked on the living room wall.
Cattlemen pass through the front door.
Their barnyard boots crisscross your Persian carpet.
You pause to chat, then paint again—

I remember you giving Moses eyes,
so he could watch Pharaoh's daughter
lift him from the Nile.

Emma, Waiting, September 22, 1827

1.

It's after midnight, on a moonless night when the holy man and his bride arrive in a one-horse wagon at the base of the hill. Up in the canopy Cumorah's katydids strum a potent meditation for honeymooners or perhaps even holy men who have been called into the night by angelic beings. The holy man hands his wife the reins, leaves her in starlight in a wagon borrowed without permission.

2.

Hoping for grace, benedictions, powers, plates, the holy man begins his steep climb into God's realm. His wife hears him rustle through Indian Pipe and Lady Fern. Beneath the katydids' clamor, she imagines the chirping of tiny shrews, interrupted by his footfall in the underlitter.

3.

On the holy man goes, higher and higher. The wife of the holy man imagines him weaving though aspen, white pine, and beech. She hears a porcupine chat out a warning. She imagines the holy man jumping aside, and, finally, when she thinks he must be somewhere near the top of the hill, she imagines the holy man parting tall millet grass, and stepping into a hill top clearing. In expectation, the wife of the holy man searches the starlit tree line for signs—low-lying clouds, phosphorescence, sudden breezes, thunder. She sees . . . nothing. Hears . . . the horse munching roadside weeds.

4.

An hour goes by. The katydids fall silent. At least, thinks the holy man's wife, at least it's the beginning of autumn. Mosquitoes and deer flies are not what they were. She stretches, tries to step down from the wagon and startles something that hisses. She retreats to her seat, where she prays for the holy man.

5.

Another hour and it's cooler now. Dew begins to collect on the bonnet and shawl of the holy man's wife. Her feet are cold. She envies deer mice nesting snugly in trunks, finches roosting close to each other. Where, she asks, where is the holy man? A hoot owl asks a different question: Who, who marries a holy man?

6.

The stars have dimmed and there is still no sign of the holy man. His wife portends her future in a litany of roadside weeds: Gypsy Weed, Henbit Nettles, Old witch Panic, Nightshade . . .

7.

Hours ago the wife of the holy man gave off hoping to hear the voice of God, but she yearns for the voice of the holy man. The reins grow heavy in her hands. No longer hearing the creak of wagon box or swish of horsetail, she dozes upright.

8.

At last, it is dawn. Songbirds trill, chirp, warble, exult: Wake up, wake up! Another holy man descends from his mount with a new covenant! The wife of the holy man stirs. Though she doesn't yet hear him, though she doesn't yet see him, she feels saplings give way to his touch, pheasants startled by beauty.

Fragment

The grey pinstripe
with yellow eyes
does not think of sparrows
dancing in sweet grass,
but leans heavily
into his future
beneath his garment bag
and brief case.
Beneath the clear
cold moon he stands
and looks for the green
rental.

What can he know beyond
that rumpled bag?
About the days and nights
that give him patterns of
expectations?
He lives and will live
in taxis, boardrooms and
stale motels.
Happy Hours.
Because he has lived,
he expects life, to be
allowed life.
See how he walks, insistent,
arrogant, never thinking
the stars could so easily
abort him,
or the wind dash
his infant brains,
or the iron bird ingest him.

Mass Transit Madonna

She looks around wondering if
The driver remembers her stop.
She does not speak to me
But bends her white neck
To check the child she holds.
Her hair was quickly gathered—
Pinned in haste against
The wind, uncorrected.
Her young eyes watching,
Gather age, take on the first,
Bolder lines of death
As though her life had crested:
Her gathering tide has turned.
On her knees are big brown eyes
Swaddled in white. They stare
From a grey plastic car seat.
Beyond them a low counterpoint
Of conversation and snatching
Laughter at the back
Of the rocking city bus
Reminds of an earlier peace.
The eyes meet mine, then sleep,
Content in their gathering life.

Mariabeeld, Izegem 1982

Wearing a veil of dark twigs
the cloistered moon wept in a tree.
A hook-nosed goddess below could feel
the bitter tears on her plaster cheek—
they drip and slide along a branch
and fall like muttered prayers on the shrine.
Everyday bells fill the air with chaos
like hounds running in the fields
and bright grass is like a mob
around the cracked walls,
but now in the soundless night
the thin light of three devout candles
waves across her tattered robe,
her chipped toes, and those peeling eyes
that stare in disbelief at the sooty words:
Dank aan Maria.

Of Two Loves

Warm, they yield
Like bread new made:
For comfort—man
Takes more than crust,
When suckles
Hot and yeasty after
Love,
After life:
There is a cost
Of words, of pain.
None take Bread
Who can be lost,
But finding life
Will hurt, will stain
The finest breast.

Cleave

Therefore shall a man leave his father and his mother,
and shall cleave unto his wife: and they shall be one flesh.
—Genesis 2:24

How do we do it
who have never done it before?

Think of Eve's hair tangled in the grass,
a raven in the tree, feathers shining.

How do we approach the subject
that burns our mouths like soap?

Think of sacrament going down,
clean as water, clean as broken bread.

How do I know who I am
and who you are?

You are Urim, I am Thummim.
We are three days of darkness.

How, after Abraham, after Joseph,
after a pedigree of plural wives?

Think of the body, the temple,
wind through the doors, foundation cracked.

Who is there to warm us?
Whose hands are in whose hands?

A Few Questions—Involving Pears—For My Newborn Son

So, how do you like the air? They way it hums on your skin, moves through your nose in quick shots, or cools the lungs with the scent of fresh pears. The power it gives to release yourself in a scream. The breath of life that comes in sharply once, and is forever after going out. How do you like it? And the light? The way it burns your eyes and cuts into your mind. The way it confuses our world with colors: the yellow-green reflected off a pear, the reds and blues absorbed, the brown shadow cast on the counter. Let it in through your thin eyelids; shut it out with the mild jut of your brow. How do you like it, son? Your ears dry and open to the noise. Shouts rumbling through the vent. The refrigerator's hum. The press and release of *pear*. The slip of our tongue shaping a voice that comes from a place we can't get at with words. Take another breath, son, open your eyes, and listen. Then tell me, how do you like it?

To a Pear

1.

Bless my eyes that they have seen you,
cold stone of green and heavy gold.
The orchard's glow has stained your skin,
good artist, now you emit the blaze

of yellow dawn, the slap of leaves,
the anger of cold branches, trunks.
Night has left its holy scars
upon your shoulders. Scorpio

has burned dark pocks onto your skin,
and shooting stars have seared their trails.
Yet blemished, you are beautiful.
You blush in brown, and make that color clean.

2.

Silent. I thought you were silent.
But you speak to me—audible words,
pear-words, a language I have just begun
to understand. *Write it*, you say,

but with what alphabet? Only Adam
knew the grammar, but he is gone,
your language with him. Accept the name
we offer, the best our tongue can take:

part of *peace* and all of *ear*. Pressure,
and release, a life in one word: *pear*.
Speak again, green god, in Adam's
vowels; I hear, and it is sweet.

3.

Touch me, and you have blessed my skin,
cold and warm at once; holding you
I think God must have hands. You fill
the space so perfectly. To cup you

is to pray. To pray is to remember
life before this life, with God
on the third day, when he squeezed
a galaxy between his palms and said:

Let there be fruit, and it was so,
so good. Your seeds, black holes,
swirl within me. I have not forgotten,
pear, you are a universe.

4.

Since when can meat quench thirst, and juice
sustain? Since when can sour
be sweet, and velvet like a razor
on the tongue? The mouth

has always longed to taste this true
and primal paradox—
Take, eat. Only you
are sin and virtue, as Eve knew.

Like her, fruit, make me wise. Give me
a swallow of cold knowledge.
Bright temple, I have fasted
and confessed. Now let me in.

Blind Man to the Healer

Sir, spare change? Well then, sit with me
if you have nothing to give. It's cool here
outside Zion's gate in the afternoon shade;
birdsong ascends from the Kidron; olive
groves soften the view of the mount.
I wasn't born blind, though I earn Caesar-heads
by saying so. I was Herod's chief executioner—
soft word for what I did. I brought more heads
to my basket than Joe of Aramathaea
has brought to his purse. Then one day
in Galilee as I returned from fishing, I stopped
on the banks of the Jordan, sweet green
it was that day, and slow. A crowd
had gathered to hear a lunatic preach.
He stood ankle-deep, clad in camel's hair
and leather. Come from the wilderness,
he spoke of vipers, fruit, stones; he said,
The axe is at the root! and threatened us with fire.
A true madman he was, dipping people
in the swirl, polluting the current with their sins.
Silly, but they did seem to come clean—
one man even white as a dove rising
out of the flow, his eyes clear as a child's.
I could never take off a head like his.
That day I started seeing things differently,
darker, I mean—I was going blind. Any light
caused me pain, even the glow of eyes
in the heads I cut off was too bright for me.
But the day they brought in that Baptist,
with his breath of locusts and honey, his wild hair,
I couldn't help but look at his eyes, long and hard.
They burned like fire, or something more painful
and pure. They were the last thing I ever saw.
Since then I take heads in the street, my eyes cold
and hard as coins. Go on, touch them and you'll see.

Some

Some light is yellow as pinewood.
Some white, coming out of snow.
Some snow is black, after a long city-winter, blistered
by the wind. Some wind is warm,
but winter keeps it locked in a stone box.
When it seeps through the cracks, they say *spring*.
When you hear it howl, it's imprisoned again.
Some prisons are good, like the prison of clothes—colors and fabrics
guarding what could hurt us most. Some women can hurt.
They can hurt for their whole lives.
Some lives are filled with fear. Some fear
can leave a hole inside of you. Some can escape
through that hole, sometimes, seep
their way out, like a sentence through the mouth saying:
Some world we live in.
Some heaven some say will come somehow.
Some ending to what we've survived for some time now.

Runaway

A bus token jingles
against the nickels and dimes
in the pocket of his Pendleton coat
as he lingers at the door
of the Salvation Army
bookstore and wonders, if he enters,
what new thing will happen to his soul?
Will it fold itself up like the city map
now lined more with creases
than with the streets he's yet to search
for someone who might know her
who might have seen the face
that haunts him like a shadow of the one
reflected in the storefront glass
looking back with empty eyes
through words that spread
like ink across his brain:
all romance twenty-five cents

Dead Horse Point

Blue fades to white where the sky ends.
It's the same in every direction.
The Colorado River is a basking snake
a thousand feet below.
From the mesa's edge I drop a stone.

It bounces once, twice, then disappears.
Its sound, too, is swallowed.
In the part of my brain
that pertains to whitened sky
I understand: everything comes to this.

Once I fueled my anger
with the history of this place: wild horses
driven to the bluff,
culled, corralled, left to die.
I nursed the irony

of their deaths by thirst
in plain view of the meandering river.
Since then I've tried to reconstruct
God's language in the glistening bones.
Their meaning escapes me.

Visions of death move through me
like wind through a church.
The desert wells up in me.
My legs grow heavy as against the sky
a solitary crow hangs crucified.

I Dream of Lima

An empty beach
in the Peruvian winter and a woman
I hardly know—
how we came here is a mystery.

A flock of birds careens
in unison above the waves,
wings flash silver,
and I am alone.

There lies across these dunes
a shanty-town,
half a million souls
fallen on the sand like Andean rain.

Drawn to the city by letters
from sons and brothers, they come
for the promise of work
and erase the road behind them.

You meet them in the streets,
the rich, furrowed earth of their faces
out of place
against the leaden Lima sky.

In barrio La Victoria,
a block from where I live and eat,
a three-legged dog sleeps in a hollow
beneath a broken sidewalk.

At night it forages.
In the heat of day it lies
curled in shadows and peers
upward as people pass like clouds.

The Dogs of Juxtlahuaca

The day they killed the dogs
in Juxtlahuaca we bought
big bags of hibiscus flowers,
five-tailed comets streaking from the earth
to our hungry lips,
color of blood, flavor of love.

Surely they knew they were starving,
the dogs of Juxtlahuaca,
yet they wagged their tails in two-four time
as if angels
played their ribs like marimbas.

Rivers of fruit swelled the village streets.
A flotsam of mangos bumped
up against a raft of bananas.
Fish, splayed and salted, schooled upstream
while flotillas of chilies
squared off with sides of aging beef.

Market-day morning brought a feast
to the dogs of Juxtlahuaca.
Town fathers in somber procession
heard confessions of hunger and served
a sacrament of strychnine and bread.

A humble stomach wastes no gift.
Soon to the music of barter and coins
the dogs of Juxtlahuaca danced convulsive jigs,
took their bows
and retired to open-eyed sleep.

Then hollowed out and light as air
they rose above the town.
All the market hushed.
We watched them circle, nose to tail,
spiraling like smoke from a burning church
through a break in the clouds, and gone.

The Spider Woman of Teotitlán

I will tell you how earth
in the hands of a woman
becomes water, and then sky;
how from pieces of sky she weaves
a history, a people, a dream.

First she takes a chicken,
or an armload of flowers
and barters for the wool of a ram.
Matted with soil, twigs and excrement,
it is a coil of Gaia's pubic hair.

Next the river swells the fleece,
a gray nimbus rising from the flow
and offered to the heavens.
It rains itself out and makes
its peace with the bleaching sun.

The wheel of life turns on a mahogany frame
planted in a swept dirt floor.
Glossy hands twist pieces of the cloud,
feed them to the wheel
and spin the threads of fate.

Nothing bleeds like the cochineal
who lays her powdery eggs in the pelvic
curves of a *nopal* then gives her life
to the alchemy of dye. In a wood-fired cauldron
boil the scarlet entrails of creation.

Now is the time to dance with the dead.
The loom and the warp
are the bones of her ancestors.
Upon them she weaves births and deaths,
ears of corn, the flight of a hummingbird.

She ties the knots of community
in patterns that repeat like the seasons and the days.
The rhythm of generations

386   Fire in the Pasture

is the over-and-under path of a wooden shuttle
worn smooth by the kiss of wool.

Vienna 1965

All day you've exhausted yourself
tracking down museums, gardens,
statues, monuments—
flexed muscles of the past.

Because you're with a friend,
you end up at the table
of someone you've never met,
a war widow living on a pension
barely enough to check starvation.

Now you hear her in the kitchen,
overboil lisping on a single burner,
distress of apron-rustle
as her flowered dress, heavy tan stockings,
utilitarian shoes,
disgorge the hollow promises:
Anschluss   Lebensraum   Deutschland Über Alles.

She sets a few slices
of black bread on the platter,
brings thin soup like an offering
and ladles it into your bowl.

How could you not savor every drop?

Wild Asparagus

Water ran down ditches to our town
from canals dug with picks, shovels, and teams.
A boy could lose a day there easy
with his cucumber boat, hand-me-down
shirt and shoes, and yesterday's games
several cloud puffs away. Summer formed a glassy
ball around a young boy's time.
For a while,
all clocks stopped ticking.

So when you came
smiling, with your sure-fire deal
about picking
wild asparagus along
the ditchbanks on both sides,
I could not grab your fingers fast enough.
You told me I should bring
willing arms for the apronloads
of wild asparagus we would stuff
ourselves with later on.
Oh, you were supposed to be old,
my mother in her cotton dress and pumps,
straddling the stream in
total confidence. You held
my breath for me in graceful jumps
from bank to bank,
piling the basket green,
stooping, picking.

Fifty years have sunk
beneath the horizon.
There remains an aching
in the steady sound
of running water lined with grass,
where ditchbanks yield
for my sweeping hand,
pockets of asparagus
standing tender-tipped and wild.

Things to Do With Bottles

How we emptied by early spring
the pine shelves that held the bottled fruit
my mother stored every summer,
Mason jars of peaches, pears, and cherries.

We milked in midwinter,
steam rising from the pail,
screened the milk into wide-mouth bottles
where it sat until the cream rose to the top.

I played *spin the bottle*
in a circle with my friends,
hoping it might stop on Linda Croft,
and I still feel that swift electric kiss.

Now I bottle words,
snatch them from pages
and stash them for tomorrow.
They struggle to the top,
press their faces against the glass
aching to break out—
rabble tumult crackle ignite
—what outrageous promises they make.

Withdrawal

Because the moon has dropped so low,
no need for a lamp in this half-spent shack
where I'll remain a while. Nothing
but mile after silent white mile, except
for the brook's jagged frown and murmur
where the ice broke through
from the weight of that magnificent elk
whose spoor has long since vanished in the snow.

I summon the sommelier with a snap
and motion him to pour
which he does with grave exactitude
before disappearing through the wall
like the resurrected Christ.
        O, Christ,
the moon's pocked flaws
magnify my aching tenfold here
where nothing shifts or thaws.

Run Sheep Run

For Freda 1914–1999

Late fall grass stands waist high and bronze,
the highway a narrow ribbon tying the landscape
to the vast Montana sky.
This will be our last dance
on earth. She has given up
all sustenance, and every day
groans with another half-truth
to keep her alive, another pocket of air.
I drive straight through.
Low clouds form a thin cloth
over the moon, bloodshot and sheer.
This is not the kind of blow
that comes from an auto accident
or sudden drowning. It is the tedious fuss
that weaves in and out until
all pills and bedsores are spent.

Her eyes flick blank, but press
for recognition. She is still
trapped in incoherence. Her heavy arm
rests against mine,
and I stroke it with my fingertips.
She plays the waiting game,
recalls childhood pastimes long since gone.
A wall clock slaps
unrelenting seconds through the room. Home's
waiting for her just beyond the sun . . .
she can hear faint voices echo
high above the back street games:
run sheep run
olly olly oxen free

The Fall

I ate the apples you've become famous for.
I didn't eat the huckleberries,
I was too late for that.
I did eat the branches, the stems,
the shriveled worms inside them.
If you believe me, I did this.
If you would believe me,
I ate more than the flesh of the apples.
I ate the core,
and the seeds because I am immune.
I ate thorns in the woods,
scraped off their skin with my teeth
and sucked until they grew dull
and swallowed.
Yesterday, I ate the wheat.
If you believe I would,
I picked and ground the wheat myself,
dusted the flour into my green bowl,
baked and ate it for dinner.
I ate the ashes because I cooked them to black
as night,
and then ate the stars.
Except for the poisonous ones,
which I planted,
concealing their bright flesh in yours.

Blue City of Rajasthan

Such a quiet shade on the edge
of desert—blue bicycle shop, blue
marching band, blue lining
royalty's garden, blue omelet shop.
Bright green chilies
and lemons hung in blue doorways.
Cows wander and wait with split hooves
on blue streets.
The old city is painted like it's not part of this world—
look at the sunset, the puzzle
of square, the blue houses in
horizontal light.
Over Jodhpur the great fort of the maharaja,
citadel of the sun,
stands on desert rock.
In a dream
it shades the clock tower, bangle bracelets,
persistent children in bare feet,
and our breakfast
of saffron lassi and fruit.
Late at night, toward the train station,
the city is emptied
and dark—no loud taxis, no traffic,
no one shouts names of spice.
In the dark, no one sells posters of movie stars.
And in the blue, these cows,
singular and white, sleepwalk
or dream in their holiness
and unrest, traveling the quiet,
toward the end of Sardar Bazaar Road.

Ganpati Guest House

1

Young man who wears a lime-green feather vest
proudly, (as he should), works the front desk.
Most mornings he grabs a beebee gun
and chases monkeys up the stairs where a large
white cow is still standing all week
at the corner, in a maze. It looks miserable. The young man

I imagine is in love with the French woman.
Men in orange, and some in white, Baba, or not, walk past
and small boys peer at us from rooms above
where we stand. Some children say this isn't the way
out. Balancing spices. Sweets.

2

Outside the guest house
men lie out white sheets on bricks to dry
in the sun, and dust, and ash.
The man next door screams at the pigeons. We debate
while we lie in bed, if it is a man, or a bird, and it turns
out, it is indeed a man screaming at the pigeons,
it seems, to save himself from something.

3

The light is extraordinary when it rises over the Ganges.
They march the dead as soon as they can,
down the alleys all day, covered in tinsel.
Chant the god's name, but it is Krishna
who is painted on the walls they pass.
He plays his flute and are we all hypnotized?
Beauty. Ladies man. A monkey gets away safely.
A monkey may have stolen Robert's book

he borrowed from the German bakery about Krishna
and Christ. We watch the kites. Another
is cut down. Squint in the sun. Blow our noses.
Now seeing a dead man. That's unbelievable, he says.
I nod. We wait. Order tea.

The Girl with No Hands

stole a silver pear
from his majesty's orchard.
And the gardener saw it, believed
she was an angel.
The way she tilted her head back
and stretched her neck to the sky,
to eat. Her hair hung like silk curtains.
And in the moonlight,
how could he not
fall in love with her?
How could he betray this love
and tell this secret
with the time to count each fruit?
Each destined
for their numbering.
It was a story the gardener couldn't
explain, but had to account for.
So, the gardener and the King waited
in hiding for the maiden
and when she appeared, hunger
was in the girl's every step.
They dared not speak,
but watched her, as moths lightly played
around their faces.
Are you of this world?
If I am a dream, then I am a dove.
Be my queen, I will make you hands,
and the gardener wept, and the king
kept what was never his to keep.

Across the Mojave Desert

The billboard reads, *In the beginning God created dot dot dot*—

following the ellipsis is a 1-800 phone number and a scripture
from the book of Genesis. We're supposed to look it up.

Immediately, the next billboard: *$5.99 LUNCH BUFFETT IN PRIMM!*

Primm—a border town just before, or after, Vegas.
A town with one lonely, insanely tall roller coaster
I rode once on a road trip in college, my eyes shut

the entire way up—when
I could have seen, as far as I could have ever seen,
across the Mojave, before the drop.

Primm—a town with names like, *Buffalo Bills,
Whiskey Pete's, and TERRIBLES Resort and Casino.*
I have been through Primm when the desert is

a thin lake surrounding casinos after a storm—

a reminder of Dali and Venice—obnoxious casino,
petrol station, mountains, entire thread of interstate floating
on a mirror.

Somewhere in the distance is a giant clock.

Today, the desert is how it is most of the time.

The Mojave looks to me
what I imagine the surface of the moon must look like, minus
blue sky and flecks of broken glass.

I have been through Primm and have seen the weekend exodus
between Las Vegas and Los Angeles.
You don't really want to see that,

because it means you are in it.

The migration should have been featured in the *National Geographic*
issue of "Great Migrations"—brake lights flicking off
and on and on and on I-15.

Right now at 8am on a Monday morning, the traffic is sparse.
Everyone here is desperate to get somewhere else.
The desert is full of cliché's like *1-800-Get Thin*, *Peggy Sue's Diner*,

and a *Texaco Fuel Station*. Signs
that say where to find various fast foods,
and an *Early Man Site* →. We fly by

a skeleton of a water park, in the middle of glorious nothing.

At a higher elevation there are Joshua trees lining the freeway,
which we all know were created in the likeness of man.

Joshua after Joshua

stands in the desert, their various arms spread
towards the sky in prayer, asking God,
what have we created?

SALLY STRATFORD

Inheritance

I wear her name
and a two carat diamond
which, like a heavy rock of salt
falls to the side between my fingers.
I'm sitting on a pink velvet chair
holding a tape recorder,
but she is asleep,
mouth open, skin loose
like pie crust draping over apples.

I want her to wake up and tell me stories
about how she slid down the banister
to meet the missionaries for dinner,
or when grandpa wouldn't let her eat,
so the green sequined dress
she wore to the country club would fit,
like a waterfall of thin emeralds.
Still, she would eat chocolate
in the shadows of her closet.
Then she would say, "It always fit."

Soon this bed will be empty,
the electric blanket smooth
over her place,
reading glasses on the table
reflecting the afternoon sun.

Mukuntaweep

I rode and rode the traffic south
until it spit me into that parking lot
wedged between red rock walls,
next to a camper, towels hanging on a tree,
baby food jars full of sand in the window.

A delicate shock, delayed for months,
overcame me. I clenched my fingers
in my hair and tried to let myself cry.
The sun set and soon the canyon
crackled with stars.
At the hot spring's turquoise water,
I dug handfuls of thermal mud
and rubbed it through my hair,
wanted to cut it off—every inch
four months of my life.

Later, hair still long and in braids
I stared at Zion Canyon in the dark.
Yazzie, the Navajo storyteller came to my porch.
He talked about the badger's bag of stars
and how coyote stole it, spreading the Milky Way.
His black hair turned silver as the moon rose.
He taught me the original name of the canyon:
Mukuntaweep. I had to practice. *Mukuntaweep*.
He left me with a story of the red-rock
that first had been mud.

I slept small in my sleeping bag
on a huge mattress,
moon leaking through the curtains.
I sat up and pulled them back
and the light spilled through,
seeping into my mattress,
like cool, clear water.

Distance

Who says I can't sit
on this London roof top
and talk to the crescent moon?
Five hundred thousand miles times
six months says I can and will
see you in every American tourist
small at the base of Parliament,
in every ardent actor.
And I will touch you
on a crowded platform
waiting for the tube
or in Hyde park with an oak
hovering over my shivering body
as the half moon moves from
branch to branch—
repainting in slow motion,
the way you always laughed
when I opened my door.

The Right Place

*But believing that it might become a healthy place
by the blessing of heaven to the saints,
and no more eligible place presenting itself,
I considered it wisdom to make an attempt to build up a city.*
—Joseph Smith

Not one has made it.
Trout launch out of Snake Creek,
flipping through the air,
vaulting up the waterfall
falling back into the foam.
I've been watching them for an hour.
It's November and the leaves
are dissolving on the ground.

Late tonight, one will make it.
She'll burst out of the water,
the moonlight trickling through the trees
catching her in the air, a flash of silvery skin.
She'll struggle up to the right place.
To clear water, gravel, and oxygen.
Dig a pocket and drop her eggs,
a spill of glowing beads.

The Empty Cistern

Silence and *grace*,
the only words I know
in either of their languages,
so I don't say much.
I stand at the small spring
and look over their valley
dotted with log houses.
The village seems abandoned.
Everyone's working the fields,
clearing the skeletons of last year's harvest
that could blow away with the dry soil.
We talk about water lines and pumps,
the cistern we built last year,
barely a dozen of us, professors,
students, a translator.
I climb up and peer into the cool cube,
dust covering the bottom.

A woman carries water down
the hill and washes clothes
with the same muscles she uses to grind corn.
Too far away to make eye contact.
I look up and the sky stretches tight
across the valley, tree line to tree line.
Then I understand how the night will come,
the sky crammed with stars
and the people will tell their stories,
each one a kernel,
alternating colors like a corn necklace,
maybe even a few about us, the gringos.

Tonight, back at Margarita's,
we will stare at the ceiling
and tell our stories,
whispers fading into the music
coming from the bar across the courtyard tile,
while the Tarahumaras sleep in their open valley.

Fire in the Pasture

The cistern alone on the hill,
without even a drop of water
steadily filling with stars.

PAUL SWENSON

Passion Play

White shirts are now required
dress for boys who bless

and pass the Supper of our Lord.
Their hearts must burn as pure

and virginal as brides, who kneel
to taste the sacrament of marriage.

Thin line between Christ's flesh and blood
and youthful sin. Boy, whose black hands

break the Wonder loaf, once wore
a mauve Dashiki as his Sunday best.

Broad chest is now opaque as chalk.
Shock, that if he shows a stripe

or hint of color at the cuffs, he's asked
to leave the table. And when he passes

the far aisle, dark eyes won't meet
the smile of that tall blonde whose

fingers crush a paper
cup to her red lips.

Holy Mary, Mother of God

See her imprint
on the tinted glass
of Seminole Finance
in Clearwater,
where cleaning chemicals,
minerals from sprinkler water,
the Florida sun,
mirror her cloth-wrapped face,
Our Lady of Guadeloupe.

On the red banks
of the Rio Grande,
pilgrims sign themselves with clay,
cross their naked torsos,
swim the river
to Our Lady of Brownville,
a crossed icon
of a whitened Madonna
in the bark of a tree.

Bend to a darker Maria
in the curve of a car fender,
at the Shrine of the Chevy Camaro;
and in the Southern Rio Grande Valley,
find an image of Jesus in a tortilla.
Feel faint when a female healer
passes a crucifix
over infected organs,
like a scalpel.

Woman on a Boat

She in her forties,
Me barely twenty.

Side-by-side on a ferry
In a Gothenberg canal.

Dark hair under dark scarf.
Eyes covered by dark glasses.

Shows up in the photo as
Woman of mystery,

Smile as wide as the sea
That would separate us.

Cheap suit, Swedish knit,
Gives me away as missionary.

Indecorous to address her
By her given name—Majbritt—

Since my hand in her conversion,
Immersion in a new religion,

Brought her from the water as
Sister Åkerborg—washed of

All her sins. Storyline
Gets thinner here. Letters

Burned with yearning for
Shining star to steer her

Life by. Don't
Know why I couldn't

Solve her questions,
Calm her fears.

Letters ceased,
Sky closed in.

Dark striations in the water
Of that Gothenberg canal

Compel a curious swell
Of old emotion. Is she

Still afloat out there,
Between the ports of

Heaven and hell?
Woman on a boat.

Nature of the Beast

The Natural Man—God's fool, Paul said.
By nature, Man (referring Genesis) finessed,
misled by Woman, devolved to stature
lower than the angels. Once fallen, perfect body,
conscious of desire. Mind perceived it flawed
and sinful, covered it in skins of animals.
But modesty did not put out the fire.

The Natural Woman—shame was not innate
to her. Refused to hearken to dictates
of her mate, or blame the serpent. For her,
felt natural in the lovely, dark and sensuous
pelts of beasts. Evicted from the garden, found
she could regard the stark & wild as beautiful.
Embraced the earth, the sky & childbirth.

The Animal (shy but fierce) drinks from instinct—
no need to think or reason. Natural Man
envies Creature's freedom, yet denies the link.
Hears exultant cry of grandeur (new thrill
of innocence and fear) pierce the wilderness.
Afraid to die—irony, like blood, seeps through.
Man works his will to hunt and kill.

The Word, so long deferred by Natural Man,
now blurred. Woman heard the whisper, ate
the fruit, discerned light from dark, bent
the arc of patriarchy. Wisdom or duty?
Natural or unnatural? Anomalies of Nature
(lion and lamb, man and man) choose to lie
down together. Muse the Nature of the Beast.

Violence, Adult Content

Do we still believe in the Apocalypse?
Not a laugh to think, that on a quiet
autumn afternoon, between lethargic sips
of decaf latté, fire may fall from heaven.
Surreal and showy, to assume that as a gloss
on prophecy, Zion's gutters soon will flow
with blood, instead of mountain water.
Who are the sufferers along the road?
Seen with naked eye, it's tricky to dismiss
anachronistic images—pale horse,
dark rider (shock to see, since bridle
trail's engorged to interstate). Can we fail
to notice that a yellow dog cannot
be found to wag its tail?

In blessed sunlight of the New Millennium,
disciples of the fateful age engage
our dread to catalog calamities in store,
enumerate the coming dead. Close
the shutters, stay indoors, but don't expect
protection from foreboding in your dreams,
or from TV scenes of global carnage.
What can it mean to worship a forgiving
God? When Jesus walked, and spoke
with sinners, prostitutes, the lame—
He promised mercy to the merciful,
the same to those who mourn; the meek,
the poor in spirit, pure in heart. He said
that those who seek, shall find.

We may awkwardly recall
(yet fail to recognize) the jealous
God of wrath, who trod a bitter
winepress of destruction of the wicked
in the testament of old. We're told
the Deity who authored slaughter
of whole cities (not a pretty sight),

became the Shepherd of One Fold.
And if He comes again at end of days
(thief in the night), some say that we
should see his crimson raiment
of the wine vat as symbol of his majesty.

Not me. I claim the gospel of Saint John,
whose Lord is one of grace, and mystery.

Middlesex Eclogues: March

Unglued, ungluing March. The river clucks,
Scudding chucked ice through where the Sudbury splays
Wide above Lee's Bridge. Hiccoughing cracks,
Edges of song: and could I catch that phrase,

Sung on the blue lip of this unsung month,
Sandy, then you might hear some glacier split
Inwardly. I split open at the warmth,
Along impacted seams where winter's plate

Tectonics jam and stall pitched reefs of speech.
Scrape then, receding ice: carve fluted grooves
On drumlin walls, incise the granite breech

With thaw-scars, the way late-winter griefs,
Retreating, pit and pock, and read by touch
How rime, the engraver, whittles and forgives.

Nightjar

And if I shrink to drain your flask of pitch?
Call you duskfeather, call you nightjar.
Up and churr then, up and hawk for moths.
Come morning, not crosswise as others do,

But flush along some branch, you'll stretch.
To nut-dun mottle, to bracken strew,
Match your plumage. Reward no twitcher
With soever a twitch. Lapsed creed, you,

You toast of no vintage, you draft
Of afterthought tipped pinging into the butt,
Nightjar. Shallow in those ruts you scored
By the footpath, your paired bald

Eggs will baffle in the sun the toddler
Tomorrow and the toddler's mother.

The Sugar Maples

In the beginning (the reasons remain dark),
The sugar maples were cast out from the garden.
Pliant once and spry, their young green bark
Tanned to nubby russet. Thirst made them harden.
Parched gusts launched their seedlings wide about.
Pinched saplings braved a pursed and dusty birth,
And, as a mean collateral against drought,
Elbowed blunted roots into angry earth.
That was how they tapped the sunken cells
That harbor all the burrowers underground,
Refugees from some distant somewhere else,
Another world, an underworld, a wound.
There was the Crannoch, clawed and shivering
With razor bristles. There was the bluff, blind
Buldrom, purling voice seductive low.
Slender and smooth and glowing at each end,
Poisonous Splee, or digging with one toe,
Delving Pendegrath. They were all survivors,
Outcast fossils of an archaic world,
Before the humans crossed the forbidden rivers
And built their ships and planted rags unfurled
On roaring coasts they claimed forever theirs.

One year out of all the stony centuries,
These maple trees relented and longed to weep.
Beseeching the maker who'd sealed shut their eyes,
They extruded, through their pores, warm gouts of sap.
These tears the maker culled into zinc pails.
He baptized with that syrup, saying, "Bloom,
Ye gathered scatterlings, come true." The scales
Fell from their eyes. He swept them with a broom
Into a china urn fired in his wrath.
What happened next was native aftermath.
He called them his new creatures, toothed their tips
Dipped red or pranked ocher run to ruddy,
And then ordained them to the gift of bleeding
Each March, and witnessing their offering

Boiled and bottled and lifted to the lips
Of children in the morning of their guilt.
Children, take your sweet time, before your erring
Brings you to those groves where it is spilt.

After the Latin

There is a table booked in both our names,
Sandy, at this burnt end of the year,
In a timbered ingle of the Wayside Inn,
    Hard by the fire.

Exactly now (as with a practiced twist
You bring the final touch of Winter Rose
To your pursed lips, and for the umpteenth time
    Apply the test

Of sitting for your portrait in the mirror,
And for the umpteenth time you pass), just now
There's bustling in the kitchens of the Inn.
    Trolleys in tow,

Platoons of waiters—Sudbury boys in white
Aprons—heft pressed linen with a snap
Above oak tables, deal out pewter plates
    And pewter cups,

While, picking out the counterpoint, brisk girls,
Making haste slowly, glide with cupping hands,
Cradling flames they stoop, then lift, to touch to
    Candle, then sconce.

From pondering ovens rolls a savory
Rumor of quail spiraling on their spits.
Glow and scent and scuttle recombine.
    The Inn awaits.

And if you ask what's the occasion—not
Our anniversary, nobody's birthday, so
Why this unlooked-for warmth amid
    December snow?—

It's this: I want you back. And if you say,
"I'm here, I never left, these twenty odd
Years," well, that's just it: I never meant
    That you should plod

Doggedly through the desert of my neglect,
Trailing as I ranged from booth to booth
At Vanity Fair. I'm done with that. I want
    You and me both

Again. I want your hand across the table,
Voice in my ears, that cadence and that timbre.
Winter's not what it used to be: it's starker
    Than I remember,

Now that we can speak in terms of years
Left to us.
        Look: no more of that. Just say
Something in that voice. Something to keep
    All that at bay.

(Horace, Odes 4.11)

An Expulsion Eclogue

A hillside. Italian late afternoon glare.

TITYRUS reclining in the shade of a beech tree, contentedly piping melodies on a hollowed reed. The picture of idyllic rural innocence.

But: enter his fellow shepherd MELIBOEUS, whose anguish intrudes upon the ideal scene. He has been expelled from his own lands, which have been confiscated by Octavian—the future Caesar Augustus—and redistributed to his soldiers as a reward for their service in far-off wars. Meliboeus is now stripped of his home and reduced to seeking some alien land in which to live out his remaining years. Most of his neighbors suffer the same fate.

So how, Meliboeus wonders, amid the upheaval, can Tityrus find the peace of mind to relax and make music in the shade?

Tityrus, it emerges, is off the hook. His own lands have been restored to him by the young Caesar himself. Tityrus had made a special journey to Rome to beg the great man's mercy. The big city was overwhelming, true; and his poor sweetheart, AMARYLLIS, had grieved during his absence; but he succeeded in securing the protection of his own lands. He and Amaryllis—so much nicer than his previous love, the domineering spendthrift GALATEA—can now enjoy the pleasures of his native acres in peace. He will regularly sacrifice to Caesar as a token of thanks.

Good news for Tityrus, free to return to his place in an ideal pastoral scene. For Meliboeus and others, though, that picture jars with the starkly photographic world of Realpolitik into which he has been exiled.

MELIBOEUS

Tityrus, limbs akimbo where
    These beeches broadly spread,
How can you sprawl there, fingering ditties
    On a hollow reed?
Here I am hauling my house on my back
    As an empire's soldiers seize
My patch of homestead, my dear pale fields,
    While there in the shade you laze,
Teaching the groves and hills to repeat
The tune of "My Dear Amaryllis So Sweet."

TITYRUS

I tell you, Meliboeus, this godsent leisure,
I owe it all to him, young upstart Caesar,
God among mortals, at least in my eyes.
Long as I live, one of my choice lambs dies
On Caesar's altar as a sacrifice.
He saved my home. If now you see these cows
Free to amble wherever they would browse,
And me to play the piper at my whim,
Well, like I said, it's all because of him.

MELIBOEUS

I'm happy for you, please, make no mistake—
       It's just your luck
Astounds me, what with everybody's farms
       Up on the block
       Or parceled out.
     Myself, I try to keep my goats
     Moving, and I keep moving, too.
     But this goat, Tityrus, tell me, how
Am I supposed to coax the girl to move,
Who's just now dropped twin kids in the tangled grove
     And left them—future of my flock—
     Dying on the naked rock?

If only I'd had eyes to read the omens.
     That time freak lightning clove my stricken oak,
And shrieking crows came gushing from its trunk,
     That was a harbinger of my bad luck.

But who's this "god" you mention, Tityrus?

TITYRUS

They'd warned me: It's not called Metropolis
For nothing. Rome. The Mother of all Cities.
Hayseed me, if I only I had known.
I'd pictured a bigger version of the town
We drive our flocks to. I'd had it all worked out:

Fire in the Pasture

As puppy is to dog, as kid to goat,
So village is to city. Ah, but not
Rome. In Rome such common sense is useless.
Compared to other cities, Rome's a cypress
Soaring above squat shrubs.

MELIOBOEUS

                                        So then how come
You felt you had to make that trip to Rome?

TITYRUS

Freedom. Tardy freedom, I admit,
Freedom that turned to me almost too late,
When my white locks strewed the barber's floor.
But now that Amaryllis calls me hers,
And Galatea's gone, freedom appears
To smile upon the sunset of my years.
It was part laziness that made me wait

To scale the ladder and improve my lot.
I don't mind telling you: I dared not wish,
While Galatea had me on her leash,
For liberty. I couldn't even hope
To set aside some savings. Many a sheep
I'd bring to market, many a cheese I'd vend
To paying villagers, but in the end
My windfalls always went the way of wind
To meet my sweetheart's whims. So I'd return
With—not exactly ready cash to burn.

MELIBOEUS

We used to wonder about your Amaryllis:
            Smitten with what grief
            She'd cry out to the gods;
Wondered for whom, when summer came to leaf,
She'd leave the ripened apples hanging
            Unplucked on groaning boughs.

She wept, she waited for you, Tityrus,
        In her empty house.
These very pines, this deep loquacious creek,
These vineyards, Tityrus, made their mournful music
        To call you back.

TITYRUS

What else could I have done to save my skin,
But snap the yoke of bondage I was in?
Where else but Rome to find, in time of need,
An earthling with the powers of a god?
It's there I saw young Caesar face to face,
To whom I dedicate twelve sacred days
Of sacrifices spiraling scented smoke.
I laid my suit before him and he spoke:
"Granted. Go back, reclaim your native space
Just as before, and rear your flocks in peace."

MELIBOEUS

Lucky in your old age, that finds you blessed
        With acreage enough,
Never to be foreclosed or repossessed,
        However rough
Your pastures, studded as they are with rocks—
    I can't help noticing—and choked
        With tangled rushes
        And clotted marshes.

At least no foreigner will introduce
Exotic plants to taint your pregnant ewes.

Lucky, as I was saying, to stake your spot
        Here in the shady cool,
Hemmed by childhood's cherished brooks
        That swell the sacred pool.
Here your neighbor's humming
        Hedge—as in the good old days,
Quilted in willow blossoms that nurse

Fire in the Pasture

Sucking, supping bees—
Will lull you into dozing as you laze.

From down here, where the pitched cliffs rise,
Pruners at their work will send
Their singing to the skies;
And there will be no end
To purling of those pigeons that you love,
Or, from the elms, the moaning turtle-dove.

TITYRUS

Sooner will antelope range in the air
And fish pant naked on the sea's parched floor;
Sooner will Germans, heedless of frontiers,
Migrate to Mesopotamia's muddy rivers;
Sooner Parthians drink from the North Sea
Than I'll forget how Caesar looked on me.

MELIBOEUS

You quip, but for the rest of us, we must
    Migrate, and it's no joke:
Some of us to dusty
    Africa, some to Scythia, some
Making away to squat along the stream
Of rapid Oxus churning clouds of chalk.
Some will even turn their backs
On civilization, cast their lot among
Wild British tribes, the planet's farthest flung.

Will I ever, after a stretch
Of years in exile, see my native land?
    Return to see, amid forlorn
    And stunted stands of shaggy corn,
My bungalow still crowned with thatch
Where once, a pauper, I had reigned?

Meantime my trim fallows
Fall to some soldier's grip,

Some rank outsider brute
Lording it over my crop.

When great men feud, look where the poor wind up:
The laborer sows for men like these to reap.
We'll take your farms, the scoundrels say, but please, before you go,
Make sure to graft your pears, and set your grape-vines in a row.

We're out of here, my lady goats, happy once, but now
We're out of here.
        Still, remember how,
Stretched out on a grotto's mossy floor,
I used to watch you dot, far off,
The rimrock of that shaggy cliff?
        Enough.

No more songs from me. And for
You goats, so much for browsing through a patch
Of flowering clovers and those bitter
        Willows, while I keep watch.

TITYRUS

Maybe so. But surely you will stay
Just this one evening, resting here with me
On this green rug of leaves? You'll be my guest:
There's mellow apples, chestnuts, freshly pressed
Cheeses galore. So stay. Already smoke
Curls from far-off. Today's work
Is over. Mountain shadows edge towards dark.

(Virgil, Eclogue 1)

Call to Repentance

Μετανοεῖτε
—*Matthew 4:17*

How often it occurs, this summons to light!
With each sunrise spilling blue and lavender inks

over the world's edge. With each call of the peony
opening its tiny fist in a spark of scarlet flame.

Dandelions seed in white like bearded prophets
and scatter their divinations hourly to the wind,

and a voice of ancient water pours over stone,
as though Christ himself had returned to speak—

Repent, repent, for the kingdom of heaven is at hand.
And what, in truth, is at hand? An unlit candle,

a sparrow falling, some few lilies bowing in a field
to accept what the wind offers, unleavened bread,

a lost coin, any number of stories too puzzling to hear—
heaven for the price of a little attention and belief,

for a *change of thought*, that Greek word for *repentance*.
So, when he slipped away quietly into a heaven lost

to the rest of the world, what wisdom could he leave
otherwise to pour himself out like water from the sky?

Parable for the Pulse of the Wrist

και εγενετο ο ιδρος αυτου
ωσει θρομβοι αιματος
—Luke 22:44

One bleak winter evening a good doctor deftly cut
the umbilical cord wrapped three times around the neck
of my firstborn to save her from strangling to death.
An intern noted the moment precisely, seven past seven,
because, like a garden hose suddenly gushing water,
the cord, once severed, whipped a circle of blood

halfway across the room against a pale yellow wall,
against the blue scrubs of those standing by the bed,
against the face of a clock fixed at seven past seven.
The splatter of blood on glass could have been a chime,
a red stripe announcing its own peculiar name for the hour.
Twenty years later on the eve of my daughter's birthday,

I recite the story again. I never tire of its strange beauty,
its happy ending returning over and over to smile at me.
This time I wonder whose blood stained the clock that night—
my daughter's or her mother's or both—a blood shared
between them, a story they traded back and forth over time.
There was a dark moment also, if stories are believed,

when blood fell in Gethsemane for this child and mother.
Another good doctor wrote a most refined Greek
translated centuries later in the authorized English:
And his sweat was as it were great drops of blood . . .
Walking to my car that night I heard those words again,
as though a sentinel of angels in a trail of streetlamps

were chanting them quietly from one century to the next,
staking a course through darkness no longer eternal.
Sharing blood, the Innocent returned our innocence.
Stains on my own blue scrubs marked the happy ending,
the eternal round, and whose blood it was etched its name
indelibly across the face of time and all who bore witness.

Confession of the Sometime Lost

How strange the way a symbol may enter your life
during the silence, the hollow space, of prayer.

After confessing a harsh word, another loss
of patience, you hear a rat scraping in the wall

and recognize the perfect emblem of your misery.
Your carcass, your very skin, is riddled with defect

the same way your house is riddled with vermin.
The scraping persists, as if the rat were gnawing

your bones instead of the ribs of the house,
scratching some deeper, unexplored rottenness.

What is it, this uneasiness, this creature within,
determined to live and multiply? It has a name.

If only you could guess it you might know peace.
You wonder if this, too, is the voice of some angel.

Devotion to the Inexplicable

Βαλε αγκιστρον
—Matthew 17:27

One morning after years of ordinary marriage
I looked into a mirror while shaving and saw inside
my box of flesh that ancient, perplexing riddle—

a man's heart—transfigured into an elegant woman.
She offered a single, white lily and then vanished,
an encounter as brief and lingering as a final kiss.

Afterward nothing was the same. All day long
the heavens opened with a mere wave of my hand,
like pulling back linen from a freshly made bed.

I touched the red glass tumblers piled in the sink
and a flock of cardinals suddenly lifted in the air.
When I read Vergil that evening I heard an angel

of living water whisper its slow river of peace.
She was a metaphor, I suppose, angling for analogy,
a hook cast for some fish with a coin in its mouth.

But why a woman first, fashioned from the heart?
And what was the flower? A poem? A prayer?
A sliver of the moon shaped like a key to heaven?

Fire in the Pasture

Latter-day Aesthetic

I once had a dream I was William Stafford
riding a bicycle to China to become a poet,

encouraged by the views of an oriental sage
cycling alongside me with the same ambition.

In China, he said, *you make good living as poet.*
True or not, we were entirely content, happy

to chase on a bicycle our dream in a dream.
What was it but a voice from another room,

a whispered oracle from some templed vision,
a truly original idea perhaps? I think of Adam,

the first in so many things, tending red peonies
in a garden, the first man to laugh, the first

to reach for a woman with love instead of lust,
the first to use words as metaphor and symbol.

Perhaps I was the first to dream of crossing
the Pacific on a bicycle in the guise of another

—a simple, animated descendent of the first
of all true originals—led from the brink of hell

to the fringes of heaven on a wave of ocean
flamed by sun and moon, believing all the while

a poem must sparkle like water for the soul
in creating the world, or prove nothing at all.

Eden

Not satisfaction,
but its proxies:
guests, food, chatter.

And then she was at my side.
She said, "Meet me in the garden."
I took this to mean,

Come with me,
and we will be buried in water,
fire, nomenclature, earth.

I waited for her, distracted—
the laughter from the house,
the ruinous clatter of dishes,

the air sick with warm sugar.
She appeared
under the heavy shadow

of a peach tree.
She said, "You've come."
I took this to mean,

I will multiply your sorrow,
spread serpents at your heels,
spit curses for your sake.

I could smell the fruit
hidden in her hands,
forbidden and necessary.

A door opened.
A voice called my name:
once, twice, gone.

She split the peach,
licked nectar
from her fingers,

and said, "Here, taste."

I took this to mean,
Here is my heart,

delicious and desirable.
See how it beats and bleeds,
how it breaks to heal itself.

Two For Samuel Beckett

1. Bethesda

We never see the angel coming,
just percussive agitation on the pool,
pockmarks without rainfall,

or stuttered wakes shouldering the air.
We watch the blind,
their visceral listening,

sifting the uneven murmur
of withered and halt,
ready to lunge at each

medicinal trickle.
Since Jesus came through
there has been much discussion

about the logistics of rising,
taking up one's bed, walking.
We saw the old man do it,

but with thighs stung by urine,
flies coating a smear
of pus and blood on stone,

and open sores generating maggots,
clarity dulls, simple faith
requires qualification.

And how much does the angel notice?
He has his work:
stir the surface, ascend.

We don't doubt there is a purpose—
some relieved, others afflicted.
And we don't deny

there is security in suffering,
always knowing what and where,
waiting for the troubling of the water.

2. The Widow Woman's Son

> Death is the mother of beauty; hence from her
> Alone, shall come fulfillment to our dreams
> And our desires.
> —Wallace Stevens

He couldn't remember death.
And he doubted
he'd get another chance,

now that the wasting flesh
of the harvest hung in traces
throughout the orchard.

He kept his eye on the curvature
of the earth and waited
for signs from the ravens.

"The women were foolish," he said.
"Upstairs laughing, spontaneous milk
from the ceiling—

all of it gone now. Good."
At night he sat in the parlor,
straining at the small pant of a moth

ruining itself on a single flame.
"Mother," he said, "thy son
still liveth." Dawn came again:

another handful of meal,
a little oil. He scratched his thigh
and knew it would not rain.

"The women were foolish," he said.
"But spring then, and I watched
as swatches of daylight slid

over their shoulders. The yellows,
soft blues, so slight they vanished
as they touched the skin."

Snow

I stood at the window with my mother
and watched a cluster of deer,
their summer red long gone.

The cracking beams of the house,
the heat rising from floor vents,
the click and toss of the dishwasher—

all of this was almost too much to bear.
But it was the snow that finished me,
the endless falling of some pure bread,

crustless and broken; how it carefully erased
all distances, quieted the mountain jays,
and melted on the windows;

how it mocked my mother's tears
as she pressed her face
against the glass and wept.

I pretended not to notice.
The deer blurred into a single stain
swallowed up in the whiteness.

Sudden Music

1.

Look at the generous spread of stars before us,
the sporadic fire of the past, the larger shadow beyond.
Look at the throw of juniper burning into nothing,

the chipped bricks, the warped wood,
the shingles bleached under a heavy moon.
Listen to the names whispered into pillows,

names we loved or never knew we loved,
names that dripped from the corners of our lips as we slept.
Listen in darkness to the sudden music of loss.

2.

Let desire escape and rise as smoke from burning cedar.
Watch it lift into the mute density of winter
and rub itself on the black layer

that separates voice from sound, breath from prayer—
smoke blurring the outline of the body
with the stillness that ensues;

smoke continuing through the nakedness
of branches, to hover in the valley,
to thin with the smoke of other desires.

3.

Consider the snow and its slow work,
dressing dead orchards, dulling our sense of what was
until we can no longer say with conviction,

"They were apple trees, it was summer."
Consider this and be content with winter: the cool wisdom
blown across the ear, the patches of bloodless grass.

Because if memory is anything it is dirty banks of snow,
or rancid ice decaying into water. And what remains
is suspect at best. It will not be able to comfort us.

4.

Look at the frost growing its white mold
on the window, clouding the periphery, focusing
our attention on that which escapes us—

on that which has always escaped us. Let it go.
Let go of the fire, the shadow, the disappearing smoke.
Let go of names dried as stains on our pillows.

Fall a little, flinch and settle into dreams just under
the surface of sleep. Listen to the muffled voices above.
They sing, "Please, please," but from here it sounds like "peace."

Capitulation: Forbidden Squirming

In sorrow shalt thou bring forth children. Right.
It's not your fault, and I will here resolve
to not blame you for blasphemy and blight
and mindless war and problems to be solved
by children we'll give birth to. (Ouch.) Unwise
misogynistic God did this, and sex
could have been fun without! but thirty Y's,
who never can tell what to do with X,
prefer me to unsquirming here remain,
their masculine embarrassment respect.
(I have not seen you till the earth in pain,
so why must ours be socially suspect?)
     If hearing me speak of the Feminine Mistake
     makes you uncomfortable—well. Try to ovulate.

First of Third

When mornings are turned quiet, and the wind
defers before the dawn, and nothing moves
to stir the sultry leaves or mutter in
the fragile grass, the Artemesian rises
with the light, into the green, recklessly
diligent. The soundlessness reminds
her not to speak unless she's spoken to.

These constant days she finds nowhere to turn,
nothing to be, no reason she should stay
or flee, or turn into the sun, or turn
and let the sun leave shadows on her back;
no final cause to dictate that she should
endure today. Such gentle madness watching
for an end should have one; green-eyed she
would be the last to tell herself to live.
But she is far beyond the telling of
herself in anything. This is the god's
decree; the days return to nothing but
the rising counter-day that follows blindly
as the day already gone descends
into the dusk, until the gods have mercy
and she melts, the echo of a soul.

Narcissus is still here. He does not know
the name of what he loves, only the face,
Apolline beauty seen with other eyes,
in other waters stilled beneath the wind.
He never found necessity before
so that he could not leave his heart
and walk away. He never loved before.
To have loved once is probably enough,
to shape, to mend, to call one's life complete;
to call one's life a long dark prelude before
death, to lose oneself, eyes lit upon
the water's azure sky and golden curls,
among the sun-soaked flowers of the spring.

She will not love again, and he will be
in love until the earth is older than the light
repeating wonder back into his eyes.

She does not see herself in polished glass,
not in the water, when the surface stills;
she stays where she can only see his face.
She sees herself in that, in his thin glance
that fell upon her once, then fell away
like yellowed leaves in yellow Alseid hair:
a moment's touch, and out they're brushed again.
He sees her as she sees herself, he hears
her as he hears himself, his eyes look past
the tumble of her eyes, and to the richer gaze
within the pool. He does not see her now.
His heart descends into the fictive spring
and she descends to hell to follow suit.
With words she could not be the first to speak,
she only has his fluted voice to call
him forth again, to call herself. But he
is gone, and she was never there.

The world behind the water could as well
be real as could the world they think to be
so tangible, and if it be such second
real, who is to say which of the real and real
is the reflection of the love that was
the love first born of an essential soul?

Between the nodding flower and its other
in reverse, its uncrossed parallel;
between the nymph's translucent skin
and bloodless heart; between the mirror she
becomes in tracing out his words, and all
the fruitless words he spills for treacherous love
that pour into the buried sky beneath,
it has become impossible to find
where this began, what cast the light between
the lovers who live in between the glass.

Chromosomes

I come, a woman, bearing only
mirrored chromosomes and lacking
all the things they told me
make a woman out of cold genetic code.

I have the shape and aches
to women by biology bestowed;
the curves above my knees were made
for making babies, but my heart
has proved a motherly mistake,
and all these years I've never prayed
to even *want* to pray the Lord God to impart
this gift of pining for posterity—

it seems then that I am no woman, here without
the gifts god gave, of feminine docility,
to women who know what they are about.

And so I do not want your chromosomes
without you, nor your tools
to build a picket fence around my home.
I do not want your obligation,
good behavior, duty to preside.
I do not need fourth-finger jewels,
proposals on a velvet blue foundation;
and if I am usually the one to call, I do not mind.
I do not want you to provide
for all my wants and wishes, wall-to-wall.

I merely want your touch among the tips
of my hair, and you
to hold my lips
in yours like it matters.

I want the nonsense in your head,
the dreams, and all the stories, shells, and shadows
and to know where I can find you in between,
that whether sunsets,

babies, monthly agony, or yearly atheism,
moves my hand to you across
the mortal marriage prism,
that your hand will be moving too.

So maybe we will go to hell
and there hang out together.

Home

Breath on glass, soft shards of night outside
the clear reflecting ghosts of light inside
the pane; the pastel of the past beside
the ruddy present day. It is, this year,
too dark to see beyond the history where
hope taught us young to cultivate despair;
beyond the solemn pale mystery,
the native image iconography,
a cross across a lifeless Christmas tree

where we, in muted scenes, were made complete
by heartfelt lies and casual deceit,
by love made loathing and, by molten heat,
made cold and whole, between the window and
the world. It is the past beneath my hand,
my fingers resting on the slow, unplanned
diffusion of our childhood in tears.
The lifetime lesson, that hope breeds despair.

The zephyr breath of wept-to-sleep nightmares,
breath on the sob of sorrow, the sulk of death,
on quiet advent prayers, unbroken breath
of mothers growing quiet, fathers deaf
to little girls and candied nights and trees
and dreams deferred by innocent degrees,
by hope, wrapped up in ribbons to appease
the gift inside thin paper hope,
despair.

Breath in air, the mist of winter life,
outside the window where the night is rife
with hope-seeded despair, now one in strife
with faith,
which like a sudden stable star,
lights long above and lingers where we are
to show the unmade Lord to us and to our
mustard-seeded family farmland, growing
hope to fertilize despair unknowing.

Fire in the Pasture

Breath on the lips of winter wind ill-blowing
year-end days from deadened years and tears
from home back to the outside now appear,
the flesh of crystals in the falling air
the polished stone of silent hearts that burn
the light back heavenward uncaught and spurn
the tear-dissolving trails of sun that turn
the lines of midnight to the silver morn.

In spring-time in the desert, God was born
to bring breath for the graceless grieving, mourn
with those still breathing undead trespass in
the parents' ignorance and dull chagrin
the children's bright and brimming filial sin

to mortal bend, below the Christmas cross to bow
to heal the both-ways broken heart and bleeding brow
        breath of the advent's uncreated vow
that we should learn to love by now.

Lingua Doctrinae

amicus, amici, amico, amicum, amico,
Amice.
The window, with its morning salty joke
of squinting scowls, unfolds a dusty yellow ray
of light on you, while I still close-eyed soak
in shadows in the middle of the room.
We resurrect the third declension, bring
the plural genitive alive, resume
linguistic worship, conjugate the Mass, and sing
our hallelujahs, pater nosters, pronoun penance
for our poor grade in repentance
for our reprobate translation of this sentence.

deus, deo, deum, deo, dive,
Dei.
I sit below the window, left of center;
you sit arch and rightly right, and see
what all the rest of us believe, and whether
it is worthy, dull, grammatically lax,
or nonsense, and your hand leaps, choking,
when we have ill-grasped the graceful syntax
of salvation, and what have we all been smoking
that we think theology the ancient tongue
of piety, apology the young
and ransomed language of the Son?

intellego, intellegere, intellectum,
Intelleximus.
If you see me smile at the fine commotion
of your indignant lexicon run loose,
it is only I am stirred by your devotion
in a faith not made a choate firstborn lamb
to the locution of our system. If I sometimes
wade too quickly into contradiction, dam
your vivid prosody before the rhyme
and reason have made art of argument,
and if my nettled morphological dissent

insists on rising, I am confident
that though your own religious phonotactics
may be the far side of the room from my intent,
the formal phonemes of my own ascent,
I doubt to disagree with the semantics
of your faith, and neither your celestial-bent pragmatics.

Talk with me

talk with me, brother
in the language we used to
with soft, close words we
would loose and let fall, like the
hush of tall grass after gusts

San Diego Bay, Night Walking

Not the fishes,
electricity,
or the even water—
unwrinkled,
black as
space.

But asteroids
through liquid
firmament—
luminous
bending,
static water
surrounding
tiny, darting bodies.

On André Derain's *Lady in a Chemise*, 1906

Your lipstick's smudged, lady—
and your sometimes yellow skin.
In lightness white;
in dark,
blue the iconic
chemise collects about your
hips. In heaps, lady—
your forward expression
lies Thinker-like on
black-twisted
knees.

Close

I once cut
open my foot
wide, scarlet
like parted lips
breathing life-blood.
Gasps ran
and fell
nearly speaking, stuttering
to bleached
concrete.
Each pulse forced
an exhale—
but no words.
I held it shut,
to silence
the blood.
You told me I
may need stitches.
This is the closest
we've been.

Baptism

We're too made of water.
Water, that
dream of playing first, then running
the cracked earth through,
of waiting.

We ask for water to drink.
It leaks through shoes,
walls, glands, hands. And in falling, filling—
a kid's toy bucket,
a garden pail, a lake.

I wish I could remember water
cold. A shudder and immersion,
was this a cleansing?
Drowning?

We take her carefully—one by
a hand, and I with a hand
covering her mouth. She floats,
floats, sinks. A weightless
fall, her left leg from her right, her
back rolling after shoulders.

From between
my fingers she gasps,
and I feel I am all there is
between her and
all that water.

Dig

I began to dream I
was soil and you
were a plant that grew
in me, root hard
as a dandelion's, leaves
pungent as rosemary,
completely without flower.
I don't know if I
went to bed with dirt
under my nails,
but I know I woke up that way,
skin scratched smooth.

Last Night's Fire

I've always felt I'm someone who
could approach her own beheading with
unvarnished resignation, no sprees of
weeping or remorse; dressed, if I were

lucky, in a murky red gown newly made by
a servant who would miss me; if not,
in a muslin shift worn fine and bleached
by countless afternoons drying on mothy bushes.

I'd acknowledge the crimes I'd committed
without feeling I should have undone them,
proclaim whatever innocence I possessed
and decline a blindfold, preferring to see

the crowd and the scaffold and what was left
of my future billowing out before me until
a man I could only hope was strong raised
a blade I could only hope was sharp and plucked

the thread of my life so fiercely that it spooled
immediately into a startling, stuck tangle, and that
was the end of that. It's what I'm doing now:
envisioning an end and walking toward it, hoping

it will be an endurable, appreciated death. I admit
I think we all deserve that, despite our collective
likeness to the sweepings of last night's fire.
But always something precious is burned with

whatever fuel warms us and boils water for
coffee in the morning and soup at night;
always, some beautiful bright trinket
that should have adorned the mantlepiece

dissolves among the coals, its smoke mixed
with the smoke of dead juniper or pine
and carried by the wind's hocus-pocus to coat
tomorrow's clouds with darkness and grime.

The Anvil of Desire

In the days when wishing was still of some use,
no one had figured out what to wish for.
At the hour when monks threw back their cowls
and drank bowls of soup flavored with one
spongy onion and a lifetime of contrition,
a shimmer emerged from the gorse and grasses
and a cat sat contentedly enclosed in a porch,
marveling not at robins or rabbits on the lawn
but at its own predatory nature. Madmen and
madwomen who were not all that mad looked up
from their after-dinner coffee or whiskey
and thought about warmth and winter and woe.
The sun gathered its fury into itself while
the moon hid in shadow and apologized
for the darkness. A small feline heart,
forged like everything else in the world on
the anvil of desire, beat without mercy or shame.

Vertigo First Thing in the Morning

You tilt your head to examine sunlight
through a glass apple, the fluid beads
inside your ears refuse to level off,
demand you flounder with them until
your stomach empties itself of apricots
eaten at breakfast. Balance is a sense
so basic we claim to have but five.
To rise from bed, to turn flips in the deep end
of a public pool, to recline against
a lover and not be sick—well, it's the
very least we can demand: not to be
reminded each time we move that balance
is precarious, life is delicate,
that hard earth rises up to meet us when we fall.

Self-Portrait as Burnt Offering

The prophet says:
I have earned a right to the voice of prophecy.
I have suffered and seen the future
and suffered by the seeing.

I am neither a prophet nor
much good at making things up as I go.
I speak in sensible tones.
I observe the present moment.
I record the moment's events.

I review the record and say,
Well, I suppose that is what happened.

I've learned this about memory: the fact that
I can't trust it doesn't mean I should foreswear it.
The same is true of weather forecasts and prayer.

Early on I discovered an elemental preference:
the story I shy from all water and earth,
the one that intrigues me air and fire.

Jehovah, angry god of an angry desert, watched
smoke ascend to heaven. In that desert
the firstborn child had to be offered
as a sacrifice, or a sacrifice made in its place.

The second child you got to keep.
Smoke is Jehovah's offering, water
his weapon. He killed first by flood.

Movement starts from the center.
Smoke ascends, water falls. In
my desert and the desert of my forebears
our offering to God is
water: sweat spilled digging
reservoirs and irrigation canals,
the water flowing in them.
My ancestors vowed to make the desert blossom.

Prosperity became an offering but not a sacrifice,
the unretainable thing God demands you keep.

The prophets of landscape say:
our dams will outlast the water they hold.

Prophecy and history flow from the present.
I learned history and doctrine; I was
seared by probability and logic but
never by prophecy and faith. My parents'
second child, I would not be kept.
I made myself the sacrifice to be offered for the first—
a resentful gift, evaporating like water in the desert,
leaving behind defiling blackness and a stench like smoke
from the charred timbers of a fallen church,
from a witch writhing in the stake's flames,
from a heap of smoldering books.
The God I was offered to can do nothing
with me but cast me away
and hope there is no other god to find me precious,
who will hand me back to my family and say,
Here, I know how to sacrifice, too.

The Afternoon Hour

For my mother

You colored me
sienna, azure,
a shape I was becoming,
a bird, perhaps,
a cloud,
a field of trees.
I don't remember much, only
the low table,
how we knelt,
how you held the crayons
like flowers,
tipping color,
a petal pouring rain.

To Stain the Sky

Three suicides
hang
on our family tree.

Aunt and grandma,
barefoot on their emaciated floor,
shared two shots,
one pool of blood
rusting the Iron Mountains red.

I don't expect you to understand.

The other was a sixteen-year-old uncle.
Family pressed and buttoned to church,
he stayed behind to tend the table,
pair knife and fork,
fold linen napkins like a prayer.
Then he found the trigger.
The horses heard,
the dogs mid-bite,
and the apple trees standing in the fields.

I won't go that way.
No,
not with a shot,
but with a spark,
retina dazzled,
striking with words,
a crack of white,
flames spinning off,
vision blazing thought.

I will fly,
go out with a
flash,
and stain the sky.

Atomic Number Sixteen

There is no word
for the snap, the bite of light,
the beginning fuse that flames like fireflies,
a multitude of them,
a chorus lit with light.

Eye it, frame it,
snap now, then shut your heart and hold
the scrap that spirals to ignition,
spinning to the end,
the moment your retinas held him, burning,
sulfurous with stars, a galaxy heat dancing
in your ears as he
wound, a snake, a quake of
sparks that flamed to your
toes.

The Science of Forgetting

The night settles
like spooned earth.

I no longer see faces,
I see trees.

The cutter is gone,
the forest has swallowed
him,

as it has
swallowed
me.

Redwood Song

There is no song for you,
none that stretches
like salvation.

The Tule River Tribe calls you
Wawona,
Toos-pung-ish,
Hea-mi-withic.

We call you
redwood.

With empty arms
and barked waves,
you swim up
an impossible distance,
skimming the skies,
cracking heaven's gate,
tying evergreen and angels.

We saw you burning, once,
passing through,
a family trip
on the lip of your groves.

We leapt out with water,
a sacrament,
all seven of us.

We didn't know you germinate
only with fire. We pressed your pines,
inhaled you like kings,
hanging on your boughs,
we, diseased beggars,
Lazarus at the
foot of such limbs.

The Dispensations

Thus need reiterates itself, the flesh
mere repetition, and all this grasping
somehow loosening our hold, and every
depth a screen, a trick, an interposing.
How much must be left for us to be here now?
In the blur of waking, it's hard some days
to know which face it is before me,
what language to invoke, from what devotion.
So now, as you step out of the car, a little
like your mother, I want to memorize
the way the angles of your hips countervail
the thrust forward of your weight, the body's
unthought impacts, as you raise your eyes
and I take my first steps toward you.

Waiting Room

Pigeon-like, unmeaning, a stream of barely
syllables from such a big girl—and eyes
that pin and read in mine that something
in them is wrong. "She'll grow out of it,"
her mother confides, leaning in a whiff
of milk and softener from the next chair:
"It's all right." And maybe it is. The girl,
now searching the box of toys, settles
on a wood puzzle, spreads the pieces out.
I hope they're all there. And when my name
is called and I rise, her eyes veering back
up at me, I want to bend down, whisper,
explain, as if my words could touch her,
as if they meant she did not have to be alone.

A Moment Ago

We were out on the deck talking with Mother,
watching the line of shadow climb the foothills,
intercepting the peaks around us one by one
as if the valley were a bowl being slowly filled
with darkness. She wore the floppy cloth hat
with the flower, having just given up therapy.
We asked what she remembered of "little"
great-grandma and others we never knew.
It was hot. An afternoon storm had splotched
here and there the laurels, startling the swallows;
a dusty trickle had formed briefly in the throats
of the gutters. Mid-recollection, she paused.
"When the day wears," she said, "or when I begin to feel
too much for myself, I think of a song I heard
my mother sing I don't know how many times
over the sink washing dishes, a child's song,
and it lifts me." It was some minutes later
that the leaves of the poplar began suddenly to rattle,
exactly as the leaves here in the darkening yard
ten years and two thousand miles away just did,
a harsh, dry sound like seeds shaken in a pod.
It is a brittle world. Over and over dusk
wells up in us; birds fly uncertainly overhead.

All That Time

I'd like, about now, a little small talk,
the grown-up kind between long agons
some summer afternoon across a table
bottling pickles or just dropping by
when what's not said is not evasion
but another language, every empty word
and nodded half-sentence a hand laid
on the arm. Such sweetness, all that time,
you around me, like the rain in the trees
I walk toward today, or like, last night,
the canopy of stars through windblown limbs,
or how, before we correct ourselves, we say
"canopy of stars" when there is only
space widening out from our arms.

The River

Names from fables, names that seemed to the child
almost to be fables: Nile, Ganges, Congo,
Amazon, Tiber, Euphrates, Colorado.
Rivers of fire and forgetfulness, of memory,
the muse's mother, paradise, hell,
crossings, discoveries. Then my own fable,
a small river of small rivers: Hobble Creek,
Provo, Jordan, Sevier, and rivers without name
all emptying into the one river, the river
in names. But—water or way, form or flow—
what are you? Archaic mover, your amnesty
oblivion, anywhere water has gathered
and found a way down, you're there, dispensing
your laws, teaching what it is to be
made of gravity and error, beyond reprieve
to be doing and doing, absently, your reasons
unknown to yourself, drawn, falling,
not pursuing, body through which bodies move,
bearing your waterlife, your darters, slitherers,
eggs, instars, your myriad, unceasing deaths,
your spilling vortices of spawn, metamorphosis,
kills. Turgid, swarming, tawny, huge,
muscular, you're a force carrying earth to the sea,
or you're a spittle of foam in the desert clay,
a washed-out gulch undercutting willows
and tamarisk, tufts a child passing in a car
imagines as refuge, home, the isles of the blest,
you're a glimmer snaking through the trees,
metallic at dawn, stilling the man's thought
on your banks, pulling him, amniotic, lachrymose,
loosening all that's coiled, as if you, not air,
not flesh, were his element. At your edges, din
of a million sobs and whispers, over stones
finding voice, on snags sometimes you sing.
Wrinkled sheet or braid or eddy scummed
with curling pollens and oils, absorbing,

disgorging, folding in and swirling out, nothing
your own and everything, tearing apart
and tumbling together, your spoils wheels, petals,
refrigerators, shopping bags, wrappers, halves
of window frames, handles, leaves, scraps
of bark, cables, trunks, limbs you've torn off
still twining in you, like limbs, or blindly bobbing,
siftings, portages, the lost and the tossed aside
and others washed up for the wrong ones
to find. Currents within currents, rippled
flashes of sky, clouds rushing beneath leaves
rushing between shadows of leaves rushing
over stones flashing with leaves. Endlessly
unwinding reel of real and unreal, figures
warped and quietly writhing, hypnotic,
I trace them as if they might lead—where?
Follow it if you're lost, they told me, but forward
or back, downward toward dispersal or up
to the source? And for what? At the end
of the searches, the fables go, an apparition,
part nymph, part matron, part hoary old man,
part beast, gapes up at you, holds out a key.
I don't hope for release. Even in my sleep
I hear it, the river pooling and surging
and purling and cleaving and cleaving.

Creation

Father

> I split the bone
> beside my heart.
> Exposed, this open grate
> now holds my mouth.
> bears a scar

Mother

> A seam holds threads
> as sinews in the
> hollow of my spine.
> A gentle finger coaxes open
> the cage of love.

Breaking Bread Above the Waters

Sunday evening flights are often full,
but one empty seat opens up the space
between me and another passenger.
Legs tightly wadded around my bags
I eye him from the side to note his early
middle age, black jeans and shirt, gobs
of gold to bedeck his hands and adorn
his neck. So much forced conversation
with strangers in the last two days, I want
now to blot out these new distractions,
potential communion with persons
knotted in yet other relations.

The walls of my book bury me until dinner
is announced. Cold chicken or hot, salad
or teriyaki. Senses stimulated we begin
to raise our heads, crumble these ranks,
roll away stones to break bread. My turn
to order. I choose chicken. Hot or cold?
she asks. I say, Hot. Before he begins to eat
my seat partner bows head and ends with hand
to cross his chest, lifts his lids and asks
if I'm from Salt Lake. He explains
he is going to school for railroad switch
training. What is there to do? I tell him
Temple Square and Mormons and Red
Iguana Killer Mexican Food and
Cathedral of the Madeline, my best tips.
He's from Chicago and I look closer
at the shining medal below his chin,
an anchor, the sea of Mary, la mère. His
two children are smart, one learns fast,
the other a smart-ass. He didn't know
you could get Mexican food in Utah, didn't
know who Mormons are, didn't know
his company cared enough to pay for him
and one other guy to part the lake back home

to discover salt out here, didn't know a life
could change with a parcel of cheap land for boys
to come play in the wide dry desert air.
I ask about his life in the City: he didn't know
the neighborhood church would go down
in graffiti, didn't know on the other hand
the Italian, Greek, Polish sections of town
would flourish. Great food, I think, that's
the reason, as I tear another bit of crust
from my roll.

Soon the meal ends, and I return to my book,
but didn't know the view outside would
pull me in. The land of a thousand lakes
has receded behind and I wonder who else
in the cabin feels the tugging sensation.
My nose pressed lightly against the hard
plexi-panel, I almost feel the two drops
of condensation streak down the inside
of the outside window, first one, then the
other, in precisely the place where two eyes
might be, as if the pane were a face, as if
it were a mirror of my face. Having lost
my place in the book, I turn to the skies
and loose a defiant heel toward heaven
to reach for the unknown holder of my
fate far below.

Make Yourself At Home

Over two years now, and still
you sit on the edge of my couch
with such politic presence,
feet planted properly, hands
folded neatly as the napkins
scheduled at your taciturn
insistence at every breaking
of bread.

I want to be
enfolded by you, overwhelmed,
flooded, wrung out by you,
smothered by your world,
the neat folds coming
only after years of tangling
and knotting ourselves around
a weighted, shifting balance,
untamed,
until we each have been
each other's time,
each other's baby
and feel each other's corners,
anticipate the cries
and know to dance in step,
dance in step, dance
to any tune
or any fret.

How Long

How long
since I last saw my younger brother grown
two heads taller but maybe that's only because
he's grown five layers thinner. Come up
from San Diego to Salt Lake City to be redeemed
dried out pockets cleaned the cobwebs of his palms
catching in my hair as he bear-hugs me whispers
"Just a month." Car retrieved by the repo man
who's glad my brother's honest now even though
it means he wants to borrow the BMW in the driveway
with the JSS license plates (dial 9 for Jesus)
so he can find a job again since the first one lined up
didn't work when they let him go and he came home
to sleep it off for a few days with milk and ashes
and the missing bread turned burnt now and then.

His eyes in my kitchen framed by a profile
of gaunt cheeks hollowed eyes and slackened pants
I ask him if he's had an AIDS test yet. Not yet they
charge for it here how long can they expect us
to come in when you have to make an appointment
two weeks ahead of time and even have to pay.
Besides I know I'm going to live forever
I just know. And Michael is lying
when he says he's got HIV he does it just
to shock me he says wrists limping stiff
against his ribs. His coat reminds me
of the images of Jews in old war films
wearing stars on their wool thickness
placed gently as lambs below fur collars.
Nobody in Utah wears coats like that.
Did they resurrect him from Auschwitz
and bring him here as my dead brother for me
to wonder how long his luck will run and how long
his nails are?

At night in bed I listen to his deafening pleas
on the phone chidings to Michael left behind
who's moving up here soon he just doesn't know it yet.
The phone bill's arrival thuds me to my feet
when I read there's a price to pay that rivals
human grief and pull to go again and not give in.
Perhaps he's used to those jobs for the cable

companies that hire phone solicitors by the dozens
because business is booming. His gift should be offered
to the Blarney stone so that twice the number
of tourists will come to finger the stitch in his side
and smell the soapy menthol in his hair. Or
perhaps twice the young-girl neighbors
ready to celebrate his birthday two months later
with admiration for his enthusiasm that inspires them
all the more as they remember their children whose fathers or grandparents
have custody and they learn to make it on their own
clean and dry. And by now Michael's here and shares
with my brother the pull-out futon in my living room
that smells like a used-up gym every time I come home
from work wishing I could do something
with my yard but knowing it's better if I help
my daughter with her homework or spin a tale
with her before it's time to sleep. Because we never know
how long.

Soul Retrieval

Here you are, sitting in the dark
Womb of the lodge, warm, almost
Unbearable at times, sweating
In the company of those
Familiar with the edges of their souls,
Hard and soft. They weep and mourn,
Laugh and dance with the shadows
That anchor them between earth and sun.

Here you are, sharing space with a shaman
Who takes the lost on journeys to find the missing
Ghosts, shapes that prove the substance
Of the body.

Here you are with healers
Who knead out the ailments lodged
In muscle and bone for the sake of the matter
In the gray mists that collect and fog about the head.

Here you are with the comforter who talks
With troubled teens and drug addicts,
Digging out the grime embedded
In the contours of that
Which has been forsaken.

Here you are looking around
Because you found you had given
Your matter away somewhere
Along the line – to school, a little blue book,
An expectation, a man,
Or a church you keep going back to, hoping
You'd find it floating
Somewhere up by the steeple or organ pipes,
Perhaps, in hopes you could channel
It back to yourself so it could move lightly
With your limbs and wishes.

Might you be like Nicodemus
Who wanted it all spelled out
In black and white, in tangibles
He could handle and read and put away
On a library shelf?
The learned priest thus missed the gray doves of Autumn—

September fury, October fire, November gentle—
Because he could not see in the dark.
Crouching on the earth, are you now ready
To exit the womb, call yourself a new name,
And wait for the moment
When you will hold a dove in your hand,
Stroke it wings close to your breast,
And thrill in the soft rhythm of heartbeat?

Acrobats

On the television, a preacher in a black suit
is talking about *grace*. His face quivers
just before the tears come, and he asks
that I awaken my faith. It is always this way,
at two o'clock on channel nine. Sometimes,
hours later, I imitate his piety
in front of the mirror

and sometimes I think of the homeless man
who crossed the street for my two dollars,
the skittish horses of his eyes
unbearably ashamed.

He said something
about food stamps
being late, an apology
of sorts. I wanted to tell him
something good,
but instead I held out the stiff bills
as if I were holding him
at gunpoint. I wanted to say that

we were
just two acrobats
swinging the same high-rise routine,
dancing it out on the sidewalk
for an audience of cars and lights.

Grace

Even Hercules spun wool
lamb-soft and delivered
by children, his bulk muscled over

a line of fine thread. Punishment
from the gods. This
is what they teach you when you ask

for more. Not divine
intervention in a cloud of smoke
but humiliation, struggle, time.

Of all virtues, this must be
the strangest to bear. Ulysses
counting waves,

time oceanic on Circe's lost isle.
Children of Israel marching
toward a land so holy

it took forty years to find.
My friend, thirty years old and held
by her mother, wrestles

from her clothes before shuffling
into the shower.
Like rain in a quiet hour: the slow

liquefaction of her mind.
All of this raw tenderness
draining from the world.

And for what? To look back and say
as He did to a world new and waiting
to decay, "It is good."

Some News About the Soul

In my solitude I speak
to the other side of myself:
quiet lark of heavy wings,
oh, supple remorse.

If you sit still enough
the birds of your body
will settle on one dark branch
and rest in chords of ceremony.

The fluttering behind our shoulders
throwing light
as from dusty lanterns
we mistake for birds.

The mackintosh tree
my father pruned last April
has now two branches that extend
toward the sparrows
like arms.

Wake

After Henry James

Always a young man in clean boots and a small white
bird churning the sky into ash. He climbs ladders,
the young man,
not towards the bird but a girl
soon to die, and he watches

the coughing, the switching of eyes,
and a long boat moored
under the parapets of Venice. By day,

a face
pressed to the glass, a window
swinging battered casts
of hat and hand and the intricate gardens
shifting their greens, he sighs. She laughs a little.

By night, tiger-faced and hungry,
the costume party reels its usual
plots: deception, the fever of loss.

We are all of us
instinctively tribal. What the labyrinth spells is
not organized chaos
or the map to forgetting
but a blueprint of the wound
we rise every day to cover.

The girl dies. The young man lifts an umbrella
to the falling sky, brushing the spent air
of the bird's flight.
After the wings, the breast opens.

Some Kind of Beginning

The alfalfa fields had their own luster
and, besides, no one came
for any harvest. Instead, as children, we drifted
in a golden sea with monarchs, my brother waving
his net like a sail. We floated past
clumps of aspen, tiny islands;
other children, on swing sets and trampolines,
were strange natives whose language
we chose not to utter. Little pilgrims
in our faded jeans and Keds
we navigated past our abandoned tree house,
past the chokecherries oozing
their droplets of blood (the sticky splendor
my mother caught and wrung
into jelly, jam, syrup), past
the knotted tree trunk crouched
like a lost ogre trying to hide at the foot
of the mountains, until we reached it:
the grave. And here we stopped,
my brothers and me,
to run, dance, laugh over the tombstone
of an almost forgotten dog. Rather,
meaning his name. Meaning
I'd rather bury my bones in the dark. Or
I'd rather lie here asleep. A tiny tombstone
reading: "Rather, a dog who deserved
far more than he got." Then,
in the quiet of chewing
our sandwiches, swallowing
green punch, we sensed the spirit
of the great dog rise up
and beg. With a reverence
befitting our Sunday School lessons,
we listened, knowing of God
and the afterlife, the inevitable judgment
of all creatures. But even then

at the mouth of the canyon
the bulldozers started their engines.
The alfalfa fields trembled.
I think it was then, without our knowing it,
that mortality came to us.
Dirt over a rough grave. The whir
of approaching machinery.
The anguish of swallowing it all for lunch
with so much laughter to spare.

DARLENE L. YOUNG

Patriarchal Blessing

The boy, sixteen, is taller than his mother, taller than
the creaky man with shining eyes and trembling hands.

Mother comes fasting, something she's good at,
years of honing her physical yearnings
into empty bowls to catch spiritual manna.
And now she is empty of all but her hope
of hearing the voice of God through this old man.
Her son, the first-fruit of her labors,
a rough-cut stone but the best she could do—
and would God touch this stone with his finger?

Her son folds into the chair with a quick glance
at her, an echo of the glance he gave her long ago
the day he stood to join his father in the font.
And maybe now the father will join them
in spirit? She, longing, glances to the corners of the room.

The trembling hands are stilled on the boy's head,
as if the words of power give them weight—
the words that dart like lightning in the air
and dance upon her eyelids. She opens them
to watch the old man, ageless, shine like sun,
his voice a whisper still but piercing bright.

The mother sits and holds the hand of God—
for once she feels she's truly not alone
in her sweet knowledge of her son's good heart.
She weeps to hear God tell her of the man
he will become, this boy she's nursed with blood
and milk, and tears,
this boy, a shining sword, a man of God.

And in the silence when the blessing's done
the son stands up and shyly takes her hand.
The old man, feeble now, stands at the door,
winking in the glitter of the stars.
For days those flashing words will dance like sparks
around her ears, behind her eyes and in the air—

as if she walked with diamonds in her hair.

Post Partum

Sucked dry, her ashy body flakes away.
She bows her head into the blessing blast,
the shower's streaming fingers pulling past
her ears and throat in webs of streaming gray.
The water, snaking down, gathers her tears
and curls past swollen breasts in milky flood
to swirl around her ankles with her blood:
she'll leak and melt until she disappears.
Her hands, unanchored, pass along her thighs,
her hips, her sagging womb. The pounding rain
can't wash the echoes of her baby's cries.
Young husband comes to watch through smudgy pane—
her edges blur. He squints and wonders why
she's staring, always staring at the drain.

How Long?

I find myself Lehi, encamped in a tent.
It's pleasant enough here, with plenty to do.
Arise, retire.
Arise, retire.
Work and pray and dance.
Retire.

I could build a house here and let go the dream
of the swaying of camels, the saltwater lapping.

But I heard a voice—and its memory has me
stretching my neck at the dry desert wind.
Still I hear only whisper of sand and tent flapping.

Arise, retire, and I used to pray
at every new dawn, "Lord is it today?"
Arise and retire. I no longer ask
but remain in my tent. You know I'll obey.

I'll make it my work to arise and retire
and cling to the ghost of the voice in the fire.
But, Lord, there's the ocean.
And what shall I do with this lack of motion?

Angels of Mercy

The Seventh Ward Relief Society
presidency argued long and soft
whether Janie Goodmansen deserved
to have the sisters bring her family meals.
It seemed that precedent was vague—
no one was sure if "boob job" qualified
as a legitimate call for aid.
Janie herself had never asked for help—
a fault they found it harder to forgive
even than the vanity behind
the worldliness of D-cup ambition.
But in the end charity did not fail.
The sisters marched on in grim duty
each evening clutching covered casseroles
(for, after all, it wasn't the children's fault).
More than once, though, by some oversight
the dessert came out a little short, as if
by some consensus they all knew
that Janie's husband, Jim, could do
without a piece of pie that night.

Washing Mother

I return for the washing.
Can't resist your need,
or else I want to atone
for leaving so eagerly
without glancing back,
back when you were whole and lively
and wanting to hold me tight.

You hold loosely now,
mind moving on,
body aching to follow.
I see the kind, huge effort you make to even
hold at all, croaking out "Yes,
I'll miss you too—"
Graceful always, but looking over my shoulder
while you say it.

I wash your frail frame,
sallow and gaunt,
holding only breath-whisper.
You're nearly gone,

flitting above me or behind,
dipping into other moments,
reaching for shadows and ghosts,
marking time.

You await without weight holy wholeness.
I watch and wait with you,
holding my breath.

Soapy water's slippery
but I must take care
not to hold too tightly
for your paper-thin skin bruises easily
these days, and your wet wrist slips silently
from my hold.

Afterword:
A Bright String of Poems

Ángel Chaparro Sáinz

When Eugene England and Dennis Clark published *Harvest: Contemporary Mormon Poems* I was thirteen years old. I had to wait five years to go to college, where I competed against teenage apathy and my hunger for adventure and successfully completed my degree. Even though Spain qualified for entrance into the European Union's Economic and Monetary Union at that time, the job market was still a challenge for a recent college graduate like me and unemployment encouraged me to go back to school. I began my PhD and I discovered who the Mormons were—though it was still two more years before I read *Harvest*.

In March 2011, Tyler Chadwick sent me an email asking if I would write an afterword for a new anthology of Mormon poetry. He mentioned *Harvest*; I went back to take a look at the collection, and its names were so familiar: Clinton F. Larson, Susan E. Howe, Carol Lynn Pearson, Emma Lou Thayne, May Swenson. I closed the book and opened the manuscript Chadwick had sent. And I started doing what Mark Strand calls eating poetry.

The first thing that surprised me about the manuscript was its variety. There are different levels of attachment to the Church, motley themes, free verse and traditional forms, personal poems, elegiac poems, experimental poems, major topics, minor topics, new images, new mappings. American poetry is decentralized, richly varied, impossible to summarize. The same applies to Mormon poetry. It would be easy enough to compartmentalize: you could divide between those who follow stanzaic forms, conventional rhyme, traditional flavor and themes (including Michael R. Collings, Karen Kelsay, Alan Rex Mitchell, Jim Papworth) and those who are experimental (including Elaine M. Craig, Simon Peter Eggertsen, Calvin Olsen, Laraine Wilkins). But that would be too easy—and too narrow, because each writer in this collection associates with the Mormon literary tradition while also exploring strange lyric terrain and spilling over into mainstream American poetry. So while it's tempting to compartmentalize these 82 poets, labelling is unrewarding.

A general overview of this volume's outpouring invokes the names and voices of the poets included in *Harvest*, as well as other well-known names and voices. Calvin Olsen's spontaneity mirrors that found in Charles Olson. Robert Frost and Maxime Kumin's observations of nature gleam in Patricia Karamesines. Raymond Carver's simplicity echoes in Laura Stott's poems. Charles Bukowski's loss of prejudice can be found in Nicole Hardy. Langston Hughes means jazz and that same music swings in Elaine Craig. Carl Sandburg was in love with flexible lines and Melissa Dalton-Bradford twists hers. Billy Collins, as poet Terry Gifford told me a couple days ago, keeps the mystery from one line to the other, and I feel the same as I read Warren Hatch. Gary Snyder goes to nature and Steven L. Peck follows. William Carlos Williams played the game of phonetics, which Alex Caldiero wins. Emily Dickinson's lyricism flows into Marie Brian. Gary Soto's aloof sentences and visual narration are like those found in S.P. Bailey. Adrienne Rich and Arwen Taylor talk about womanhood. May Swenson and Neil Aitken discuss death. Linda Pastan and Deja Earley speak from the depths of the quotidian; I would call them surgeons of the routine. C.K. Williams purifies ordinary things and Matthew James Babcock does the same from different angles, using new tones and with a tendency for little details, such as might be found in an airport reflection room. I could go on, but won't, only to mention that many of these poets seem to focus on the specific detail as a source for the poem, making the poem's core something real or tangible through which to distil profound emotions.

This collection's current, assorted and composite nature is also highlighted by the experimental nature of certain poems. From Alex Caldiero's dissection of the language of emotion to Elaine Craig's visual poetry branches to the snaky, chaotic Calvin Olsen—who seems to write as if onboard a capsizing ship—to John Talbot's use of dramatic techniques, the experimentation is blatant. But there is also a subtle overturning of rhythm, rhyming, diction, musical syncopation, irony and images in the other poets gathered here. Lance Larsen is a master of brand-new images. Natasha Loewen explores a wide range of personal metaphors. Tyler Chadwick is to rhythm what Emil Zatopek was to athletics. Helen Walker Jones masters time; Joe Plicka, perspective; Laura Stott, sarcasm; Sally Straford, momentum; Javen Tanner, syntax; Holly Welker, strength; Philip White, rhythm; Sunni Brown Wilkinson, collocation; Darlene Young, symbolism; Danny Nelson, rhyming; Timothy Liu and Shannon Castleton, line-cutting. Music is basic to Michael Hicks' line. Jon Ogden is funky. Michael Collings is able to broadcast static onto the page. Marilyn Bushman-Carlton, Laura Nielson Baxter, Danielle Beazer Dubrasky, Deja Earley, Elizabeth Garcia, David Passey, and Elisa Pulido all slip peculiar voices, tones, or vibrations into their poetry.

As illustrated above, the poets of *Fire in the Pasture* have developed and experiment with techniques and content that both express uniqueness and that tie them to a Mormon foundation as they draw lines to connect outsider and insider perspectives and sources. This tendency to seek interplay with and to establish connections and dialogue among various perspectives and sources—from candid revisions of the pioneering period to the stress put on relationships with nature, with other humans, with God—encompasses the whole collection. This mirrors the ever-present theme of connection in the Mormon religious tradition. And from this exploration of the connections among human beings and between humans and nature, we can draw significant metaphors that complicate the identities and voices of the poets gathered here.

Danielle Beazer Dubrasky frames her family relationships in terms of the desert's beauty. Sarah Dunster links human experience and nature through references to Native-American culture. Aaron Guile's internal rhyming patterns give a rhythm so personal and alluring that the reader is persuaded to follow him in his diving and whale-seeing. Patricia Karamesines is delicious, carnal; she follows the rhythms of nature in pursuit of communion and relief. Karen Kelsay uses stanzaic form to link nature and remembrance. Jim Papworth watches and discerns the flying of birds. Steven Peck is sage from Moab, juncos in winter, a coyote-man mapping a different geography. Laura Stott shares pregnant, colorful images of the Mojave Desert, with a penetrating insight into the ironic sociology of the postmodern migration from Las Vegas to Los Angeles. Holly Welker digs in the soil of her body. Amber Watson states that "we're too made of water" and language is affective water in her poetry. And Warren Hatch offers the beautiful metaphor of grafting. This method of plant propagation where the tissues of one plant are fused with those of another symbolizes the connections among human systems, time, and space that modulate this collection.

Maybe the most complex of these connections is the one between each poet and Mormonism. The Mormonness of these poems is evident in how some poets rely on recurrent topics within Mormon culture or how they develop and revise diverse tenets of the Mormon gospel, such as death, sin, Joseph Smith, pioneering, baptism. Sometimes this means a change in style, in the cadence of language, but I perceive a peculiar approach to these topics, an approach showing personal and dynamic introspection and evaluation rather than exposition. Neil Aitken and Sharlee Mullins Glenn approach death, the first as a personal challenge and as joined to movement and travel, the second, by slipping into sorrow and impotency. With a strong spiritual tone, Mark D. Bennion evokes the distance between living and remembering. Elizabeth Garcia follows a common pattern found in this collection with her musings on original sin, but she does it from the perspective of gender roles. Sarah E. Page turns back to Eve and the apple, but from an uncommon angle. Doug Talley talks about repentance, but he is really saying something else. Alan Rex Mitchell imagines Joseph Smith tending a garden and thinking about the West. Jonathon Penny not only talks about rites and dialogue as a healthy performance of religion, he also reshapes Joseph Smith. Elisa Pulido writes sharply about the Church's pioneering days. Elizabeth Pinborough submerges readers in the volatility of a sensible woman's spiritual experiences. Paul Swenson offers an explicit missionary poem. Sunni Brown Wilkinson writes about grace, Darlene Young, a patriarchal blessing. Laura Hamblin solemnly, but controversially, approaches baptism.

And while all of these poets deal with spirituality, faith or the gospel on different levels and with different objectives, it is always with complexity, a lack of fixation, and as an exercise in paradox. As Scott Cameron says, "truth is not static; it collides." This collision gives *Fire in the Pasture* a superb diversity, and it explains the narrowness of making divisions. As Jonathon Penny says, "This is a rather wretched place, / All things considered: / More paradox than paradise." Paradox dissolves boundaries and contraries; it opens toward possibility and complexity without forcing us to choose between extremes.

N. Colwell Snell speaks about "bottl[ing] words," which is a good metaphor for how desperately we try to catch and retain, evoke and revive experience. But there are things impossible to bottle. You cannot bottle the Missouri River. And you cannot bottle poems. Poems are fluid; they connect, they unify, they prompt discovery. From this collection, I won't keep any bottle, but a string—a "bright string of poems." Not a string to bind with, but through which to telephone dear friends and family with tin can receivers. A tightrope to cross so we might embrace on the other side. A "gossamer" veil strung between "Thee and me," "earth and sky" (as Judith Curtis says) through which each poet in this collection reaches a hand to welcome us into the intimate communion of minds, bodies and souls offered in what Laura Hamblin calls "a room made of poetry."

Contributor Notes

Neil Aitken is the author of *The Lost Country of Sight*, winner of the 2007 Philip Levine Prize for Poetry, and the founding editor of *Boxcar Poetry Review*. His poems have appeared in *Barn Owl Review*, *Crab Orchard Review*, *Ninth Letter*, *Iron Horse Literary Review*, and elsewhere. A former computer programmer, he is presently pursuing a PhD in literature and creative writing at the University of Southern California.

Claire Åkebrand is a Swede who grew up in Germany. She has a BA in English from Brigham Young University and plans on obtaining a PhD in Creative Writing. Claire has the unusual luck of being married to her favorite poet.

Matthew James Babcock teaches composition, literature, and creative writing at BYU–Idaho in Rexburg. He holds a PhD in Literature and Criticism from Indiana University of Pennsylvania. His book, *Private Fire: The Ecopoetry and Prose of Robert Francis*, was published by the University of Delaware Press in 2011. He is a Dorothy Sargent Rosenberg Poetry Prize recipient, and Press 53 chose his novella, *He Wanted to a Be a Cartoonist for The New Yorker*, as one of two first-prize winners in its 2010 Open Awards competition. Among other places, his writing has appeared in *Terrain*, *Spoon River Poetry Anthology*, *The Rejected Quarterly*, *Quiddity*, and *Dispensation: Latter-day Fiction*.

Sometimes **S.P. Bailey** wishes he were an English gentleman some 200 years ago. He would like to spend his mornings with his children and dogs tending to the estate, afternoons reading and writing (and practicing law), evenings by candlelight with his beautiful wife, Andrea, Friday nights dancing at balls he would throw for everyone in the county, and Saturdays shooting things from his horse with Fitzwilliam Darcy, Colonel Brandon, and the rest. Alas, Shawn was born in Utah circa 1976, and he has no estate, horses, or dogs.

Laura Nielson Baxter was born and raised in Utah County and loves the people who live there despite all their quirks. She received her BA in English with emphases in Literary Studies and Creative Writing as well as a degree in Art from Utah Valley University. She has a passion for all things art, enjoys the outdoors, and loves having adventures with the most awesome husband ever invented, Kirk. Laura regularly shares many projects, including her poetry, on her blog, lauranielsonbaxter.blogspot.com.

In 2000, **Mark D. Bennion** graduated with his MFA from the University of Montana. Since that time, he has taught writing and literature courses at Brigham

Young University—Idaho. His poetry has appeared in various journals, including *Aethlon*, *caesura*, *The Comstock Review*, *Irreantum*, and *RHINO*. He is also author of the collection *Psalm & Selah: A Poetic Journey through The Book of Mormon* (Parables Publishing, 2009). In addition to writing poetry, Mark collects baseball cards, plays racquetball nearly every week, and enjoys Korean cuisine. He and his wife, Kristine, are the parents of five children.

James Best lives in Brooklyn, New York, with his wife, Valerie, and their terminally ill bonsai, Moonlight Graham. He attended NYU's MFA in Creative Writing and now writes for television to support his poetry habit. His poems have been published in *RATTLE*, *Paterson Literary Review*, *Cold Mountain Review*, *South Carolina Review*, *Limestone*, and other places. Also, he writes copy for t-shirts for American Eagle and Converse, shoots short films and web series, and publishes humor essays. He has plans to live forever.

Lisa Bickmore's work has appeared in *Quarterly West*, *Tar River Poetry*, *Caketrain*, and elsewhere. Her book, *Haste*, was published by Signature Books in 1994. She teaches writing in Salt Lake City.

Will Bishop was born and raised in Boise, Idaho. After a two-year stint as an LDS missionary in Spain's Canary Islands he earned both a Bachelor's and Master's degree in Humanities from Brigham Young University. He currently lives in Lawrence, KS, where he is working towards a PhD in American Studies from the University of Kansas.

Sara Blaisdell's non-fiction and poetry have appeared in *ZYZZYVA*, *The Chariton Review*, *Literature and Belief*, *The West Wind Review*, *Sophia*, and on public radio's *This American Life*. She works at a dog daycare in Virginia.

Marie Brian lives in Woodland Hills, Utah, with her husband and three kids. She spends her time generating awkward moments with her family, reading low-brow literature, and creating subversive embroidery in the name of her online pseudonym, The Cotton Floozy.

Joanna Brooks grew up in a conservative Mormon home in the orange groves of Orange County, California, during the Cold War. She is now a national voice on Mormon thought, politics, and culture. Her prize-winning poems and essays have appeared in *Dialogue*, *Sunstone*, and other literary journals. For more, visit joannabrooks.org.

Gideon Burton has taught in the English department at BYU since 1994 and has been active in the LDS literary scene, teaching LDS literature, creating the Mormon Literature & Creative Arts database, writing on Mormon film, and promoting the Association for Mormon Letters. For many years he has composed a daily sonnet, many on religious themes. His most recent can be found at OpenSourceSonnets.blogspot.com.

Marilyn Bushman-Carlton has been a Utah Arts Council Artist-in-Residence, UAC Artist Grant recipient, and prize winner in the UAC Original Writing Competition. She is the author of *on keeping things small* (Signature Books, 1995), *Cheat Grass* (Pearle M. Olsen Publication Award, 1999), and *Her Side of It* (Signature Books, 2010). The chapbook version of *Her Side of It* was a finalist in the 2005 Jessie Bryce Niles Chapbook Contest at *The Comstock Review*, and the book received the Association for Mormon Letters' Award for Poetry in 2011. She contributed to *Discoveries: Two Centuries of Poems by Mormon Women* and *To Rejoice as Women: Talks from the 1994 Women's Conference*. Her work has been featured in *Earth's Daughters*, *Ellipsis*, *Exponent II*, and *Iris*, among other periodicals and anthologies.

Polyartist, sonosopher, and scholar of humanities, **Alex Caldiero** makes things that appear as language or images or music, and then again as the shape of your own mind. Caldiero is the author of numerous publications, visual and text-sound works, including *Body / Dreams / Organs* (Elik Press, 2005), *Poetry is Wanted Here!* (Dream Garden Press, 2010), and *Sound Weave*, a poetry-music CD with Theta Naught (Differential Records, 2006). He is featured in *Dictionary of the Avant-Gardes* (Routledge, London/NY) and is the subject of the experimental documentary *The Sonosopher: Caldiero in life . . . in Sound*. Alex is Poet/Artist-in-Residence at Utah Valley University.

In 2009 and 2010, **Scott Cameron** received awards for his poetry from the Dorothy Sargent Rosenberg Poetry Prizes. He received his Ph.D. in English from Boston University and currently teaches English at Brigham Young University—Idaho.

Shannon Castleton has published poems in journals such as *Northwest Review*, *Crab Orchard Review*, *Ellipsis*, and *Literature and Belief*. She has taught writing classes at BYU, Salt Lake Community College, and Westminster College, where she also worked as the advisor to the literary magazine, *Ellipsis*. Currently, Shannon lives in the Philadelphia area with her husband and their four daughters.

Tyler Chadwick lives in Pocatello, Idaho, with his wife, Jessica, and their four daughters. His poems have appeared in *Metaphor*, *Dialogue*, *Irreantum*, *Salome*, *Black Rock & Sage*, *Wilderness Interface Zone*, and *Victorian Violet Press Poetry Journal*. In 2009, he received the Ford Swetnam Poetry Prize and in 2010 he was nominated for a Pushcart Prize.

Ángel Chaparro Sáinz was born in Barakaldo, Spain, in 1976. He holds a degree in English Philology from the University of the Basque Country (Universidad del

País Vasco—Euskal Herriko Unibertsitatea) and he recently received summa cum laude marks from the same university for his dissertation "Contemporary Mormon Literature: Phyllis Barber's Writing." He is presently teaching at the University of the Basque Country. His research deals mostly with Western American Literature, ecocriticism and feminist studies, even though he is also interested in a variety of topics dealing with poetry, popular music and minority literatures.

Elaine Wright Christensen has two collections of poetry: *At the Edges* and *I Have Learned 5 Things*. Her poems have appeared in numerous journals, including *Ensign*, *Weber Studies*, *Ellipsis*, *Dialogue*, *Petroglyphs*, and *The Comstock Review*, where she placed first in the Muriel Craft Bailey Memorial Award judged by Stephen Dobyns. She has also published poems in anthologies, such as *The Cancer Poetry Project*, *Encore* (a collection of prize winning poems for the National Federation of State Poetry Societies), *Discoveries: Two Centuries of Poems by Mormon Women*, and recently, *New Poets of the American West*. She has been nominated for a Pushcart prize. In 2007 she was a finalist in the Utah Arts Literary Contest and was selected for the Bite Size Poet of the Month in November 2010. Elaine received a BA in German and English from Utah State University. Living in Sandy, Utah, she is the mother of five, the grandmother of eleven.

Michael R. Collings, Emeritus Professor of English at Pepperdine University (Malibu, California), has been publishing literary and bibliographic studies; articles, chapters and reviews; novels and short stories; poetry; and other works for over thirty-five years. His academic studies emphasized such writers as Stephen King, Orson Scott Card, Dean R. Koontz, and other science fiction, fantasy, and horror authors—he is considered a leading authority on both King and Card. His creative works similarly address mainstream, science fiction, fantasy, and horror audiences, although several of his novels and volumes of poetry directly explore LDS themes. His twelve-book Renaissance-style epic, *The Nephiad*, is one of a handful of LDS verse epics published over the past century-and-a-half. He is now retired and lives with his wife, Judi, in his native state of Idaho.

Elaine M. Craig enjoys a varied life. In addition to an interest in poetry reading and writing, she has been a thesaurus editor, a professional butterfly catcher, a bike mechanic, and a geologic map colorer. She enjoys singing, catamaran sailing, the outdoors, and making many types of things—although sometimes not dinner. Elaine has several times had the opportunity of collaborating with composer David H. Sargent on solo and choir compositions. Their song cycle, *Notes*, premiered in 2010 and was published by Mormon Artists Group. Elaine and her husband live in Utah; they have three children.

Judith Curtis has English degrees from BYU, Boston University, and completed the Creative Writing Certificate program at Phoenix Community College. In addition to writing poetry, directing memoir groups, and writing stories for her grandchildren, she is a Master Gardener and a volunteer at the Desert Botanical Garden in Phoenix. She has had poems published in *Irreantum*, *Dialogue*, *Segullah*, *Exponent II*, and *Wilderness Interface Zone*; and she participated in the Mormon Women Writers tour in 2010 that was organized by Dr. Joanna Brooks and Dr. Holly Welker. She is currently poetry editor for *Exponent II*.

Melissa Dalton-Bradford resides in Singapore with her husband, Randall, and the two youngest of their four children, Dalton Haakon and Luc William. (Their daughter, Claire, studies at BYU-Provo.) This is the sixth international address she has called home, having lived in Hong Kong, Vienna, Oslo, Paris and Munich. She took a BA in German and an MA in comparative literature from BYU, and taught German, humanities, English and writing at the university level. In addition to serving actively in local church congregations everywhere she's lived (and thereby learning their languages), Melissa has been cataloguing this unusual trajectory in the written word. She is currently expanding her poetry and essay portfolio, (her work can be found in *Segullah* and *Irreantum*), compiling an extensive grief anthology, and completing a memoir on her firstborn, Parker.

William DeFord lives in Grand Junction, Colorado. His poems have been published in *Tar River Poetry* and *Red Rock Review*.

Danielle Beazer Dubrasky has received a Virginia Center for Creative Arts Fellowship. Her manuscript, *Drift Migrations*, was a finalist for the 2010 White Pines Press Poetry Prize. She also received the 2006 Utah Arts Council First Place Award for a book-length collection of poems. Her poetry has been published in *ECOllective*, *Tar River Poetry*, *Weber Studies*, *CityArts*, *Petroglyph*, *Irreantum*, and *Dialogue*. Her publications include *Persephone Awakened* (a poetry chapbook). She teaches creative writing at Southern Utah University.

Sarah Duffy was born in New York City on January 18, 1978. Spending most of her youth between New York and Southern California, she eventually moved to Utah in 1997 and graduated from Brigham Young University with a BA in English in 2011. She currently resides in Provo, Utah, and works for a non-profit organization. Her poetry has appeared in *Inscape* and *Tar River Poetry*. Her favorite poets are constantly changing, but more recently they include Li-Young Lee, Jay Hopler, and Jane Hirshfield—to name a few of many.

Since she was a child, **Sarah Dunster**'s journals have been littered with poems and stories. Literature and writing keep her sane as a stay-at-home mother of many small children. Sarah's poems have been published on *Wilderness Interface Zone*. This spring, her poem, "Three Miles with Ghandi," was awarded an honorable mention in *Segullah*'s spring contests, and her short fiction piece, "Back North," took first place. Sarah loves the association of other LDS writers and artists that she has gained over the last few years.

Deja Earley's poems and essays have previously appeared or are forthcoming in journals like *Arts and Letters, Borderlands*, and *Lilliput Review*, and three of her poems were recently included in *The Southern Poetry Anthology, Volume II: Mississippi*. She has received honors in several writing contests, including the 2008 Joan Johnson Award in poetry, the 2004–2005 Parley A. and Ruth J. Christensen Award, and first place in *Sunstone*'s 2011 Eugene England Memorial Personal Essay Contest. She completed a PhD in English and Creative Writing at the University of Southern Mississippi and moved to the Boston area, where she works as a development editor at Bedford/St Martin's Press.

Simon Peter Eggertsen was born in Kansas, raised in Utah and schooled in Virginia and England; he now lives in Montreal. He has degrees in literature, language and law. His pedigree in poetry is recent. His work has been published, or will be, in *Nimrod, Vallum* (Canada), *Atlanta Review, Dialogue, Irreantum, The Caribbean Writer, New Millennium Writings*, and elsewhere. He has won an International Publishing Prize (Atlanta Review, 2009), been named a finalist for the Pablo Neruda Prize in Poetry (Nimrod International, 2009), was Runner-up for the Little Red Tree International Poetry Prize (2010), and had two poems selected as finalists for the New Millennium Writings Awards #29 (2010).

Kristen Eliason received her MFA from the University of Notre Dame, where she spent an additional year in residence as the 2008 Nicholas Sparks Prize recipient. Kristen's work has appeared in *DIAGRAM, Scrivener Creative Review, Six Little Things, Two Review, Reed Magazine, Makeout Creek, Juked*, and others.

Lisa Ottesen Fillerup lives in Heber Valley, Utah, where she is best known for speeding while delivering hot cinnamon rolls to friends and neighbors. Though she handles a mean red KitchenAid mixer, she also loves to hike, read the funnies, write poems and find treasures at the local thrift store. She and her sculptor husband, Peter, are the parents of six children.

Elizabeth Garcia lives with her husband in Atlanta, Georgia, where she taught Literature and Composition for six years before deciding to write poetry full-time until children come along. Her poems have appeared in *Borderline, Segullah, Eudaimonia Poetry Review*, and *Irreantum*, which nominated her for a Pushcart Prize. She also serves as an Associate Editor for FutureCycle Press, as Assistant Editor for the Georgia Poetry Society's *Reach of Song*, and on the poetry board for *Segullah*.

Sharlee Mullins Glenn is a writer of poetry, essays, short stories, and criticism. Her work has appeared in periodicals as varied as *The Southern Literary Journal*, *BYU Studies*, *Irreantum*, *Segullah*, and *Women's Studies*. She holds a Master's degree in Humanities from Brigham Young University and taught there for a number of years. She is also a nationally published, award-winning author of children's books. Sharlee lives with her husband and children in Pleasant Grove, Utah.

Aaron Guile is the clichéd eternal student, trying to graduate while raising three children alone. He is an English major at Utah Valley University; hopefully he will graduate in 2012 after twenty-five years of trying. He lives in Provo, Utah, with two of his children, a paper-strewn desk, and his beloved, overfilled book-shelf.

Laura Hamblin received her Ph.D. in creative writing/poetry from the University of Denver. She is a full-professor at Utah Valley University where she has received awards including the Faculty Ethics Fellow, the Dean's Faculty Creative Award, and the Faculty Excellence Award. She teaches women's literature, the history and theory of the genre of poetry, composition, and topic classes including seminars on Martin Buber and William Blake. Hamblin is part of the faculty who put together Utah Valley University's new Peace and Justice Studies Program. Her book of poetry, *The Eyes of a Flounder*, was published by Signature Books in 2005. From 2007–08 Hamblin lived in Amman, Jordan, where she gathered oral histories of Iraqi women refugees.

Nicole Hardy is the author of two poetry collections: *This Blonde* and *Mud Flap Girl's XX Guide to Facial Profiling*, which was published as part of *Main Street Rag*'s 2006 Editor's Choice chapbook series. She earned her MFA at the Bennington College Writing Seminars and was nominated for a 2007 Pushcart Prize. Her work has appeared in journals including *Nimrod*, *The Red Wheelbarrow*, and *Meridian Anthology of Contemporary Poetry*, as well as *The New York Times*' "Modern Love" column. Her memoir, *Fallen*, is forthcoming from Hyperion.

Warren Hatch's poetry has been published in *Prairie Schooner*, *Western Humanities Review* and elsewhere. His first collection of poetry, *Mapping the Bones of the World* (2007), is available from Signature Books. Warren teaches technical communication and nature writing at Utah Valley University where he is also Associate Director of the Capitol Reef Field Station.

Michael Hicks is Professor of Music at Brigham Young University. Author of four historical books for University of Illinois Press, he has just completed four years as editor of the journal *American Music*. His poetry has been published in *Dialogue*, *BYU Studies*, *Literature and Belief*, *Sunstone*, and in the recent anthologies *Cadence of Hooves: A Celebration of Horses* and *New Poets of the American West*.

Susan Elizabeth Howe is an associate professor of English at Brigham Young University. She holds a Ph.D. from the University of Denver and an M.A. from the University of Utah. She has directed the BYU Reading Series and been a reviewer and contributing editor for *Tar River Poetry*, the poetry editor of *Dialogue: A Journal of Mormon Thought* and *Literature and Belief*, the managing editor of the *Denver Quarterly*, and the editor of *Exponent II*. Her poems have appeared in *Poetry*, *The New Yorker*, *Shenandoah*, *Southwest Review*, and other journals. Her first collection, *Stone Spirits*, won the publication award of the Redd Center for Western Studies. She co-edited the collection *Discoveries: Two Centuries of Poems by Mormon Women*, which has been released in a second edition. Her next collection, *Woman & Snake*, will be published by Signature Books in 2012. She and her husband, Cless Young, live in Ephraim, Utah.

E.S. (Sarah) Jenkins received her MA in English from Brigham Young University in 2008. After writing a thesis on contemporary American poetry, she turned her attention to writing contemporary American poetry, completing an MFA at Northwestern University in 2011.

President of Utah State Poetry Society 2009–2011, **LaVerna B. Johnson** enjoys sharing poetry and encouraging young poets. She is a co-founder and first president of Redrock Writers (www.redrockwriters.org). She has served as a Utah State Poetry Society board member, president of the Dixie Poets chapter, originator and first director of Poetry In the Park (www.zionpark.org), as editor of the UTSPS publication, *Panorama*, editor of Redrock's Chaparral Poetry Forum, and on the editorial board of Utah Sings. Her work has been published in *Panorama*, *Irreantum*, *Nine One One*, *Encore*, *Utah Sings*, *Heritage Writers Anniversary Book*, *Southern Quill*, online at www.cowboypoetry.com/lavernab, in three chapbooks and numerous newspapers and magazines.

Helen Walker Jones has received the Association for Mormon Letters short story award, *Sunstone*'s annual fiction prize, first-place in the Utah Arts Council fiction competition and *Dialogue*'s fiction prize. A Pushcart Prize nominee and a finalist in the Iowa Short Fiction Contest, she has published in Harper's, *Wisconsin Review*, *Gargoyle*, *Richmond Quarterly*, *Florida Review*, *Indiana Review*, *Chariton Review*, *Cimarron Review*, *Apalachee Quarterly*, *Nebraska Review*, and many others. She and her husband, Walter, live in Salt Lake City.

Patricia Karamesines has won many awards for her poetry, essays, and fiction, including from the University of Arizona, the Utah Arts Council, and the Utah Wilderness Association. She is the author of *The Pictograph Murders* (Signature Books, 2004), which received the Association for Mormon Letters' 2004 Award for the Novel. She writes for the Mormon arts and culture blog, *A Motley Vision* (www.motleyvision.org), and runs the nature writing blog, *Wilderness Interface Zone* (wilderness.motleyvision.org).

Karen Kelsay is a three-time Pushcart Prize nominee and the editor of *Victorian Violet Press*, an online poetry magazine. Her poems have been featured in *The New Formalist*, *The Raintown Review*, *The Flea*, *The Lyric*, *14 by 14*, *The HyperTexts* and *Lucid Rhythms*. She lives with her British husband in Orange County, California.

Lance Larsen is the author of three poetry collections, most recently *Backyard Alchemy*. Recipient of a Pushcart prize and an NEA fellowship in poetry, he teaches at BYU and is married to mixed-media artist Jacqui Biggs Larsen.

Timothy Liu is the author of eight books of poems, most recently *Polytheogamy* and *Bending the Mind around the Dream's Blown Fuse*. He lives in Manhattan.

Natasha Loewen is a mother of four, an English student, and a writer living in Victoria, BC. She has been published in Canadian literary journals and recently won a scholastic award and publication for her poetry. She plans to attend art school one day, and perhaps live as a gypsy, travelling to and also fro, speaking English of all sorts, very mediocre French, and about twenty Italian words.

P.D. Mallamo lives in Kansas City with wife and children, and has just completed a master's degree in exercise physiology at the University of Kansas. He writes the Sunday ward bulletin. Everything else is scribbled in the margins.

Casualene Meyer (Richardson) was born in Seattle and attended BYU (BA, 1991; MA, 1994) and The University of Southern Mississippi (PhD, 1996). Poetry editor for *BYU Studies* and a mother of seven, she lives with her family in Madison, South Dakota.

Alan Rex Mitchell was raised in rural Oregon and educated at Utah State University and the University of California Riverside. His numerous scientific journal articles, reports, and columns have been concerned with theoretical and practical agro-environmental practices. He is recovering from having worked for universities, state, and federal agencies, and is now politically libertarian, culturally omnivorous, and philosophically anti-nihilist. His missionary novel, *Angel of the Danube* (Cedar Fort, 2000), prompted Richard H. Cracroft to call him the Mormon Saul Bellow. In addition to poetry, he has written about religion and economics, and started a publishing company, Greenjacket Books. He lives with his wife and occasional children in the wilderness of Utah's west desert.

Danny Nelson's short stories, columns, and poetry have appeared in publications such as *The Collegiate Post*, *Rio Grande Review*, and *Inscape*. He is a major contributor to *The Fob Bible*, published in 2009 by Peculiar Pages. He lives in Seattle, where he pursues a PhD in English Literature.

Glen Nelson's poetry has predominantly been published in collaboration with composers. He has written three operas with Murray Boren and six song cycles and individual songs set to music by a number of fine-art composers. Four of his poems in this anthology were composed by Boren into a cycle for baritone and piano titled, "Pop Art Songs." In addition to poetry, Nelson is a ghostwriter and editor whose books have appeared repeatedly on *The New York Times*' bestseller list. He owns and operates Mormon Artists Group, a company based in New York City that commissions and publishes work from LDS artists. To date, they have produced 21 projects with 76 Mormon artists in a wide variety of media.

Dave Nielsen was born in Salt Lake City, Utah. He attended BYU, where he received a master's degree in English. Currently, he is a student at the University of Cincinnati, pursuing a PhD in English. He is the brother of poet and essayist, Shannon Castleton, whose work also appears in this anthology.

Marilyn Nielson received the Gordon B. Hinckley Presidential Scholarship from Brigham Young University, and graduated Magna Cum Laude in 2002, with a double major in Music and Home Economics and a minor in English. As a student, she won the Academy of American Poets prize and several other poetry prizes. For her Honors Thesis, she composed a set of Art Songs for soprano and piano, with text by T.S. Eliot. She has won First Place for both Poetry and Personal Essay in the BYU Studies contest, and her poetry and personal essays have been published in, among other publications, *BYU Studies*, *BYU Magazine*, and *Inscape*. She has also been a staff writer for the Spanish Fork News. Marilyn and her husband, Sam, live in South Jordan, Utah, and are the parents of five young children.

Jon Ogden has a master's degree in rhetoric and composition from Brigham Young University. He lives in Provo with his wife and son.

Calvin Olsen received his B.A. in English from Brigham Young University and is now completing his MFA in Poetry at Boston University. He received a 2011 Robert Pinsky Global Fellowship and recently returned from the Iberian Peninsula, where he completed a translation project on the poetry of Alberto de Lacerda. His poetry has appeared in *The Honeyland Review*, *Clarion*, and *SWAMP*. He currently works as an editorial assistant at *AGNI magazine*.

Sarah Elizabeth Page graduated Cum Laude from Brigham Young University in 2007 with a degree in English and an emphasis in creative writing. She is currently pursuing her Masters of Science and Certification in Secondary English at Southern Connecticut State University. When not scribbling novels or taking pictures of the ragged aster and other weeds running rampant in her garden, she enjoys getting lost on long walks in the Naugatuck State Forest.

James (Jim) Papworth teaches at Brigham Young University—Idaho. He helps Anne, who is (at the time of this writing) feverishly trying to finish her dissertation before Christmas 2011, raise their two young sons and a couple of 20-somethings who still find comfort in the nest. Jim loves the outdoors, especially fly fishing and back-packing. He appreciates *Irreantum*, *Perspective*, and *Cold Drill Press* for publishing some of his poems.

David Passey has worked as a lawyer in New York City since 1999. During his undergraduate studies at Brigham Young University, he won BYU's annual poetry contest twice and received a grant from the university for his work as a poet. In 2009 he was the winner of the annual *BYU Studies* poetry contest.

Steven L. Peck works as an associate professor of Biology at Brigham Young University where he teaches the History and Philosophy of Biology. His poetry has appeared in *Dialogue*, *Bellowing Ark*, *BYU Studies*, *Irreantum*, *Red Rock Review*, *Glyphs III*, *Tales of the Talisman*, *Victorian Violet Press Poetry Journal*, and *Wilderness Interface Zone*. His chapbook of poetry, *Flyfishing in Middle Earth*, was published by the American Tolkien Society. In 2011, he was nominated for the Science Fiction Poetry Association's Rhysling Award. He lives in Pleasant Grove, Utah, with his wife, Lori Peck.

Jonathon Penny teaches English literature at UAE University in Al Ain, United Arab Emirates, where he lives with Wendy and their three giant sons. He has only recently started publishing poetry—at *Gangway Magazine*, *Wilderness Interface Zone*, and in *Dialogue*. He is at work on several projects under the nom de plume "Professor Pennywhistle," which he expects will be published soon and to much fanfare and critical acclaim. Samples of that work can be found at professorpennywhistle.wordpress.com.

Elizabeth Pinborough is a BYU alumna and graduated with her master's degree in religion and literature from Yale University in May 2011. Art is her greatest love, and she spends her happiest hours drawing, painting, photographing, and writing creatively. Women's history captivates her, and she comes from a line of strong, faithful women. She is a member of the *Exponent II* staff and is a contributor to the Mormon Women Project.

Joe Plicka is the former editor of *Quarter After Eight*, a journal of innovative prose. His work recently appeared in *Bananafish*, *Anti*, and *Fringe Magazine* and was nominated for a Pushcart Prize. He currently lives and teaches in Athens, Ohio, where he is working on various novels and short fictions.

Elisa Pulido's writing has appeared in numerous journals in the U.S, including, *River Styx, The Ledge, The North American Review, Margie, Another Chicago Magazine, The Tor House Newsletter, The New Guard, Litteral Latté* and *RHINO*. Her work has also appeared in *Interchange* and *The New Welsh Review* in the U.K. She is an honorary member of Academi Cardiff, the national literary society of Wales. She has an MFA in writing from the School of the Art Institute of Chicago and is currently finishing coursework for a doctoral degree in Religions of North America at Claremont Graduate University's School of Religion. In 2010, she participated in "Our Visions, Our Voices: A Mormon Women's Literary Tour," and organized a Religions in Conversation Conference at CGU on the theme, "Poetry and Religion—Finding Religious Realities through Sacred Verse." The conference brought together scholars, poets, and performers of liturgical verse from eight world religions. She has served as a missionary in the Switzerland, Zurich mission and is currently a church service missionary to the San Clemente Stake Singles' Ward.

Will Reger was born and raised in the St. Louis, Missouri area. He began writing poetry in his 7th grade P.E. class to entertain his friends, and then never quite stopped. He later served a mission in Belgium and went on to earn two bachelor's degrees from BYU in Russian Language and Literature and European Studies, followed by a Masters and Ph.D. from the University of Illinois in medieval Russian history. He is currently a professor of history at Illinois State University and the author of several articles on mercenaries, serving also as the editor of the *Military Encyclopedia of Russia and Eurasia*. Despite these distractions, he continues to be devoted to the short story, often scribbling an occasional poem in the margins of his notebooks when the fever comes upon him. He lives in Champaign, Illinois, with his wife, Mary, and their two youngest children.

Jim Richards completed a Ph.D. in literature and creative writing at the University of Houston in 2003 and has since taught at BYU–Idaho. His poems have appeared in *Prairie Schooner, Poet Lore, The Texas Review*, and *Contemporary American Voices*. He currently serves as poetry editor of *Irreantum*.

Casey Jex Smith has shown his work in galleries across the United States. His book *Church Drawings* is available in a limited run from Mormon Artists Group. He is married to the artist Amanda Michelle Smith. Visit him at caseyjexsmith.com.

John W. Schouten is a poet, a novelist, a consumer researcher and a marketing professor at the University of Portland. He has authored two books to date: a textbook, *Sustainable Marketing* (Prentice Hall, 2011), and a novel, *Notes from the Lightning God* (BeWrite Books, 2009).

N. Colwell Snell graduated from the University of Utah with a BA in English. He was named the 2007 Utah State Poetry Society Poet of the Year. His manuscript, *Hand Me My Shadow,* won the 2007 Pearle M. Olsen Book Award, the 2007 City Weekly Arts Award for Best Poetry Collection, and was runner-up in the 2007 Utah Center for the Book award. He was nominated for a Pushcart Prize in 2005, and his poetry won 1st Runner-up in the 2006 William Faulkner-William Wisdom poetry competition. His poetry has been published in *Bay Area Poets' Coalition*, *California Quarterly*, *Comstock Review*, *Weber Studies*, and elsewhere. He lives in Salt Lake City.

Laura Stott grew up in Draper, Utah and currently lives with her husband, Jake, in Los Angeles, California. She attended graduate school at Eastern Washington University in Spokane where she received her MFA in Creative Writing, Poetry. She has been an adjunct instructor at Weber State University for the past six years and has spent most of her summer months in the small town of Skagway, Alaska. Her poetry has been published in various publications. Laura is currently looking to publish her full-length manuscript of poems.

Sally Stratford's poems have been published in *Dialogue* and *Tar River Poetry*. She received her bachelor of arts in English from BYU. She plays guitar and upright bass in a bluegrass band, and is an accomplished fine art and documentary photographer. She lives in Grand Junction, Colorado, with her husband, Willie DeFord, and their two children.

Paul Swenson is a Utah journalist whose writing morphed into poetry in the 1990s under the lingering influence of his sister, May Swenson, one of the most anthologized American poets of the 20th Century. His first poetry collection, *Iced at the Ward/Burned at the Stake*, was published in 2003 by Signature Books. His second, *In Sleep*, is due in Spring 2012 from Dream Garden Press.

John Talbot is the author of two books of poetry, *The Well-Tempered Tantrum* (David Robert Books, 2004) and *Rough Translation* (2012). His poems appear in *Poetry*, *TheYale Review*, *The American Scholar*, *The Iowa Review*, *Literary Imagination*, *The Southern Review*, *Arion*, *Southwest Review*, and many other journals both in America and Britain. His verse translations from Ancient Greek and Latin appear widely, including in a recent Norton anthology of Greek poetry. He writes on poetry and translation for *The New Criterion*, *TheYale Review*, and *TheWeekly Standard*, publishes chapters and articles on Greek, Latin, and English literature in scholarly books and journals, and collaborates in larger projects, such as *The Oxford History of Literary Translation in English* and the forthcoming *Oxford History of Classical Reception in English Literature*, both from Oxford University Press. His third book, a study of English poets' uses of ancient meters, will be published by the London firm Duckworth.

Doug Talley received a BFA in Creative Writing from Bowling Green State University and a JD from the University of Akron. Early in his career he practiced law with a firm in Akron, Ohio, and presently works as an executive in a small consulting company. For several years he edited a poetry column for an on-line publication, *MeridianMagazine.com*. His poems and essays have appeared in various literary journals, including *The American Scholar*, *Christianity and Literature*, and *Irreantum*, and in 2009 his work was nominated for a Pushcart Prize. His poetry collection, *Adam's Dream*, was released in 2011 from Parables Publishing. He and his wife, April, live in Copley, Ohio, where they both continue to write and raise their family.

Javen Tanner's poems have appeared in *Roanoke Review*, *The Midwest Quarterly*, *Southwestern American Literature*, *Dialogue*, *The Raintown Review*, and several other journals and magazines. His chapbook, *Curses for Your Sake*, was published in 2006 by the Mormon Artists Group in New York City. In Manhattan, Javen worked as Associate Artistic Director of Handcart Ensemble, and co-produced and/or acted in Two Yeats Plays: *The Cat and the Moon* and *The Only Jealousy of Emer*, and the New York premiere's of Seamus Heaney's *The Burial at Thebes*, Ted Hughes' translation of *Alcestis*, and Simon Armitage's adaptation of *The Odyssey*. He is currently the Artistic Director of The Sting & Honey Company in Salt Lake City.

Arwen Taylor studies medieval literature and the history of the English language, and spends most of her professional time writing dissertation chapters. She hopes, however, to someday finish grad school and get back to writing unpublishable novels. Her poetry and fiction have appeared previously in *The Fob Bible*.

Amber Smith Watson is a Creative Writing MFA student at Brigham Young University. Her creative work has appeared in *Touchstones*, Utah Valley University's journal of literature and art, and *Cutbank*, the University of Montana's literary journal, and it will appear in *The Normal School* fall 2011. Native to Columbus, Ohio, Amber now lives in Pleasant Grove, Utah, with her husband, Jeff, her children, Elaina and Carter, her dog Copper, and a tank full of fish.

Holly Welker was born and raised in southeastern Arizona, the descendant of dour Mormon pioneers who moved south from the Great Salt Lake Valley shortly after arriving in it. Having relocated to Salt Lake City a few years ago, she is surprised at how much she loves the city. She has an MFA in poetry from the University of Arizona and a PhD in contemporary American literature from the University of Iowa. Her poetry and prose have appeared in such publications as *Alaska Quarterly Review*, *Best American Essays*, *Bitch*, *Black Warrior Review*, *The Cream*

City Review, Dialogue: A Journal of Mormon Thought, Gargoyle, The Guardian, Gulf Coast, Hayden's Ferry Review, Image, The Iowa Review, Iron Horse Literary Review, Other Voices, New York Times, PMS, Poetry International, Poetry Northwest, The Spoon River Poetry Review, Sunstone and TriQuarterly.

Terresa Wellborn is is a bricoleur, librarian, and cartographer of words. She is fond of the color blue, rock gardens, and chocolate chip waffles. She has a BA in English Literature from Brigham Young University and a MLIS degree from San Jose State University. Her writing has appeared in *Segullah* and is forthcoming in *Monsters and Mormons* and *Inscape*. She is writing her way to a book.

Philip White's poems have won a Puschart Prize and have been published in *The New Republic, Slate, Poetry, Ploughshares, AGNI, Poetry Daily*, and elsewhere. His first book, *The Clearing*, won the Walt McDonald prize. He teaches Shakespeare at Centre College in Danville, Kentucky.

Laraine Wilkins prided herself in being an intellectual, gaining a bachelor's and master's degree in German literature from Brigham Young University and doing additional graduate work at Harvard University. She was the editor of the Mormon literary journal *Irreantum* from 2004–2006. Laraine loved writing and spending time in the outdoors, especially the desert. In 2006, at the age of 41, she died in an automobile accident.

Born and raised in Cache Valley, **Sunni Brown Wilkinson** currently teaches English and writing at Weber State University. She received an MFA from Eastern Washington University. Her work has been published in *Red Rock Review, Tar River Poetry, Southern Indiana Review*, and *Weber: The Contemporary West*, among other publications. She lives and gardens in Ogden and loves hiking the trails there with her husband and sons.

Darlene Young has published in *Irreantum, Dialogue, Exponent II, Victorian Violet Press Poetry Journal, Segullah*, and several anthologies. She currently serves as secretary for the Association for Mormon Letters. She lives in South Jordan with her husband and four sons.

Acknowledgments

Neil Aitken. "Pointer," *diode* (May 2009). "Conditional," *ReDactions* 8/9 (2007). "Letter Fifty," *DMQ Review* (2007). "Burials" and "The Art of Forgetting," *The Lost Country of Sight* (Tallahassee, FL: Anhinga Press, 2008). Used with permission of the poet and Anhinga Press.

Claire Åkebrand. "October Plush" and "House," *Splash of Red* (12 Feb. 2010). "Thief in the Night," *Inscape* (Fall 2008). Used with permission of the poet.

Matthew James Babcock. "Moose Remembered," *Terrain* 25 (2010). "The Transient Rains of April Thirteenth," *PANK Magazine* 4.8 (2009). "Daughters and Geese," *Weber Studies* 22.2 (2005). "Jerusalem Artichoke," *Irreantum* 12.1 (2010). "Inch," Winner, Dorothy Sargent Rosenberg Prize, 2008. Used with permission of the poet.

S.P. Bailey. "Reliquary" and "Prayer," *BYU Studies* 45.3 (2006). "Sisyphus" and "Ripple Rock," *Dialogue: A Journal of Mormon Thought* 43.3 (2010). Used with permission of the poet.

Mark D. Bennion. "Our Only Summer in Black Earth, Wisconsin," *Perspective* 1.1 (2001). "Joseph Smith," *BYU Studies* 40.1 (2001). "Dear Father, Love, Abish," "Swollen," and "Triptych," *Psalm & Selah: a Poetic Journey through The Book of Mormon* (Woodsboro, MD: Parables Publishing, 2009). Used with permission of the poet and Parables Publishing.

James Best. "Wayne," *Slipstream* 28 (2008). "Expiration Dates," *Rattle* 30 (Winter 2008). "Contingency #4: White Out," *Dialogue: A Journal of Mormon Thought* 43.2 (2010). Used with permission of the poet.

Lisa Bickmore. "Autumn Sutra," *Sugar House Review* 2 (2010). "Where No One Follows," *Frontiers: A Journal of Women Studies* 22.1 (2001). "Dog Aria," featured in the Utah Arts Council Series of Bite Size Poems (May 2010). Used with permission of the poet.

Will Bishop. "*Moses und Aron*" and "When I Do Go On My Honeymoon," *The Fob Bible* (El Cerrito, CA: Peculiar Pages, 2009). Used with permission of the poet and Peculiar Pages.

Sara Blaisdell. "You Rise from the Exhibit," *The Chariton Review* 30 (2007). "Closer," *West Wind Review* 24. (2005). "Ophelia," *Literature and Belief* 23.2 (2004). Used with permission of the poet.

Marie Brian. "Orisons," *Dialogue: A Journal of Mormon Thought* 39.3 (2006). "Spindrift," *Segullah* 2.1 (Spring 2006). "Pangaea Lost," *Popcorn Popping* (6 Nov. 2006). Used with permission of the poet.

Joanna Brooks. "Invocation/Benediction," *Exponent II* (Dec. 2010). Used with permission of the poet.

Gideon Burton. "I Promise," "Her Fingers Knew the Alphabets of Rain," "Red Wheelbarrow," "Beacon," and "Salt and Blood" are licensed under a Creative Commons Attribution 3.0 Unported License. Feel free to copy, imitate, remix, or redistribute them (just give attribution).

Marilyn Bushman-Carlton. "Goodbye," *BYU Studies* 48.1 (2009). "Nothing We Needed To Know," "Prayer for a Grandchild," "The Smell of a Baby," and "So She Wouldn't Fail," *Her Side of It* (Salt Lake City, UT: Signature Books, 2010). Used with permission of the poet.

Alex Caldiero. "It Occurs To Me," *I Am Not Only: only Bruce Conner did not say this* (Salt Lake City, UT: Alex Caldiero, 2008). "Almost a Song," *Body/Dreams/Organs* (Salt Lake City, UT: Elik Press, 2005). "Love Adoration Amour Devotion," "Keep Listening," and "Analfabetismo," *Poetry is Wanted Here!* (Salt Lake City, UT: Dream Garden Press, 2010). Used with permission of the poet.

Scott Cameron. "We Think We Know the World When We Divide," *Irreantum* 12.2 (2010). Used with permission of the poet.

Shannon Castleton. "Telling My Husband His Death," *Northwest Review* 39.2 (2001). Used with permission of the poet.

Tyler Chadwick. "Fruit," *Dialogue: A Journal of Mormon Thought* 39.2 (2006). "On *Stand of Trees* by J. Kirk Richards," *Wilderness Interface Zone* (29 Oct. 2009). "Two Poems on Fatherhood," *Irreantum* 9.2/10.1 (2007–8). "For the Man in the Red Jacket," *Mormon Artist* C1 (Nov. 2009). Used with permission of the poet.

Elaine Wright Christensen. "Tornado," *The Comstock Review* (Fall 2000), Winner, Muriel Craft Bailey Award. "Sermon on Manchac Swamp," *Encore: Prize Poems of the NFSPS 2000*, ed. Budd Powell (Dallas, TX: Great Impressions, 2000). "Still Life," *The Comstock Review* (Spring 2001). "A Little Night Music," *The Comstock Review* (Fall 2000). Used with permission of the poet.

Michael R. Collings. "For Grace Isabella," *Strong Verse* (28 July 2005). "Pomegranates," *Strong Verse* (7 March 2007). "Damon Again," *Irreantum* 11.1–2 (2009). "At Midnight" and "Cosmology," *In the Void: Poems of Science Fiction, Myth and Fantasy, & Horror* (Rockville, MD: Borgo/Wildside Press, 2009). Used with permission of the poet and Borgo/Wildside Press.

Judith Curtis. "Maybes at Sixty," *Exponent II* (Winter 2003). "Building on Ruins," *Passages: The Maricopa County Community College Creative Writing Competition* (2005–6). "Reflections on Darkness and Light," *Dialogue: A Journal of Mormon Thought* 39.4 (2006). Used with permission of the poet.

Melissa Dalton-Bradford. "Early Harvest," *Segullah* 4.3 (Fall/Winter 2008). "Sailing to Manti," *Segullah* 3.2 (Summer 2007). "Pieta," "Bottled Fruit," and "House for Rent," *Irreantum* 12.2 (2010). Used with permission of the poet.

William DeFord. "St. Teresa of Avila as Middle Manager" and "A Story of Two Raindrops and a Wooden Frame," *Red Rock Review* 15 (Spring 2004). Used with permission of the poet.

Danielle Beazer Dubrasky. "Legacy," *Dialogue: A Journal of Mormon Thought* 37.3–4 (2001). "The Meadow" and "Descent," *Persephone Awakened* (Parowan, UT: Woodhenge Press, 2003). Used with permission of the poet.

Sarah Duffy. "Oceanside," *Tar River Poetry* 48.2 (Spring 2009). Used with permission of the poet.

Sarah Dunster. "Gaius," *Dialogue: A Journal of Mormon Thought* 44.2 (2011). Used with permission of the poet.

Deja Earley. "I Teach Six-Year-Olds about Jesus in Sunday School," *Dialogue: A Journal of Mormon Thought* 40.3 (2007). "In the Hall While They Take Chest X-rays," *Diagram* 10.4 (2010). "The Unfortunate Marriage," *Shampoo* 32 (2008). Used with permission of the poet.

Simon Peter Eggertsen. "Felucca at Maadi," *Irreantum* 12.1 (2010). "poetry on the 'fridge door,'" *Dialogue: A Journal of Mormon Thought* 40.1 (2007). "Lisa Gherardini Might Be Pregnant," *New Millennium Writings* 20 (2010–11). "Twelve Questions in One Long Sentence," *Salt River Review* 11.2 (2008). "Things Missed," *Dialogue: A Journal of Mormon Thought* 43.3 (2010). Used with permission of the poet.

Kristen Eliason. "The User's Guide to Onomatopoetic Elegies," *Juked* (Jan. 2008). "abandonment for two," *The Bend* 4 (2007). "arms upon arms to an earth," *Diagram* 9.1 (2009). Used with permission of the poet.

Lisa Ottesen Fillerup. "To Kent, My Brother," *Irreantum* 3.2 (2001). "The Blue Jacket," *Irreantum* 12.2 (2010). Used with permission of the poet.

Elizabeth Garcia. "Adjusting" and "God as Intern," *Irreantum* 12.2 (2010). "In the Mountains of Gilead: Jephthah's Daughter," *Segullah* 5.1 (2009). "The Semantics of Blessings," *Segullah* 4.2 (2008). Used with permission of the poet.

Sharlee Mullins Glenn. "Raison d'être," *Irreantum* 3.1 (Spring 2001). "Ye Shall Be as the Gods," *Irreantum* 7.3 (2005). "Somewhere," *Segullah* 1.2 (Fall 2005). "Blood and Milk," *The Mother in Me: Real-World Reflections on Growing into Motherhood*, ed. Kathryn Lynard Soper (Salt Lake City, UT: Deseret Book, 2008). Used with permission of the poet.

Aaron Guile. "Tonkas," *Dialogue: A Journal of Mormon Thought* 39.3 (2006). Used with permission of the poet.

Laura Hamblin. "Celibacy at Forty-two (III)," "Red-tailed Outside Scipio," and "To Baptize," *The Eyes of a Flounder* (Salt Lake City, UT: Signature Books, 2005). Used with permission of the poet.

Nicole Hardy. "Mud Flap Girl on Being Hard To Get" and "Mud Flap Girl on Birth and Venus," *Mud Flap Girl's XX Guide to Facial Profiling* (Charlotte, NC: Main Street Rag, 2006). "Living Alone," "Made for TV," and "Lost and Found," *This Blonde* (Charlotte, NC: Main Street Rag, 2009). Used with permission of the poet amd Main Street Rag.

Warren Hatch. "The Fine and Dying Art of Shaping Light into Words," "Northern Cross," and "The Voice of Water Here," *Mapping the Bones of the World* (Salt Lake City, UT: Signature Books, 2007). "Red Shift" and "Sparrows and Boys," *Irreantum* 12.2 (2010). Used with permission of the poet.

Michael Hicks. "Faith Healing" and "Family Tree," *Dialogue: A Journal of Mormon Thought* 38.4 (2005). "Jesus' Final Oration at The Last Supper," *Literature and Belief* 26.1 (2006). "Museum of Ancient Life," *BYU Studies* 43.2 (2004). "Deluge." *BYU Studies* 41.2 (2002). Used with permission of the poet.

E.S. Jenkins. "Weary," *The Fob Bible* (El Cerrito, CA: Peculiar Pages, 2009). Used with permission of the poet and Peculiar Pages.

LaVerna B. Johnson. "Tonight You Died," *Panorama* 19.1 (May 2000). "Oleander Snow from Yucca Flat," *Encore: Prize Poems of the NFSPS 2009,* ed. Valerie Martin Bailey (San Antonio, TX: NFSPS, 2009). "Memorial Service," *Panorama* 26.1 (May 2007). Used with permission of the poet.

Helen Walker Jones. "The Holding Room," "Guest Room," and "Sheep Ranch Near Hillspring," *Dialogue: A Journal of Mormon Thought* 39.1 (2006). "The Accompanist," *Timber Creek Review* 9.2 (2003). "Restaurant in Naples," *Timber Creek Review* 8.3 (2002). Used with permission of the poet.

Patricia Karamesines. "The Pear Tree," *Victorian Violet Press Poetry Journal* 3 (2010). "Glaucus," *Dialogue: A Journal of Mormon Thought* 41.3 (2008). "The Orchid

Grower," *Dialogue: A Journal of Mormon Thought* 38.4 (2005). "The Peach," *Dialogue: A Journal of Mormon Thought* 38.3 (2005). Used with permission of the poet.

Karen Kelsay. "In Spite of Her," *In Spite of Her* (Flutter Press, 2010). Used with permission of the poet and Flutter Press.

Lance Larsen. "Vineyard," *In All Their Animal Brilliance* (Tampa, FL: The University of Tampa Press, 2005). "To the Lost One-third," *Backyard Alchemy* (Tampa, FL: The University of Tampa Press, 2005). "Why Do You Keep Putting Animals in Your Poems?" *The Best American Poetry 2009*, eds. David Wagoner and David Lehman (New York City: Scribner Poetry, 2009). "To the Ode," *Prairie Schooner* 83.4 (2009). Portions of "Backyard Georgics" were published in *Poetry* (November 2010). Used with permission of the poet and The University of Tampa Press.

Timothy Liu. "The Model," *For Dust Thou Art* (Carbondale, IL: Southern Illinois University Press, 2005). "Elegy for a Poet Whose Books I Didn't Think Were Worth Re-Reading, Not Until Now," *AGNI Online* (2010). "Sunnyside Road," *AGNI Online* (2008). "Next Day," *Shampoo* 4 (2001). Used with permission of the poet and Southern Illinois University Press.

P.D. Mallamo. "Salt Lake City cemetery, Jewish Section," *Dialogue: A Journal of Mormon Thought* 41.4 (2008). "Oz Chronicle #3" and "Oz Chronicle #4," *Otoliths: A Magazine of Many E-Things* 16 (2010). Used with permission of the poet.

Casualene Meyer. "Earth Writing," *BYU Studies* 39.1 (2000). Used with permission of the poet.

Alan Rex Mitchell. "Road to Carthage Sonnet," "Joseph's Soliloquy," and "Stephen Markham's Complaint," *The Road to Carthage* (Vernon, UT: Greenjacket Books, 2010). Used with permission of the poet.

Danny Nelson. "The Short Books" and "Jacob to Esau," *The Fob Bible* (El Cerrito, CA: Peculiar Pages), 2009. Used with permission of the poet and Peculiar Pages.

David Nielsen. "Internship at a Large Firm," *Tar River Poetry* 44.2 (2005). "My Daughter's Favorite Bedtime Story" and "Working a Turkey Pen," *Willow Springs* 57 (2006). "To Rosie, Not Yet Three," *Garbanzo!* 6 (2009). "After This Life," *The Cream City Review* 28.2 (2004).

Marilyn Nielson. "Marie Curie, Dying," *Inscape* (2002). "After Eden." *BYU Studies* 41.2 (2002). "Sheep," *BYU Studies* 44.2 (2005). Used with permission of the poet.

Jon Ogden. "Creationism: Five Theories," *Inscape* (Fall 2006). "Prayer Cap," *Inscape* (Winter 2006). "Benediction," *Folio* (Spring 2010). Used with permission of the poet.

Sarah E. Page. "Coring the Apple," *Mormon Artist* C1 (Nov. 2009). Used with permission of the poet.

Jim Papworth. "Postcard" and "Above Henry's Lake: Mid-November," *Perspective* 3.1 (2003). "Above the Aspen," *Perspective* 6.2 (2006). "Welder: Falling," *Irreantum* 12.1 (2010). Used with permission of the poet.

David Passey. "City Dog," *BYU Studies* 49.4 (2010). Used with permission of the poet.

Steven L. Peck. "Sage," *Red Rock Review* 22 (Spring 2008). "Winter Gifts," *Victorian Violet Press Poetry Journal* 5 (2010). "The Slaying of the Trickster God," *Wilderness Interface Zone* (17 Nov. 2010). Used with permission of the poet.

Jonathon Penny. "The Soil's the Earth's Best Mother," *Wilderness Interface Zone* (11 Jan. 2011). "Thorns and Thistles and Briars," *Wilderness Interface Zone* (28 Mar. 2011). Used with permission of the poet.

Elizabeth Pinborough. "A Sister Shaker's Hymnal," *Dialogue: A Journal of Mormon Thought* 42.2 (2009). Used with permission of the poet.

Joe Plicka. "True Love," *Inscape* (Winter 2006). "hymn to a thing that I knew and still know to some degree," *Anti-poetry* 4 (2009). Used with permission of the poet.

Elisa Pulido. "Dog Walking at Night in a New Neighborhood," *Zocalo Public Square* (19 April 2010). "On the Mormon Trail, June 1848," *Tor House Newsletter* (Winter 2008). "Herman and Laurie in Retrospect," *The New Guard* 1 (2011). "Revelation," *National Writers Union, Chapter 7* (2006). Used with permission of the poet.

Jim Richards. "Cleave," *Literature and Belief* 23.1 (2003). "A Few Questions—Involving Pears—for My Newborn Son," *BYU Studies* 39.1 (2000). "To a Pear" and "Some," *Meridian Magazine Online* (2003). "Blind Man to the Healer," *Perspective* 5.2 (2005). Used with permission of the poet.

John W. Schouten. "Runaway" and "Dead Horse Point," *Consumption Markets and Culture* 12.4 (2009). "I Dream of Lima," *Consumption Markets and Culture* 10.4 (2007). "The Dogs of Juxtlahuaca" and "The Spider Woman of Teotitlán," *Consumption Markets and Culture* 6.2 (2003). Used with permission of the poet.

N. Colwell Snell. "Vienna 1965," *Weber Studies* 23.3 (2007). "Wild Asparagus," *California Quarterly* 26.4 (2000) and *Oasis Journal* (2004). "Withdrawal," *Encore:*

Prize Poems of the NFSPS 2001, ed. Budd Powell (Dallas, TX: Great Impressions, 2001). "Run Sheep Run," Finalist, 2005 Faulkner-Wisdom Poetry Competition. Used with permission of the poet.

Laura Stott. "The Fall," *Weber Studies* 22.1 (2004). "Blue City of Rajasthan" and "Across the Mojave Desert," *Literature and Belief* 31.1 (2011). "Ganpati Guest House," *ReDactions* 12 (2009). "The Girl with No Hands," *Eclipse* 21 (2010). Used with permission of the poet.

Sally Stratford. "Inheritance" and "The Right Place," *Dialogue: A Journal of Mormon Thought* 36.3 (2003). "Mukuntaweep" and "Distance," *Tar River Poetry* 40.1 (2000). "The Empty Cistern," *Dialogue: A Journal of Mormon Thought* 36.1 (2003). Used with permission of the poet.

Paul Swenson. "Passion Play" and "Holy Mary, Mother of God," *Iced at the Ward, Burned at the Stake* (Salt Lake City, UT: Signature Books, 2003). Used with permission of the poet.

John Talbot. "Middlesex Eclogues: March," *Atlanta Review* 13.1 (2006), as "III (from *Middlesex Calendar*)." "Nightjar," *The Yale Review* (Forthcoming). "After the Latin," *The New Criterion*. "An Expulsion Eclogue," *Literary Imagination* 12.1 (2010), as "Eclogue I: Virgil." Used with permission of the poet.

Doug Talley. "Finding Place," *Irreantum* 11.1–2 (2009). "Call to Repentance," *Ancient Paths* 14 (2007). "Parable for the Pulse of the Wrist," *Meridian Magazine Online* (January 2005). "Confession of the Sometime Lost," *Literature and Belief* 23.2 (2003), as "Confession." "Devotion to the Inexplicable," *Bellowing Ark* 25.5 (2009). Used with permission of the poet.

Javen Tanner. "Eden," "Two for Samuel Beckett," "Snow," and "Sudden Music," *Curses For Your Sake* (New York City: Mormon Artists Group, 2006). Used with permission of the poet.

Arwen Taylor. "Capitulation: Forbidden Squirming" and "*Lingua Doctrinae*," *The Fob Bible* (El Cerrito, CA: Peculiar Pages, 2009). Used with permission of the poet and Peculiar Pages.

Holly Welker. "Dig," *Dialogue: A Journal of Mormon Thought* 34.3–4 (2001). "Last Night's Fire," *Image: Art, Faith, Mystery* 64 (2009–10). "The Anvil of Desire," *Literature and Belief* 26.1 (2006). "Vertigo First Thing in the Morning," *The Cream City Review* 28.2 (2004). "Self-Portrait as Burnt Offering," *Dialogue: A Journal of Mormon Thought* 42.4 (2009). Used with permission of the poet.

Philip White. "A Moment Ago," *Slate* (31 Oct. 2006). "All That Time," *Ploughshares* 36.4 (2010–11). "The River," *The Cincinnati Review* 5.1 (2008). Used with permission of the poet.

Laraine Wilkins. "Breaking Bread above the Waters," "Make Yourself at Home," and "How Long," *Weber Studies* 17.3 (2000). "Soul Retrieval," *Irreantum* 8.1 (2006). Used with permission of Lena Schoemaker, the poet's daughter.

Sunni Brown Wilkinson. "Acrobats," *Weber: The Contemporary West* 25.2 (2009). "Some News about the Soul," *Exponent II* 27.3 (2005). "Wake," *Weber Studies* 22.3 (2006). "Some Kind of Beginning," *Dialogue: A Journal of Mormon Thought* 42.2 (2009). Used with permission of the poet.

Darlene Young. "Patriarchal Blessing," *Dialogue: A Journal of Mormon Thought* 40.4 (2007). "Postpartum" and "How Long?" *Irreantum* 9.2 (2007). "Angels of Mercy," *Segullah* 3.1 (Spring 2007). "Washing Mother," *Dialogue: A Journal of Mormon Thought* 39.3 (2006). Used with permission of the poet.

Index of Other Mormon Poets

The following list includes names of people associated with Mormonism who have published poems in various places since 2000. It is by no means a comprehensive list; but, when taken with the names of the poets published in *Fire in the Pasture*, it represents an expansive index of published Mormon poets.

CPSIA information can be obtained at www.ICGtesting.com
Printed in the USA
LVOW081821080313

323402LV00008B/818/P

lowed all high school and College sports. I remember receiving a pair of track shoes for my birthday when I was fifteen, a subtle hint from Dad. I was never really gifted as an athlete. The next gift I remember from Dad was when I graduated high school. He gave me a twenty-dollar bill and a suit case—another subtle hint.

From there, I attended Utah State University, majoring in education. I attended fall quarter at USU before leaving for Fort Ord California for my six months active duty serving in the National Guard. I returned to Milford after my six months of training and was looking for a job. I found work at Bryce Canyon National Park working as a dishwasher in the Bryce Canyon Inn. Bryce Canyon became my favorite place in the world. I spent ten summers at Bryce Canyon working in every capacity. I worked as a bus boy in the dining room, prep cook in the pantry, bell hop, bell captain, dining room manager, assistant manager of the lodge, and finally three summers as the lodge manager. The lodge employed about 120 people for the summer months, opening in early June and closing shortly after Labor Day. Wages were low due to the fact that meals and lodging were provided to the employees as part of the contract. Most of the employees supplemented their wages by earning tips. Tips were pretty good. Working as a bell boy, we were paid thirty-two cents and hour, because the company had to match the wages of a like position in the county. There were no other bell boys in the county so they could pay us whatever they determined. We made up for the low wages by making good money in tips.

Bryce Lodge Employees, 1971

State Show

Bell Boys

As employees of the Lodge, everyone was expected to participate in the evening entertainment. The Lodge employed a program manager who directed several shows that included *Girls, Girls, Girls, State Show, Vaudeville*, and a variety show. These shows played nightly in rotation, so that each one was performed twice a week. We had great fun entertaining the dudes (as we referred to the guests). State Show was by far the best program we performed. It's a song-and-dance routine about the states in the U.S., written by Mirriam Stallings. We received a standing ovation every time we performed State Show. In addition to the employee shows, we were expected to participate in "sing-a-way" every morning when the tour buses were loaded and ready to depart the lodge. All of the lodge employees would gather on the front porch and sing to the dudes. Sing-a-way would sometimes culminate in what we called "kiss-a-way," when one of the employees was returning home after the summer season was ending.

We hold a Bryce reunion every five years, and have done so since the 1980s. We always perform State Show as the culminating activity of the reunion. Our last reunion was held in 2015; we had more than eighty former employees in attendance. We performed State Show again with some minor modifications of the dance steps due to the aging condition of the performers.

Bryce Canyon was the meeting place for many budding romances. Many of the employees found their soul mate working at the inn or lodge and later were married. It is amazing how the couples now have sons with the first name of Bryce.

I received my bachelor's degree from Southern Utah State College (now Southern Utah University) in June of 1970. I went back to Bryce Canyon for the third year as the manager of the lodge. Because I graduated with a secondary teaching endorsement, I was looking for a teaching job when I went to Bryce. Oddly enough, there was a glut of teachers graduating that year in education, and my majors, psychology and sociology, were not highly sought after. So in the back of my mind there was, "What if I don't get a teaching job?"

So I started work at Bryce Canyon, thinking that I had a few months to sort out my options. It was a great summer. Many of my dear friends were returning to Bryce. I was 24 years old, unattached, and had much going for me.

Early in August, I met a couple who worked at a small private college located in Sherman, Texas, just south of the Oklahoma border. Austin College was a prestigious school with an enrollment of about 1,200. It was a Presbyterian school and ranked very high in its academic standing. Tony Weight was the dean of students at Austin College and told me about an opening at a men's dormitory for the director of Dean Hall. It paid about $400.00 a month plus room and board. She asked me if I was interested in applying for the position. It took me about ten seconds to answer in the affirmative.

Two weeks later, I found myself sitting in the airport in Las Vegas in 100-degree-plus weather waiting for a flight to Dallas, Texas. I was pretty nervous and had no idea how to prepare for the upcoming interview.

Tony and her husband Shirl met my plane in Dallas and drove me the fifty miles to Sherman for the interview. There were five staff members who interviewed me for the position. Mr. Stanley Cobb was directing the interview as he was head of the housing department for the college. I guess I must have made a good impression, because they offered me the job before I departed to catch my plane back to Las Vegas.

I finished my contract at Bryce Canyon, and reported for my new job right after Labor Day. I loaded everything I owned in my black 1967 Mercury Cougar and headed off for a new adventure some 1,200 miles away.

Austin College was a great experience. I was the head resident in a dormitory with 400 male students, mostly freshmen. The majority were rich kids who'd attended private boarding schools for most of their lives. They all drove fancy cars and had trust funds that would choke a horse. They'd learned every trick in the book, and re-wrote the ones that didn't exist. I can't remember ever getting a full night of sleep. I had trouble with understanding the terminology used by the "Texans." For instance, they would always say things like, "I'm fixin' to carry Tom over to the Ad building." I'd respond with, "You don't have to carry me; I can walk." Then there was the sir thing. They always called me sir. I was only a few years older than most of them, and didn't think I deserved that kind of respect. When I would go to the service station to get gas, the attendant would always ask, "Do you want me check your all?" I would answer, "What's my all? Then I'd get this look like, "Are you from this planet?" So finally the dorm residents gave me a Texas Dictionary. That sort of solved the problem.

The big mistake I made at the beginning of the school year was to tell the dorm residents that I was their new mother. Of course, from that day until I left, I was Mother Tom. At the end of the school year they gave me a pen that had Mother Tom engraved on it.

The school year moved along rapidly, and soon I found myself looking at January term. January term was unique in that students took only one class. It was all day, every day for the entire month of January. Many students left campus to study abroad such topics as Medieval Art, Witchcraft, Scuba Diving, or some other exotic subject. I was chosen to teach a course in operant conditioning in white rats because of my background in experimental psychology. The class was small and consisted of only ten students. We used a paperback text on operant conditioning. It was very interesting and rewarding to everyone except the rats. As I recall, some of the rats were very hard to train and learned bad behaviors because of student mistakes. Some of the problems resulted in rats that were very resistant to extinction, because the new behaviors they learned were very rewarding, such as self stimulation. When the class ended, I was told to gas the rats and put them down the garbage disposal. It was such a waste of talented rats who could press a bar for food using many different schedules of reinforcement.

Before School ended in Mid-May, I was asked to renew my contract with the option of working on a master's degree at no cost to me. It was very tempting, but I opted not to return the following year and take my chances at finding a teaching job in Utah. I had a couple of other offers from the private sector from fathers of the students who attended Austin College. They too were very tempting, but I couldn't wait to get back home in Utah.

CHAPTER TWO
MOVING FORWARD

I returned to Bryce Canyon that summer where I felt comfortable and at home among the great Ponderosa Pines with the faint scent of vanilla coming from their core. Again, it was a wonderful summer at Bryce, but many of my friends had moved on and had started their career somewhere, and Bryce Canyon wasn't a part of their life anymore.

My opportunity came in the middle of September of 1971 when my college advisor called me and told me about a teaching job in the field of special education in Cedar City. Congress had recently passed Public Law 94-142, which required school districts to provide education for students with disabilities. The five-county association of governments in Southwest Utah submitted a proposal to form a class for students with severe disabilities and house them in the old nursing home located next to the old hospital in the heart of Cedar City. The students came from towns within the five counties. They were brought to the group home on Sunday afternoon by their parents, and the kids remained there until Friday afternoon, returning home for the weekend. The house parents were a young couple attending the university and majoring in psychology. This pilot program operated successfully for four years. Because there was pressure on local school districts to provide better services locally, the students were served in their home districts, and the program was discontinued. I stayed on as the special education teacher in Iron County.

While in my senior year at SUSC, I did a practicum working with three students with disabilities in a pilot program housed on the campus. Several psychology students were involved in the program, offering an opportunity to practice some of the techniques we learned in the academic and lab courses. I especially liked working with one of the students in the program. Lisa was a student with severe autism. She provided me with some interesting insight and experience. It was because of this experience that my college advisor, Dr. Kupfer, thought I might be a good candidate for the job.

I drove to Cedar City for the interview, again not knowing how to prepare for questions I might be expected to field. I met with Dr. Morris, the Iron County School District Superintendent, and Dr. Forsythe, the elementary Director who explained to me the details of the job for which I was applying. Since this was plowing new ground, neither of them could give me much information or a job description. I'm sure I was the only candidate applying for the position, because they called and offered me the job before I arrived home from the interview.

I started on an entirely new career on October 1, 1971. My classroom was located in the old junior high school in the heart of Cedar City. My classroom just happened to be the same classroom where I attended second grade years earlier with my favorite teacher, Mrs. Brown, who inspired me to become a teacher in the first place. When I attended school there, it was the old West Elementary School.

I was given a few days to gather materials, furnishings, and work on curriculum. What curriculum? There was no curriculum. Plowing new ground provided me with the opportunity to create my own curriculum. Part of the collaboration that proceeded the decision to form a classroom for students with disabilities involved the psychology department at the university. Because the classroom would provide great opportunities for budding psychologists, several practicum classes were being offered as part of the college curriculum. This meant that I would have upwards of twelve college students helping me every day to do something none of us knew anything about. In addition, I was given a full-time teaching assistant to help in the classroom. Luckily, Arlene had prior experience working with students with disabilities. She had worked in a special school located in Salt Lake City.

As soon as we could, Arlene and I arranged a trip to Salt Lake to visit with teachers and administrators about curriculum and classroom management. We spent two days making copies of everything we could get our hands on, and making notes on what we couldn't copy.

Our class consisted of twelve students ranging in age from five to twenty-two. Lisa and Krissy were from Milford. Krissy had Down syndrome and was a delight. She was well-mannered and eager to learn. Lisa was one of the students I worked with in my psychology practicum. She had many behaviors that required extensive shaping. Curtis, Jodie, and Robert came from Tropic, a small town in Garfield County. All three had delays in learning and had never attended school. All three advanced well in a structured environment. Tammi was from Kanab, located in Kane County, and had Down syndrome. She had attended public school where she was basically tended to and had little formal instruction. Kelly came from Hurricane, in Washington County. He had Down syndrome and suffered with several medical conditions. Susan and Brooks were from Parowan in Iron County. Susan had Down syndrome and was also diabetic. Brooks was brain damaged and had attended public school in Parowan. Scott, Tamra, and Alan lived in Cedar City. Scott was intellectually disabled, as was Alan. Tamra was autistic.

We were off and running. Every day was a great adventure, and most of those adventures I'd rather not have again. How do you plan curriculum for students ranging from ages five to twenty-two, with disabilities ranging from severe autism to mild developmental delays?

Our classroom was located on 300 West and Center Street in Cedar City. The room was one that had been used for storage and hadn't been occupied for several years. It was basically a box with no storage, no outside door, just a bank of windows on one side and chalk boards on the other walls. The heating system was radiators under the windows. It was freezing cold or extremely hot, and generally nothing in between. The restrooms were way down the hall. We had to share them with the junior high students, who were always mouthy and rude when we took our kids to the restroom. Many times we were interrupted when junior high students would open the door and yell "retard," and running away. We could expect it during the class change every hour.

We ate lunch in the old lunchroom downstairs affectionately referred to as the dungeon. It was in the basement where there were no windows, and it was always dark and smelly. We got some pretty funny looks when we graced the lunchroom with our band of misfits. But the lunch ladies liked us, so it didn't matter.

Each week, we held a lengthy staff meeting with university professors, college students, and me. We discussed everything from behavior modification to toilet training, and everything in between. Usually we got bogged down with discipline and how to chart behaviors we'd never seen before. Just imagine six college students taking data on one autistic student who has a fetish for purses and flips out every time a woman enters the room carrying a purse. We tried many approaches to extinguish that behavior. We used a purse for reinforcement for good behavior. We went to the local thrift store and bought all of the purses we could find. We put them in a corner, and when Lisa worked extra hard, we would give her time with the purses. Her eyes would roll back and she would be trancelike as she felt the texture of each purse. One day, Mrs. Chatterly, a third grade teacher, walked through our room and was attacked by Lisa. She grabbed Mrs. Chatterly's purse and ran to the corner. We had to do some negotiating with Lisa to get the purse back. We also spent a great deal of time helping Lisa use a fork and spoon in the lunchroom. She ate everything with her hands. We finally shaped her behavior enough that she would eat mashed potatoes with a spoon or fork. Then when we told her to eat the carrot and celery sticks with her hands, she looked at us like we were nuts. *One Flew Over the Cuckoo's Nest* looked like a fairy tale.

There were days when I wondered if these kids went home and plotted against us. I can imagine their secret meetings cooking up some new way to shock and terrify us. We developed a token economy in the classroom and used poker chips to reinforce good behavior and task completion. We kept the tokens in metal cans that were attached to a board. As we dropped the tokens in the can, we made sure there was an audible sound to reinforce the positive behavior that earned the token. The students loved collecting the tokens each day. We kept a log of tokens earned and emptied the cans each day to prevent stealing. On Fridays, we counted the tokens right before lunch. Those students who had earned twenty-five or more tokens were rewarded with the privilege of going to the college pool to swim for the afternoon. Those who had not earned enough tokens had to go to the pool and watch, rather than swim. It was amazing how hard the kids worked on Fridays if they didn't have enough tokens to swim.

The pool provided some great opportunities for physical exercise, and also some situations that were hysterical. I remember one time when Emery hadn't earned enough tokens to swim. We were in the pool and looked up to see a naked blimp running from the dressing room and jumping in the pool. Emery was fifteen years old with Down syndrome and weighed 250 pounds. He couldn't stand sitting on the bench watching. It was really fun to gather him up and get him back to the dressing room trying to cover him up with a towel.

Another time, I remember when Susan wasn't swimming because she wasn't feeling well. She was sitting in the observation area watching. The observation area was located in a balcony on the east side of the pool. She was trying to get my attention, and I didn't see her. She kept leaning over the balcony, waving her arms and yelling. She leaned over too far and fell to the pool deck, breaking both legs. It was about the twentieth of December and it was freezing cold outside. We called an ambulance, and in the excitement of getting Susan stabilized and loaded in the ambulance, I didn't have an opportunity to put on any clothing. I ended up riding in the ambulance to the hospital in my swimming suit. When we arrived at the emergency room, you can imagine the look on the faces of the hospital personnel when we came wheeling Susan in and me half naked. She ended up in a body cast and missed about six months of school. Her situation was complicated, as she was a diabetic and needed constant care. She had to be monitored all the time because she was also double jointed and kept trying to wiggle out of the cast.

Speaking of the swimming pool. It was spring, and the weather was nice. We were at the pool, and some of the college girls and instructors were laying out on the pavement outside the pool. I was talking with them through the glass. They said to me "Why don't you come out?" I asked them how to get there, and they told me to go through the girls' dressing room. I told them I couldn't do that. They said that nobody was in there and that their girls were in the pool. So I went in the girls' dressing room. When I rounded the corner, I met a college girl coming out of the shower. She just happened to be one of our college helpers. I quickly made an exit. The next time I saw her, I was so embarrassed that I didn't know what to say. So I quickly said the first thing that came to mind. "You look different in clothes." She wasn't impressed.

Every time I had a question about curriculum or core standards, I would go to the district office and ask for some help. Most of the time, I got the same answer: "We don't have a clue, buddy; you're on your own." I did get some help from the regional special education consultant, Creig Ingram. He was good to find curriculum for me and direct me to resources relating to developmental delays and behavior. Creig also planted the seeds for our involvement in the Special Olympics.

CHAPTER THREE
MOVING RIGHT ALONG

We had such a successful first year as a new special ed unit that we were re-warded with a real classroom at the South Elementary School. The room had everything that was lacking at the previous school, including younger students who didn't make fun of us. Our classroom was located in the lower west wing of the school next to Jean Moore and her special ed class who were classified as EMR (Educable Mentally Retarded). My students were classified as TMR (Trainable Mentally Retarded). The EMR students were higher functioning. These classifications were changed later to Intellectually Handicapped and

Learning Disabled. Jean and I became fast friends and did a great deal of team teaching. She loved to teach art, reading, and social studies. I loved to teach P.E. and anything that was active. So we grouped all of the students and taught to our strengths.

Linda Wilson was a new kindergarten teacher who taught across the patio from us, and we did a lot of activities with her class trying to develop some interactions with normal functioning students. The kindergarten students were perfect because they weren't conditioned to biases and didn't think our kids were weird. It was fun to see how those young students bonded with our much larger and strange-acting students.

Linda was expecting her first child, and we spent a lot of time teasing her. One day, she wore a dress that had a pleated skirt. Jean lovingly referred to her as "cupcake," and that became her new nickname.

Linda was always nagging at me for not wearing a tie to school. I tried it a few times but had a rough time of it because the kids always tried to swing on it and choke the life out of me, or I would dip it in the paint or glue or something. One day, Linda made a hideous-looking tie out of paper and sent one of her students to give it to me to wear. Attached to the tie was a note that said, "You look terrible. Wear this." We had a program in the gym that day, and when we all brought our classes for the program, we saw the principal, Mr. Adams, wearing the paper tie. He always wore a black bowtie, and that day he wore the new paper tie in addition to the bowtie to the program. When Linda saw him wearing the tie, she was horrified and went to the student who was supposed to give the tie to me. She asked him if he had given the tie to Mr. Walker. He said "Yes, I gave the tie to Mr. Walker, and he's wearing it now."

Linda asked, "What did you say to him when you gave him the tie?"

He said, "Mrs. Wilson said you look awful and she wants you to wear this tie." Of course, Linda was horrified. And guess who got the last laugh?

Linda and Jean were always trying to line me up with a date because they thought they were better at picking out women for me to go out with than I was. They went so far as placing an ad in the local newspaper trying to give me some women to date. They gave all of my qualifications, including the fact that I drove a 260Z sports car. The ad ran for about a week, and I had several phone calls. Mr. Adams heard about the ad and came to ask me about it. Of course I didn't know anything about it, and he immediately knew the source of the ad. He spoke to Jean and Linda and said, "That's one strike."

It seems like Linda, Jean and I were always in hot water because we continually had something going on around the school. That year, when I came to work on my birthday, I found that my office and all of my teaching curriculum had been cleaned out. I had nothing to teach with that day. I was panicked and didn't know what I was going to do. Then I had a great thought—I decided that I would take my students to each classroom and drop them off one by one, letting the teacher know that they could have them in their classroom until I got my furniture and teaching materials back. It was amazing how quickly I had things returned to me. I think I even got things that weren't mine.

When Halloween came around, the students were all excited and wanted to dress up along with all of the other kids in the school. On Halloween Day, we always had a parade through the school and walked through every classroom. When the parade came to our classroom, we joined in at the end of the parade, and the kids were really excited.

Emery didn't have a costume, so we went to the school kitchen and gathered up an apron, chef hat, rolling pin, and potato masher. He went as the Pillsbury Doughboy. When we came to a fourth grade classroom and paraded through, the teacher, Mr. Ence, started to laugh at Emery's costume. Emery took offense to his laughter and cooled him with the rolling pin. Another year at Halloween, we all dressed up as Ghengis Kahn and the Mongoloids.

That night, I took the class trick-or-treating through the neighborhood near the group home because all of my students were away from home. We had a great time until we came to a house where an older woman lived. She was happy to see us and gave everyone candy. She would say, "One for you and one for you and one for you," and when she came to me, she said, "And one for daddy." Talk about offended. Here I was, twenty-four years old, unmarried, and with twelve kids ranging in age from five to fifteen. The woman must have been blind or thought I was a real mover.

That year, we added some new students: Jeffery, a boy with Down syndrome, aged fourteen, Kelly, another boy with Down syndrome, aged eight, and Rosie, a delightful seven-year-old Native American girl with autism.

Jeffery was really into hand flapping and spinning on the floor. He'd developed self-stimulating behaviors that were extremely hard to extinguish. We tried to teach him by replacing the flapping with acceptable behaviors. He would get wound up and spin on the floor while yelling hallelujah over and over again. One time I took him to the bathroom and put him on the toilet. I went back to the classroom to check on the other kids and got distracted. When I returned to the bathroom about twenty minutes later, he was just sitting there with fifty yards of toilet paper unwound from the roll, waving it back and forth in a trance and singing hallelujah. He was very good at getting up and running away from the classroom. He would gallop all over the school with one of us chasing close behind. He got to be known around the school as the running flapper.

Rosie was a cute little Native American girl who looked normal and was always dressed to the nines. She resisted being touched by anyone, and would cower back whenever anyone came near. She always stayed a good distance from everyone. One day, I was helping one of the boys at the drinking fountain when she came up behind me and put her arms around me from the back. I thought that finally she was coming around. Then, to my surprise, she bit me on the behind and hung on. We did a war dance around the room for several minutes before she finally let go. I had a welt on my backside for several weeks.

Kelly was a frail boy who had poor circulation due to a congenital heart problem. His fingertips, lips, and ears were always blue, and he had very little energy. He came from a very good home where his mom and dad took good care of him.

During that school year we received a new student, Alan. He was fifteen, nearly six feet tall, and had a very loud voice. He had autistic characteristics and focused on one thing only: the war in Vietnam. Every day he would go off on the other kids, chasing them around, frightening them, and telling them he was going to take them to Cambodia. He became so violent that his parents had to send him away to a secure facility. He was so frightening to everyone in the school that other teachers and students would walk outside and around our room rather than walk through on their way down the hall.

Trudi, another girl with Down syndrome, was very spirited, and gave us a workout every day. Every morning, she would run in from the bus and say to me, "Walkit, (that's what she called me) sit down n' shut up, I need talk you now." So I would sit down and listen to her. Soon she would jump up give me a kiss and off she would go. She loved Mike, another boy with Down syndrome. She would tell me daily that they were going to get married at McDonald's and go on a honeymoon in Awahee (Hawaii). One time, she wanted to teach the reading lesson, and was making everyone tow the mark. She soon got out of hand because she was too assertive, and I was taking her for a little time out. She started hugging me and telling me she loved me. I told her that was okay and that I loved her too but that she was still getting a time out. She said, "That used to work on you." A few years ago, Trudi had a tumor on the brain. Her family was very concerned and asked me to come and give Trudi a blessing before the surgery. I gave Trudi a blessing and we were all engaged in small talk when Trudi said, "Walkit, I'll give you a call when I get home and we'll do lunch." And that she did.

Mike was Trudi's boyfriend. He and Trudi were an item. Mike was also quite a character. He loved Mrs. Melling, who taught fourth grade down the hall. He called her "Smelling." Mrs. Melling always had a Tab (Coke product) with her or hidden somewhere in her classroom. Mike loved to visit her classroom and find her Tab and guzzle it. When he returned to my classroom he would say, "Smelling Coke." I tried to have Mike say "Mrs. Melling" when he saw her instead of "Smelling." We worked on it, and finally, Mike would greet her with "Mrs. Smelling." She said, "Kings X, I would rather be smelling Coke." When we were practicing for a Special Olympics gymnastics competition, we would go to the university, and one of the staff would work with us on technique. One day, Mike picked up a Coke cup and downed the contents while we were there. Later, Mike was feeling a little sick, and I smelled mint coming from him and inquired of one of the college helpers about the contents of the Coke cup. He told me that a "cowboy" had been there chewing tobacco and was spitting in the cup that Mike drank. That cured Mike of drinking other peoples' drinks.

Naomi, another girl with Down syndrome, used to role play a lot, pretending she was the teacher, and would try to boss everyone around. Often I would say to her, "Who died and made you boss?" One day I was talking to her sister Tressa, who was a special ed teacher. Tressa told me that Naomi was visiting at her house and went to one of her daughter's bedrooms and locked the door so she could play with the dolls. Tressa knocked on the door several times and told her to come out. Finally, Naomi opened the door, put her hands on her hips, and said, "So, who died and made you boss?" I wonder where she heard that statement?

Tammy, a beautiful young girl with autism, gave us many days of wonderment. She had some very interesting behaviors, and we were never able to shape them. We quickly learned that we could never force her to do anything. We would try to encourage her and let her take her time at everything. She loved the National Geographic Magazine. We stocked the classroom with as many as we could find. We used them as a reinforcer. She would spend hours flipping through the pages and saying "Oo, aha." When we went to the lunchroom, we would have to give her time to touch bricks in the hall, in the same routine every time, or she would freak out. When we would enter a building with a double entrance, she would not go in. Even if we covered her eyes and tried to carry her, she would not go in. We would have to look for another entrance. When getting on the bus at the end of the day, she would stand there for a long time with one foot on the first step of the bus and the other foot on the ground. She would rock back and forth and finally get on the bus. Often she would get irritated with the younger students and would make a low, guttural sound. The little ones knew to run for cover or she would be after them. She also liked to run away from school. We had to keep a close watch on her at all times, or she would run away. When she ran, it was always the same route. She would run through the parking lot, down the street, and run into a couple of houses in the neighborhood on her way to the university. I would run after her, and the neighbors would stand back and watch as we ran through their house, encouraging me with a smile and some kind of a treat. The run would usually end at the university dormitory playground. She would giggle and then would let me take her back to school. When she became an adolescent and was having her first female period, she ran out of the restroom screaming, "Band Aid, Band Aid!" How do you explain to her what had happened?

One night, I received a phone call from the local police. They told me there was a naked girl running down the railroad tracks. Yep, it was Tammy. I got many phone calls from the police every time there was someone who acted a little different and they suspected they were disabled. The suspects were not always one my students. One time, a student at the school came up to me and said, "You don't look too bad to me." I inquired of him what he meant. He said, "My mom told me you were the retarded teacher; you don't look too bad to me." A great compliment, I think.

One morning, Tammy didn't come to school. We thought she was sick, and didn't think much of it. Later in the day, one of the district maintenance workers brought her to the room all dirty and wet. When I inquired as to what had happened, the worker told me they were working under the school on a broken pipe. They had to leave to get parts, and when they came back, they found Tammy under the building and playing in the mud. Tammy got off the bus that morning and took a shortcut to our room, where she got distracted and ended up under the building.

Stephanie was a high-functioning girl with Down syndrome. She and I had been working hard for some time reading and sounding out words and practicing rhyming verbs. She was getting pretty tired and looked me in the eye and said, "Walker, put a thock in it." This was inspiration for the title of this book. She had a frontal lisp and had a hard time with the "s" sound. Stephanie liked to pull up her shirt and pat herself on the stomach. She got quite a reaction from everyone. One day, we determined that every time she exhibited that behavior, we would put another tee shirt on her. It didn't take long before she was wearing twelve tee shirts and she looked like a middle linebacker. The technique worked. It's called overcorrection. Stephanie was also a runner. She often ran out of the room and down the hall or outside. We corrected this behavior by running to the fence with her every time she ran away. Both Stephanie and I got to be in pretty good shape from all the running we did. Stephanie's father was a lawyer, and every time I tried to discipline her, she would say, "You touch me and we'll sue."

Dusty was an eleven-year-old boy with Cerebral Palsy. He came in the middle of the school year and had some difficult behaviors for us to manage. He would sit down and refuse to do anything. It took all of our best behavior modification techniques to help him learn to behave. He had a bad habit of hitting women in the chest. We warned all of the women in the school about this behavior, and they were on their guard when they were around him. The women who worked with him learned to put their hand up on their chest in order to deflect any of his advances. One day, we had a visit from some personnel from the Utah State Office of Education. One of the women from the state was talking with me when Dusty laid her out before I could warn her of his behavior. I didn't care much for her, so it was somewhat of a payback, and I wanted to cheer.

Rod was a very active boy with Down syndrome. He was about eight or nine years old when he came to my classroom. Rod's family was very supportive and great to work with. They told me many stories about Rod that made me appreciate what they went through daily. He loved to run away from the classroom and hide from us. We had to be aware of him all of the time. He was so cute and loveable that it was very hard to discipline him. One day, he couldn't be found, so I started looking for him. Not finding him anywhere in the school, I went outside and finally located him in the custodian's truck. He was at the wheel pulling it back and forth, completely engaged. He was surprised to see me, but he kept on with his fantasy. I discovered that he'd eaten the custodian's lunch that was in a lunch box on the seat of the truck. I got to buy the custodian lunch that day, and he always locked his truck after that.

Another time when Rod was missing, I went right to the parking lot. I found my truck against the fence about fifty yards from where I parked it. Rod got in my truck and pulled it out of gear, causing it to roll across the parking lot and in to the fence. When I found him he asked, "Where's your lunch?" I never left my truck unlocked again. I'm a slow learner.

Alan and John David liked to team up and drive us up the wall with their antics. They got on a kick making bodily sounds, when they would cup their hand over their armpit and pump their arm downward. They would do this and get all of the other students going. One day, I'd had enough. When they started their routine, I announced to them we were going to have arm day. They thought that was great and asked me what arm day was. I told them they would be able to do their arm trick all day long. They thought it was great and started out enthusiastically. Soon it became old and they wanted to quit. I told them, "No, this is arm day, and you get to do it all day." By lunch they were worn out, and we never saw that behavior again.

I could always tell what John David had watched on TV the night before by the way he dressed at school. He was Michael Jackson with his gold pants, white glove, and leopard jacket, or Indiana Jones with his hat and whip. One day, the optometrist came to do vision screening. He asked John for his name. John said, "I am Michael Jackson." The doctor wrote it down and John said, "Well, duh." He had some good spin moves and could moon walk with the best, so he did some of his moves for the doctor. He was not impressed.

I used the overcorrection technique on Marge, a student with multiple disabilities. She was in a wheelchair and developed the behavior of screaming every day during the lunch hour after she'd eaten. We tried everything to extinguish the behavior, but nothing worked. Finally, one day we turned on the tape player and recorded everyone screaming for about five minutes. That day, after lunch, when Marge started screaming, I took her in the restroom and turned on the tape. After a short session, Marge quit screaming and never did it again.

On Wednesdays, we did a little home economics in the classroom. Our room was equipped with a kitchenette: it had a stove, refrigerator, and sink. We did some simple cooking and baking to teach the students how to fix food for themselves. We also made it a habit of sharing our creations with the faculty and staff of the school. Every time we offered our food to one of the school employees, they would say, "Did your kids touch this?" We got pretty good at caramel popcorn and brownies. One Wednesday, we tried to make taffy. We demonstrated to the students how you have to pull it after it's cooked in order to get the bubbles out and cut it in bite-sized pieces. When we gave Stephanie some taffy to pull, she tried it and then got queasy and threw up on all of us. We didn't try taffy again.

Classroom. Mr. Walker

23

CHAPTER FOUR
SPECIAL OLYMPICS

In 1972, we became involved in all aspects of Special Olympics, from gymnastics to track and field, swimming, and run, dribble, and shoot. With the help of representatives from the state level, we were able to incorporate Special Olympics in our daily routine and enhance the abilities of our students. In 1972, we hosted the area Spring Games in Cedar City sponsored by Southern Utah University. The events consisted of track and field events: 50-meter dash, long jump, softball throw, 400-meter relay, 100-meter run, and other events. All of the Special Olympians from Southern Utah participated in our area games. Teams came from St. George fifty miles away, Garfield County a hundred miles away, and Beaver County fifty miles away. At first, there were only about thirty participants, but as teams became more organized, the numbers grew to about a hundred and fifty participants.

Every spring, we'd have the support of the university PE department as they encouraged P.E. majors to work with us as practicum students. They were great to help with skills development, and they became good friends and role models for our kids. On the day of the area games, they would completely organize and staff each event so we could focus on getting the special Olympians to the various events.

The university also helped us by providing student nurses who were working on a bachelor's degree in nursing. These ladies were great to support and help wherever and whenever needed. They also became good friends with our students.

One year, I will never forget an experience with one of the women P.E. students who was shooting the starting pistol for the races. We were doing the fifty-meter run, and things were going well. All of a sudden, it was evident that this young woman was having problems. I went over to see if I could help. I asked her if everything was alright. She turned around and looked at me with tears streaming down her face. She said, "I can't see to shoot the gun." She was crying so hard that she was unable to function because she was so touched by the effort of these special Olympians.

State Games 2